Forging the Past

Great Comics Artists Series
M. Thomas Inge, General Editor

Forging the Past
Seth and the Art of Memory

Daniel Marrone

University Press of Mississippi / Jackson

www.upress.state.ms.us

The University Press of Mississippi is a member of the Association of American University Presses.

Images © Seth//Gregory Gallant

A version of chapter 3, "Pictures at a Remove: Seth's Drawn Photographs," appeared in *ImageTexT* 8.4 (2016).

A portion of chapter 7, "Forging Histories: Ghost Worlds and Invented Communities," appeared as "Seth's Ironic Identities: Forging Canadian History" in *Canadian Review of Comparative Literature* 43.1 (March 2016).

Copyright © 2016 by University Press of Mississippi
All rights reserved

First printing 2016
∞
Library of Congress Cataloging-in-Publication Data

Names: Marrone, Daniel, 1983– author.
Title: Forging the past : Seth and the art of memory / Daniel Marrone.
Description: Jackson : University Press of Mississippi, 2016. | Series: Great comics artists series | Includes bibliographical references and index.
Identifiers: LCCN 2016007767 | ISBN 9781496807311 (hardback)
Subjects: LCSH: Seth, 1962– —Criticism and interpretation. | Comic books, strips, etc.—Canada—History and criticism. | BISAC: LITERARY CRITICISM /
  Comics & Graphic Novels. | BIOGRAPHY & AUTOBIOGRAPHY / Artists,
  Architects, Photographers. | SOCIAL SCIENCE / Popular Culture.
Classification: LCC PN6733.S48 Z73 2016 | DDC 741.5/971—dc23 LC record available at http://lccn.loc.gov/2016007767

British Library Cataloging-in-Publication Data available

Contents

Acknowledgments vii

Introduction 3

1 Style and the Appearance of Authenticity 19

2 Return, Repetition, and Other Ambivalent Impulses 41

3 Pictures at a Remove: Seth's Drawn Photographs 59

4 The Rhetoric of Failure 79

5 Collection and Recollection 97

6 Dense and Porous: Browsing, Parataxis, and the Texture of Comics 121

7 Forging Histories: Ghost Worlds and Invented Communities 149

Conclusion 179

Appendix: Interview with Seth 185

Notes 221

Bibliography 225

Index 231

Acknowledgments

Sincerest thanks to Barry Curtis and Roger Sabin for their generous encouragement, astute advice, and attention to detail.

I am also deeply indebted to Seth for being such a gracious and willing participant in this work, for donating hard-to-find back issues of *Palookaville*, and particularly for inviting me into his home to talk about comics.

Special thanks to Sarah Pinder for her constant support.

Forging the Past

Introduction

> For all of us there is a twilight zone between history and memory.
> —Eric Hobsbawm, *The Age of Empire*

Seth has a way of sneaking up on the reader. His work seems so familiar, so much a product of a certain reassuring tradition of visual culture, that its inventiveness may come as a surprise. This is not a matter of easy incongruity—cartoon form, literary content—but a far more subtle and discreet exploration of a complex medium. In much of his work, Seth offers readers a strange kind of hospitality, inviting them to dwell in the shifting terrain between history and memory.

In such a space, where history and memory overlap, the latter often rushes in to fill the gaps left by the former. Seth's work is deeply engaged in this process, what Walter Benjamin calls "the mysterious work of remembrance—which is really the capacity for endless interpolation into what has been" (*Reflections* 16). It is possible to conceive of cartooning in similar terms: as both a practice and a capacity related to the excavation of the past. Seth suggests that "the whole process of cartooning is dealing with memory" (Taylor 15), a claim that goes a long way toward setting the parameters for much of this investigation. Although this book takes a cue from Eric Hobsbawm, its primary historiographic touchstone is Linda Hutcheon, whose focus is not history but literature. Hutcheon provides a remarkably apt description of Seth's work when she uses the term "historiographic metafiction," which, she says, questions "how we know the past, how we *make* sense of it" (*Canadian Postmodern* 22, emphasis in original). This investigation seeks, in a number of different ways, to address one principal question: How does Seth make the past?

To a certain extent, this book began with a suspicion about longing for the past in comics. Could the ostensible prevalence of nostalgia in many of the most popular and critically acclaimed comics be more than a mere trend or coincidence? The abundance of memoirs, period pieces, carefully researched chronicles, and otherwise historically inflected work—to say nothing of the longing for a lost home that defines superheroes as familiar as Superman and Batman—seems to suggest that comics as a medium might be particularly suited to wrestling with nostalgia. Cartoonists like Chris Ware, Ben Katchor, and Seth himself have identified the significance of longing for the past in their work—and, perhaps even more often, have had this significance thrust reductively upon them. However, with the notable exception of Charles Hatfield's work in this area ("Same as It Never Was"; "It's Not the House I Lived In"), the relationship between nostalgia and comics remains largely untheorized. Precisely because Seth's interest in the past can be mistaken for unadulterated longing, his body of work becomes an ideal site for redressing the somewhat impoverished understanding of nostalgia in contemporary comics. In this book, I locate his attitudes toward the past along a spectrum of "ambivalent longing"—in which the ambivalence is just as important as the longing.

I sometimes refer to the various iterations of this ambivalent longing simply as nostalgia, using the word as a kind of shorthand for a family of phenomena concerned with homecoming, return, and repetition. As Svetlana Boym recounts in *The Future of Nostalgia*, the word "nostalgia" was coined by Swiss physician Johannes Hofer in 1688 to diagnose a homesickness so acute it could lead to nausea, fever, and even cardiac arrest (3–4). Due to its obsessive tendency, Boym characterizes the condition as a mania: the sufferer, invariably a Swiss soldier in these early instances, compulsively returned to thoughts of home (4). A physical return home to Switzerland was the most reliable cure at first, but as nostalgia evolved and spread across Europe over the eighteenth century, the "mania of longing" became increasingly difficult to treat, even as its physical symptoms fell away (6). By the nineteenth century, the affliction was far more fashionable than incapacitating, embraced as a romantic attitude, which Boym summarizes as a Cartesian proposition: "I long therefore I am" (13). A Swiss invention with Greek roots, "nostalgia" literally translates as an ache (*algia*) for the return home (*nostos*)—although Boym offers a more evocative and precise definition: "a longing for a home that no longer exists or has never existed" (xiii).

The fictive, imagined home is at the center of much of Seth's work, as is its implicit analogue, the nation. (In some instances, the nation becomes an explicit concern, most obviously in a work like *The Great Northern Brotherhood of Canadian Cartoonists*.) The longstanding national implications of nostalgia—which Hofer considered a patriotic illness (Boym 4)—help to account for the subtle correlation between Seth's imagined homes and his invented communities. Of course, nostalgia is as much about a return to the past as the return home: Boym calls it a "historical emotion" (7), a reaction to "the modern conception of unrepeatable and irreversible time" (13). Nostalgia tends to obscure the distinction between geographical and historical origins, operating at once spatially and temporally. Boym identifies a strain of "restorative nostalgia," which aligns itself with the notion of tradition (often national or regional tradition) and which attempts to realize "a transhistorical reconstruction of the lost home" (xviii). She contrasts this with a "reflective nostalgia" that "dwells on the ambivalences of human longing and belonging and does not shy away from the contradictions of modernity" (xviii). Seth exemplifies this nostalgic mode in his work, which is often preoccupied with precisely these ambivalences and contradictions. Where restorative nostalgia reacts against such contradictions, reflective nostalgia embraces them—in both cases, ambivalence is at the root of longing for the past.

Ultimately, the past is inaccessible, except through memory and history, which are familiar and yet fundamentally enigmatic practices that attempt to make present a fundamental absence. Keith Jenkins offers this reminder: "History is a discourse about, but categorically different from, the past" (6). Anachronism becomes an inevitable starting point for even the most dispassionate history, which can only view the past from a present moment, obscuring what has been even as it tries to bring it into focus. This is the essential, ambivalent operation of history: to juxtapose time, to set time against itself, creating continuities and discontinuities, constructing linear chronological progressions. Echoing Jenkins, Alun Munslow suggests that "because history is not the same as the past, the notion of correspondence has to be replaced with the logic of narrative representation" (15). Without dismissing history as artificial, Seth's work draws attention to the narrative representation of the past and reveals the extent to which the making of history is an act of great artifice.

There is likewise no shortage of artifice in the making of memory, which may be considered a medium or art in its own right. "It may seem odd to speak of memory as a medium," W. J. T. Mitchell writes in *Picture Theory*, "but the term seems appropriate in a number of senses. Since antiquity, memory has been figured not just as a disembodied, invisible power, but as a specific technology, a mechanism, a material and semiotic process subject to artifice and alteration" (191–92).

Memory as a Medium

A familiar story retold in brief:

The lyric poet Simonides of Ceos, dining at the house of an aristocrat, is called away moments before the roof of the banquet hall collapses, killing everyone at the table. In his absence, the house becomes a ruin, a crypt, the guests crushed beyond recognition. When it comes time to properly bury the dead, Simonides finds that he is able to recall the seating arrangement at the feast and identifies each body based solely on its location in the rubble. In doing so, he stumbles upon the method of loci, a classical "art of memory" in which recollection is aided by the visualization of a spatial order.

This canonical anecdote (most famously recounted by Cicero in *De Oratore*) becomes something of a prototype for imagining relationships to the past—and it almost permits a conflation of memory and recollection. To parse these related terms, it may be useful to draw on Aristotle's distinction between the two, which David Krell succinctly summarizes in this way: "Memory as such [Aristotle] classifies as an affection or pathos; recollection or reminiscence he celebrates as an activity" (13). Seth's remarks about the process of cartooning suggest that in some sense comics, too, constitute an art of memory, a reminiscent activity—and one that is strangely kindred to the method of loci in terms of the primacy of visual representation and spatial arrangement. The typical comics page consists of images arranged in highly structured spatial configurations, and Seth's work in particular is often preoccupied with recollection and imagined spaces.

One of Mitchell's primary contentions is that "all media are mixed media, and all representations are heterogeneous" (5). This is particularly true of the representations found in comics, which often seem to exemplify the kind of heterogeneous combination—"imagetext"—that interests Mitchell. Seth's dense, composite work certainly constitutes an imagetext, not only as comics but also as an exercise in the medium of memory. "Memory, in short, is an imagetext," Mitchell says, "a double-coded system of mental storage and retrieval" (192). The medium of memory and the medium of comics are both imagetexts, and together they reach a height of craft and inventiveness in Seth's work.

The Structure of Comics

One of the underlying suggestions of this book is that comics are in some way homologous to memory—that the fundamental operation of comics, as a visual medium, mobilizes and makes space for narrative interpolations in a way that not only is comparable to but in a certain sense mimics the historical interpolations of memory. Consequently, this investigation must always be moving toward an adaptable, carefully considered understanding of the operation and structure of comics. This understanding is strongly informed by the work of Thierry Groensteen and Charles Hatfield, and also draws on Scott McCloud's popular book *Understanding Comics*.

Groensteen is among those who conceive of comics "as a language ... an original ensemble of productive mechanisms of meaning" (*System of Comics* 2). I generally reserve the term "language" for verbal expression, preferring to identify comics as a medium. However, I also suggest, in chapter 2, that language may be understood as "a system of segregations" (which is consistent with Groensteen's description of comics as a system that constitutes a distinct language). Hatfield sometimes refers to comics as a "form"—although I do not adopt his usage of that term, I do occasionally distinguish between comics as a medium and the cartoon as a unique visual form. Similarly, Jeet Heer and Kent Worcester refer to the "cluster of related forms" associated with the umbrella term "comics" (*Comics Studies Reader* 13).

Groensteen considers the panel to be the irreducible unit of what he calls the language of comics, which he characterizes as a system of fragmentary components (*System of Comics* 5). Comics require the reader's active cooperation, he writes, because they "offer the reader a story that is full of holes, which appear as gaps in the meaning" (10). The media historian John Durham Peters argues that gaps, often considered the hallmark of degraded communication, are in fact indispensable to it. He observes that the more suspended and indiscriminate the form of communication—in other words, the greater the distance between sender and receiver—the more "the audience bears the hermeneutic burden" (124). This distance, however, does not become an impediment to communication and the production of meaning. As Peters asserts, the "gaps at the heart of communication are not its ruins, but its distinctive feature" (130). The chapters to follow return again and again to the distinctive gaps at the heart of Seth's work.

Moving from communication in general to the more specific field of literature, Roman Ingarden's ontological investigation *The Literary Work of Art* provides a narrower theoretical framework that can be aligned with formal studies of comics. Like Groensteen and other comics theorists, Ingarden emphasizes the contribution of the reader, saying that "during his reading and his aesthetic apprehension of the work, the reader usually *goes beyond* what is simply presented by the text (or projected by it) and in various respects *completes*" what has been represented (252, emphasis in original). In literature, the interpretative obligation produced by the unavoidable gap between author and reader takes an inconspicuous and more particularized form: gaps in the representation of the narrative world. Ingarden observes that "while reading a work we are not conscious of any 'gaps,' of any 'spots of indeterminacy,' in the represented objects" (251).

Jeff Mitscherling explains that spots of indeterminacy "belong to the peculiar mode of being of the literary text and in fact make possible the creation of its 'reality'" (106). This "mode of being" is what distinguishes literary works from other narrative arts. Certainly there are spots of indeterminacy in any narrative, but other media are less suspended than literature for two immediately discernible reasons: (1) words on a page are static, and (2) words do not represent by means of physical resemblance. Both of these characteristics demand that the reader be the sole animator of the text during the act of reading; although it has been conceived by an author, the represented world of the literary work is set in motion by the reader's attention. Comics have a literary mode of being all their own: although they share with traditional literature a fundamental immobility, they also operate by means of image-based representation that depends on resemblance.

The two characteristics of traditional literature are easily reconceived as the two principal differences between words and images, which Robin Varnum and Christina Gibbons identify in the introduction to their 2001 anthology *The Language of Comics: Word and Image*. The first is that "images resemble the objects they represent," whereas "words represent objects only by virtue of custom or convention" (xi). In the eighteenth century, Gotthold Lessing observed the second key difference: whereas "words must be spoken or written one after the other in time and are apprehended sequentially, the elements of an image are arranged side by side in space and are apprehended all at once" (Varnum and Gibbons xi). Comics, however, disrupt the decisiveness of such distinctions: the cartoon mode of representation simultaneously resembles the objects it represents and relies heavily on convention; and the panels of a comic may be apprehended sequentially or all at once (not infrequently, both kinds of perception compete and cooperate on the page). Seth's comics take full advantage of the particular tensions and capacities of the medium, and discreetly test the limits of cartooning conventions.

Varnum and Gibbons's introductory remarks also include an incisive assessment of Scott McCloud's contribution to the field and the "great heuristic value" of *Understanding Comics* (Varnum and Gibbons xiii). McCloud's familiar definition of "sequential art"[1] relies on the word "juxtaposed"—meaning adjacent, consecutive in space—to differentiate comics from film, video, and animation, which are similarly sequential, but only temporally (McCloud 7–9). McCloud also offers a detailed account of the function of the gutter— "that space *between* the panels" (66, emphasis in original)—along with the closely related phenomenon of "closure," which allows the reader to "mentally construct a continuous, unified reality" (67). However, as cogent as *Understanding Comics* often is, it is nevertheless an autodidactic work that exists in relative isolation from other theories of signs and representation.

By contrast, European scholarship has a history of theoretical approaches to comics, as Varnum and Gibbons point out (xiii). In *The System of Comics*, Groensteen unmistakably engages with semiotic theory and brings it to bear on comics, ultimately advancing a new semiotic theory of the medium that is striking in its simultaneous specificity and applicability. Groensteen describes his book's principal theoretical frameworks as "macro-semiotic" (6): the *spatio-topical system*, namely the distinctive potentialities of space and place on the comics page, is governed by *arthrology*, Groensteen's designation for the various relations among comics images.

Despite marked methodological differences, Groensteen's work is by no means incommensurate with McCloud's; indeed, there is considerable correspondence between the two. Both emphasize "the active cooperation provided by the reader" (Groensteen, *System of Comics* 10), which McCloud generally terms "closure."[2] For Groensteen, the panel is "the base unit of the comics system" (*System of Comics* 34), a contention that is complemented by McCloud's chapter on the gutter, which identifies various types of "panel-to-panel transitions" (McCloud 70). The panel and the gutter are necessarily interdependent, and "it is between the panels that the pertinent contextual rapports establish themselves with respect to narration" (Groensteen, *System of Comics* 107). One of the distinguishing features of comics is that structuring gaps not only are conceptual—as in the gaps of communication or literary spots of indeterminacy—but also match the representational concreteness of the medium.

It is possible to make several assertions: (1) the comics panel is not equivalent to either the frame or the shot of moving image media; (2) the panel cannot be treated as a picture or painting, particularly when it is in juxtaposition with other panels; and (3) the image-based representational contents of a panel are not equivalent to the units of traditional literature (i.e., the letter, the word, etc.). This last point may seem especially self-evident, but it still calls for some elaboration. How should the contents of the panel be conceived, if they cannot be compared to the components of traditional literature? In McCloud's straightforward but not unsophisticated account, the constituent element of comics is the "cartoon"—a particular iconic mode that represents reality by means of "amplification through simplification" (30). (The term "icon" is used by McCloud to designate both words and images; Will Eisner similarly suggests that, in comics, "text reads as an image" [2].) Operating as "a vacuum into which our identity and awareness are pulled" (McCloud 36), the cartoon induces a certain kind of perception that sets comics apart from other visual forms like painting and illustration. McCloud describes the cartoon as both "a way of drawing" and "a way of seeing" (31), an account that is congruent with Groensteen's contention that "comics lean toward a work of *narrative drawing*, and its images generally present intrinsic qualities that are not those of the illustration or the picture" (*System of Comics* 105, emphasis in original).

To this understanding of the substance of comics, Hatfield adds a description that is credible, straightforward, and far-reaching: comics, he states, are "heterogeneous in form, involving the co-presence and interaction of various codes" (*Alternative Comics* 36). Although almost any medium might be plausibly characterized as "heterogeneous" (as Mitchell would be quick to point out), Hatfield's sturdy definition addresses the distinctive formal amalgamation inherent in comics. The complexity of this system demands a specific kind of reading. As Hatfield puts it, "the reader's role is crucial, and requires the invocation of learned competencies; the relationships between pictures are a matter of convention, not inherent connectedness" (*Alternative Comics* 41). By convention, the gaps between images invite a particular response (which the cartoonist guides by means of manipulation of verbal and visual cues), but it is ultimately the reader who makes the connections moment to moment to arrive at the illusion of a seamless whole.

In many ways, it is the discontinuity of the comics page that affords the medium its great formal flexibility: with such a wide range of available techniques, the cartoonist is able to suit form to narrative in a way most writers cannot. No particular combination of elements is necessary to tell a story in comics because the exclusion of an element—for instance, speech balloons or panel frames—generates a specific kind of gap, which the reader will have little trouble assimilating into a field of information that is by nature already full of gaps. The surface of Seth's page is only very rarely an unbroken, monumental unit, and in such cases usually for the purposes of rhythmic punctuation, to contrast the more fragmented and porous pages that precede and follow it (this technique is deployed to particular effect in his book *George Sprott*).

Most comics pages comprise a network of panels that invite a specific kind of participation from the reader—at once separate and linked, the panels lend themselves to multiple ways of being read. A single image, as Hatfield notes, functions simultaneously "as a 'moment' in an imagined sequence of events, and as a graphic element in an atemporal design" (*Alternative Comics* 48). In terms of the significance of page layout and its effect on the reader's experience of the "flow" or "rhythm" of panels, it is clear that "comics exploit *format* as a signifier in itself" (52, emphasis in original). Like Groensteen, Hatfield describes the system of comics at a macrosemiotic level and is able to broaden the terms of discussion without becoming vague or imprecise:

"Comics involve a tension between the experience of reading in sequence and the format or shape of the object being read. In other words, the art of comics entails a tense relationship between perceived time and perceived space" (*Alternative Comics* 52). This tension among codes and between modes of perception lends comics their uniquely changeable coherence and at the same time accommodates a range of reading strategies. Just as there is no single template for a comics page, there is ultimately no "right" way to read a comics page: "There is simply no consistent formula for resolving the tensions intrinsic to the experience" (66).

An Open and Inductive Approach

In her book *Nostalgia: Sanctuary of Meaning*, Janelle L. Wilson offers this astute advice: "Attempting to grasp the meaning and experience of nostalgia requires an open and inductive approach" (19). Likewise ambivalence, which this investigation identifies as the source of not only nostalgia but also the uncanny, the Gothic, and a wide array of other aesthetic/literary phenomena related to the seemingly inevitable return of the repressed. This premise—which, needless to say, owes a great deal to Freud's understanding of ambivalent impulses—finds its full elaboration in chapter 2 and informs every chapter to some extent. Although the phrase "ambivalent impulses" and its attendant ideas come from Freud, my overall approach to ambivalence and the return of the repressed is not strictly psychoanalytic. It would be more accurate to say that it is a literary approach of Freudian extraction, of the sort that Francesco Orlando pursues in his study *Obsolete Objects in the Literary Imagination* (which takes on a central role in chapter 4). Ultimately, this investigation does not regard psychoanalysis as a fundamentally coherent system of thought that must be adopted in its entirety. Especially in a literary context, the discipline may be more useful in fragments, which is to say as an occasional tactic rather than an overarching strategy.

Following Wilson's advice, I aim to pursue an open and inductive approach, to rigorously clarify, classify, and interpret the complex network of literary and historical operations at work in Seth's comics, but at the same time to be flexible, to preserve certain spots of indeterminacy, to allow for theoretical detours, to not always resolve every ambiguity that presents itself. Various chapters borrow and at times even deform certain concepts to illuminate an aspect of Seth's work. For instance, chapter 5 includes a somewhat abbreviated account of Jacques Derrida's notion of the crypt as a point of reference for better understanding how collections operate as receptacles for the past.

Similarly, chapter 6 makes unusually literal use of Gilles Deleuze's dense philosophical work *The Fold*. Such digressions help to ventilate the larger arguments of the sections in which they appear.

Seth's own comments also help to round out the discussion. In August 2011, I visited Seth at his home in Guelph, Ontario, for an informal, occasionally meandering, but ultimately quite fruitful interview (the transcript of which is included here as an appendix). Unless otherwise indicated, all remarks attributed to Seth throughout this book come from that interview, which does not become a dominant source text but which does certainly lead to fresh avenues of inquiry. This book does not treat Seth as the ultimate authority on his own work or accept his comments as incontestable, but his reflections are certainly subtle and perceptive enough to warrant sustained analysis. (The interview also suggests some interesting topics that are *not* taken up in the chapters, for instance, the future of the book as a cultural object and the ways in which a cartoonist cultivates a sense of silence in comics.)

This investigation does not generally attempt to draw parallels between Seth's life and his work, and it never assumes his fiction to be veiled memoir. His biographical details are as follows: born Gregory Gallant in 1962 in the southern Ontario town of Clinton, he moved to Toronto in the early 1980s to attend art school and stayed in the city for nearly twenty years, before eventually settling in Guelph.[3] Even in those instances when his stories are patently (or playfully) autobiographical, particular knowledge of his personal life does little to extend an appreciation or understanding of the work. However, this is not to say that his extraliterary circumstances, or indeed his personal opinions, do not have a place in this investigation. His remarks about his own work, and the cultural context out of which that work emerged, are important parts of this study, even if they do not constitute its focus. At the center of this investigation is Seth's authorial role as a forger of histories.

My analysis focuses almost exclusively on Seth's longer stories, those book-length works that he both conceived and illustrated. Seth's first professional comics experience—prior to publishing his own work in the series *Palookaville*—was as an artist for the Vortex Comics series *Mister X*.[4] He speaks of this job as a kind of "apprenticeship period" during which he was not only refining his technical drawing ability but also discovering those cartoonists who would have a great influence on his subsequent work (see page 189). In 1990, he was one of the first authors to publish with Drawn and Quarterly, at the time a barely established outfit based in Montreal and now one of the most highly regarded alternative comics publishers in North America. Arguably, Drawn and Quarterly represents a continuation of the avant-garde comics publishing tradition epitomized by Art Spiegelman and Françoise Mouly's pioneering magazine *Raw*, which was a fixture of alternative comics throughout the 1980s. Seth's work is rooted in this cultural context, which favors the output of comics auteurs whom the reader imagines working in isolation in a studio (this is in fact how Seth works; see page 187). As one of Drawn and Quarterly's flagship authors, Seth shares with his publisher a trajectory from smaller-scale, independent fringe to literary comics establishment.

Palookaville (initially *Palooka-ville*) is Seth's long-running comic book series, which in 2010 abandoned its magazine format in favor of a hardcover compendium-style book that includes essays and sketchbook extracts along with ongoing comics stories. Seth's first book-length narrative, *It's a Good Life, If You Don't Weaken*, appeared in issues 4 through 9 of *Palookaville* before being published as a standalone "picture-novella" in 1996. The story weaves together two autobiographical plots, with Seth's day-to-day life in Toronto set alongside his search for a little-known Canadian gag cartoonist, John "Kalo" Kalloway. He ultimately discovers that the cartoonist died years ago, having given up cartooning to raise a family. *It's a Good Life* closes with reproductions of all extant Kalo gags collected by Seth over the years. Convincing as these reproductions are, however, John Kalloway is in fact a complete invention—as perhaps are any number of the ostensibly autobiographical incidents depicted in the book.

For nearly twenty years, *Palookaville* was home to *Clyde Fans*, a family saga about two brothers, Simon and Abraham Matchcard, who attempt to manage the electric fan company founded by their long-dead father, Clyde. A story in five parts, *Clyde Fans* shifts among different time periods, locations, and narrative points of view: part 1 takes place in 1997 in the Matchcard family home (which includes the Clyde Fans storefront), with Abe directly addressing the reader, reminiscing about the business, now defunct, and about Simon, now dead; part 2 is set in 1957 and follows Simon on an unsuccessful sales trip to the small town of Dominion City; part 3 finds Simon back in the Matchcard home, now in 1966, and centers on his mother's growing dementia and his own fragile mental state; part 4 skips ahead to 1975, tracing the beginning of the end of the family business; and part 5 concludes with a revealing return to 1957. *Clyde Fans: Book 1* (2004) collects issues 10 through 15 of *Palookaville*.

The ongoing serialization of *Clyde Fans* in *Palookaville* has run parallel to the publication of book-length narratives begun in other formats—for instance, in Seth's personal sketchbook. *Wimbledon Green: The Greatest Comic Book Collector in the World* (2005) is Seth's first sketchbook story, a lively send-up of the world of comic book collecting that boasts a sprawling cast of collectors, cartoonists, sellers, and other peripheral figures, all orbiting around the title character. One of the book's many notable features is the inclusion of sample comics from Wimbledon Green's collection. Seth's polished and stately follow-up, *George Sprott: 1894–1975* (2009), offers a quietly unpredictable biography of a small-town hero known for his decades-long lecture series and local TV show, in which he revisits arctic expeditions from early in his life. Much of the book first appeared serially, in weekly installments, in the *New York Times Magazine* from September 2006 to March 2007. *George Sprott* is distinguished from Seth's other work by the presence of an unseen omniscient narrator. Seth's most recent book, *The Great Northern Brotherhood of Canadian Cartoonists* (2011), is another nonserialized narrative that began in his sketchbook. In some respects a companion volume to *Wimbledon Green*, this book comprises numerous appraisals of metafictional comics and detailed portrayals of the brotherhood's sprawling clubhouse.

Along with comic books, picture-novellas, and sketchbook stories, Seth is also known for a range of other endeavors, among them: cover illustrations for the *New Yorker*, book designs, installations in art galleries, a float in a parade, and occasional pieces for Canadian newspapers and magazines (sometimes in comics form, sometimes not). Also notable are his nonnarrative books, such as *Vernacular Drawings* (2001), a "Consolidated and Abridged" selection of full-size pages culled from six sketchbooks, and *Forty Cartoon Books of Interest* (2006), a compact annotated bibliography of idiosyncratic works from Seth's personal comic book collection.

In the scope and substance of his work, Seth is perhaps the foremost contemporary cartoonist in Canada, arguably more visible than his friend and colleague Chester Brown, and with a higher literary profile than an artist like Bryan Lee O'Malley (whose extremely popular *Scott Pilgrim* comics were adapted into a 2010 film). Of course, this kind of fuzzy ranking reveals very little about the actual literary significance of Seth's work and its place in the comics landscape, broad subjects that will gradually come into focus over the course of this book. Some sense of Seth's comics cohort can, however, be gleaned from his more autobiographical work and even from the telling dedications that appear in his books. Seth has dedicated books not only to Chester Brown (who appears as a character in *It's a Good Life*) but also to his contemporaries Joe Matt and Chris Ware. Their work, as well as that of Daniel Clowes, offers many useful points of comparison that help to bring out various aspects of Seth's narratives.

Seth has been the subject of numerous journalistic profiles and interviews over the course of his career, but in-depth academic work is in comparatively short supply. Charles Hatfield was one of the first to take a scholarly interest, giving a paper on Seth and "the problem of nostalgia" at the 2002 annual conference of the Popular Culture Association. (This was something of a follow-up to his 2001 paper for the PCA, which addressed the significance of nostalgia in contemporary comics as a whole.) Hatfield anticipates many of the avenues of inquiry that I pursue in this investigation, from the importance of irony and ambivalence in nostalgic comics to the structural affinity between comic book narratives and collection. Of particular note is Hatfield's conclusion that Seth's work represents "a signal moment in comics' ongoing dialogue with itself." Katie Mullins similarly frames Seth's work as an act of "autocritique," arguing that *It's a Good Life* addresses the shortcomings of the mainstream comics tradition by means of its female characters ("Questioning Comics").

Jared Gardner, in his 2006 article "Archives, Collectors, and the New Media Work of Comics," examines the increasing presence of archives in a range of contemporary comics narratives (by Seth, Clowes, and others). He observes that *Wimbledon Green* "goes so far as to playfully imagine the collector and the superhero as one and the same" (799). His arguments, which are occasionally at cross-purposes to many of the claims I make, are specifically addressed in chapters 5 and 7. Candida Rifkind takes a more biographical approach to Seth's work in "Drawn from Memory: Comics Artists and Intergenerational Auto/biography" (2008). One of her focal points is father-son relationships, and she appropriately selects as objects of study Spiegelman's *Maus*, Ware's *Jimmy Corrigan*, and Seth's collaboration with his father, *Bannock, Beans, and Black Tea: Memories of a Prince Edward Island Childhood during the Depression* (2004). This collaboration also makes a brief appearance in Paul Buhle's 2007 article "History and Comics," in the context of a comparison between oral and graphic history (316).

To date, the most robust engagement with Seth's work appears in Simon Grennan's article "Demonstrating *Discours*: Two Comic Strip Projects in Self-Constraint" (2012), which applies a narratological approach to *Clyde Fans*. Grennan's methodology seems to run parallel to that of this investigation, without substantively corresponding to or conflicting with it. Chapter 1 provides a summary of Grennan's comics narratology and attempts to put it in context with an argument about how Seth's style reflects a particular type of ambivalent longing.

This study of Seth's work is distinguished primarily by its length and breadth, but it also aims to make an original contribution to comics studies at a broader theoretical level, perhaps most of all through its unique application of the term "interpolation." Interpolation, in the most neutral sense of the word, is simply the insertion of something additional between existing parts, often the introduction of new matter into a preexisting text. In developing a particular understanding of the relationship between comics and memory, however, interpolation takes on a more specific meaning.

Walter Benjamin describes remembrance as "the capacity for endless interpolation into what has been." This book reconceives that comparison as more than just a metaphor: following Mitchell's understanding of imagetext, I propose a relation between interpolation into the past (as described by Benjamin) and the reader's capacity for interpolation into the comics text (as theorized by Groensteen and others). According to this account, there is a significant structural similarity between the medium of memory and the medium of comics—to such an extent that the latter serves as an ideal vessel for the former. In this investigation, the term *interpolation* encapsulates these complex relations, referring to the memory-inflected filling of gaps and construction of meaning that comics pages invite the reader to undertake.

Interpolation has another connotation that seems relevant in light of Seth's approach to storytelling: to interpolate can also mean to surreptitiously insert spurious or forged material into an authentic document. Seth frequently engages in this kind of authorial interpolation, but, for the sake of clarity, I do not lump his historical interventions and forgeries together with the intangible mental processes of the reader's interpolation (although the interpolating mechanism is understood to be comparable). Instead, these playful forgeries are identified as instances of historiographic metafiction. For the most part, *interpolation* is reserved for those acts of meaning-making carried out by the comics reader, which are sometimes specifically designated as acts of *readerly interpolation*. Generally, this investigation names ambivalence as the prevailing logic of literature (if not the governing principle of all communication). Interpolation, as I have defined it, concerns an ambivalent impulse related to the past—an ambivalent nostalgia—that is characteristic of what Mitchell calls "the composite imagetext structure of memory," which parallels the imagetext structure of comics.

Any discussion of the behavior and responses of "the reader" relies on my own readings, reactions, observations, and speculations—in short, my own personal encounter with Seth's work. My role in this investigation is to be a kind of ideal reader (a "Model Reader," as Umberto Eco might have it), one who is especially receptive to Seth's evocations of the past and who is eager to dwell in the space between history and memory. With this in mind, I aim to offer a comprehensive but by no means definitive account of Seth's work.

Each chapter contributes to an overarching argument about ambivalence, longing for the past, and the way in which Seth's work induces the reader to fill narrative gaps. Chapter 1, "Style and the Appearance of Authenticity," considers the materiality and appearance of Seth's work (with particular attention to the influence of Peter Arno on Seth's cartooning style) in an attempt to understand how a sense of authenticity becomes legible to the reader. Chapter 2,

"Return, Repetition, and Other Ambivalent Impulses," begins with Zygmunt Bauman's account of ambivalence, delineates the relation of ambivalence to modernity and ambiguity, and elaborates the role of Freud's thinking in this investigation through a consideration of the uncanny. Chapter 3, "Pictures at a Remove: Seth's Drawn Photographs," closely examines Seth's drawn photographs, comparing the ways in which comics and photography relate to their represented realities in terms of time, narrative, duration, and framing. Chapter 4, "The Rhetoric of Failure," traces the frequent revaluation of success and failure in Seth's narratives, placing Seth in a Chekhovian tradition of storytelling and drawing on Francesco Orlando's study of obsolete objects in literature. Chapter 5, "Collection and Recollection," focuses on *Wimbledon Green* and *Clyde Fans*, drawing together arguments about ambivalence, narratives of the past, and the fortification of identity through the process of collecting. Chapter 6, "Dense and Porous: Browsing, Parataxis, and the Texture of Comics," offers a multifaceted account of the distinctive texture of comics, exploring the simultaneous fragmentation and coherence of the comics page as well as addressing exceptional cases like the single-panel gag cartoon and the foldout page. Chapter 7, "Forging Histories: Ghost Worlds and Invented Communities," explores Seth's invented worlds and interior landscapes, making particular use of Hutcheon's concepts of the heterocosm and historiographic metafiction as well as certain frameworks from Hayden White's landmark work *Metahistory* (specifically, the notion of a "metahistorical consciousness").

Seth's ironic, humorous, and metafictional approaches to the past reveal a deep ambivalence, in certain instances even a self-reflexive meta-ambivalence. He nimbly mobilizes history, (auto)biography, anecdote, documentary, and other parallel modes; this investigation seeks to understand the ways in which his appropriation of such historicizing discourses substantiates the powerful evocations of longing, loss, and memory that characterize his fiction. Memory is here conceived not just as an invisible, ubiquitous mental phenomenon that reflects our experience of time and relation to the past but as a medium, an art—and one that is in some significant ways akin to the medium of comics. It is this affinity that enables Seth to so effectively turn the medium of memory on itself, using it as an instrument to examine the processes of making the past.

1

Style and the Appearance of Authenticity

The most immediately compelling feature of Seth's work is its appearance, those physical elements that combine to form a strong, instant impression of what may be generally termed "style." This is hardly unusual in the medium of comics, which conveys so much by visual means; even alongside other contemporary comics, however, Seth's books often stand out as carefully designed book-objects. It comes as no surprise that he is also a sought-after designer for other people's books, a parallel profession that has superseded his work as a jobbing magazine illustrator. Much more than just the external package, however, what I refer to in this chapter as style includes page design and panel layout, shading and color scheme, treatment of fictive, diegetic space, and of course the actual drawing itself, which in Seth's case strongly recalls a bygone era of cartooning. Although he does not attempt to slavishly reproduce the technique of any particular cartoonist from the so-called Golden Age of American comics, Seth conjures a consistent surface that seems uncannily familiar, reassuring, and authentic in its evocation of this visual history. This is not style in the sense of something opposed to substance or meaning but rather, as Susan Sontag predicts, style as a kind of "totality" (*Against Interpretation* 17). Style is understood to encompass and sometimes even dictate substance.

Still, as Sontag points out, even to invoke the term "style" is to imply something that is somehow separable from what might commonly (and with a pretense of neutrality) be referred to as "content." Implicit in this chapter is an argument that such a separation may be considered an acceptable and even productive theoretical maneuver, particularly in the analysis of a visual narrative medium like comics. At the same time, however, style in comics is more than just the sum of its parts, more than the choices made by a cartoonist between various interchangeable elements. Style is connected to what

Thierry Groensteen calls the "medium-related pleasure" of comics, which he rightly maintains cannot be reduced to a simple combination of narrative and artistic pleasures ("Why" 10). The medium-related pleasure of Seth's comics is often bound up with a sense of history, craft, and that nearly intangible quality, authenticity. The word "authenticity" accommodates a great deal of connotative slippage, which this chapter attempts to preserve even as it draws out particular meanings. Likewise "appearance." The discussion of "the appearance of authenticity" represents an effort to parse a sometimes elusive set of concerns: not only what Seth's style looks like and how it operates, but also the process by which it becomes perceptible to the reader.

The Specter of Authenticity

In her contribution to *The Concept of Style* (edited by Berel Lang), Svetlana Alpers observes that "style, as engaged in the study of art, has always had a radically historical bias" (137). That is to say, the concept of style has traditionally been an instrument of art historians used to classify and chronologize their object of study. With this in mind, Seth's relationship to the past already begins to come more into focus: part of the reason his period evocations are so compelling is that he is using style as a historicizing discourse, as art historians do, but in a manner that is at once nonspecific and almost overdetermined. By "nonspecific" I mean the ambiguity of his style—it evokes the past, but not any particular past, a past that exists only on the surface of his page. By "overdetermined" I mean the indiscriminateness of his style—it is applied uniformly to every part of a narrative, regardless of the actual year in which the story takes place.

Alpers's is one of the less fastidious essays in *The Concept of Style*, which is a dense and wide-ranging anthology full of careful terminological distinctions and schematic proposals that are often at odds with each other. Can all these schemas really be equally useful? Ultimately, the most intricate theories seem to collapse under the weight of their various taxonomies, typologies, and neologisms; less prescriptive contributions fare better. For instance, Kendall L. Walton asks, "Are styles attributes of objects, or of actions?" (72). She suggests that the two are intimately connected, but favors the latter. Her approach takes into account the way in which a work is made, "the act of creating it," and draws a sharp distinction between art objects and natural objects (for instance, sunsets) (73–74). This understanding of style as the product of an artist's process, constituted by actions, dovetails with one of Sontag's formulations: "If art is the supreme game which the will plays with itself, 'style' consists of the set of rules by which this game is played" (*Against Interpretation* 33).

Simon Grennan sees Seth's work in terms of such representational constraints or rules, which he claims may be summarized as "*nothing un–North American, nothing post-1959*" (296, emphasis in original). Arguing for an alternative approach to comics narratology, Grennan uses *Clyde Fans* to highlight the relation between what Émile Benveniste refers to as *histoire*, "what is told," and *discours*, "the situation in which enunciation is made" (Grennan 296). He persuasively suggests that Seth "uses a history of specific past forms of expression to self-consciously form his own" and that the reader's experience "parallels this adoption of past forms" (300). Within this framework, however, Seth's style is understood as the product of an appropriated *discours*: "We see Seth's attempts to act within constraint, by adopting a complex *discours* other than his own, whilst simultaneously recognizing that he is Seth, drawing in the twenty-first century and not a comic strip artist of the 1940s" (313). Why Grennan considers the *discours* of Seth's work to be "other than his own" is not entirely clear; arguably, both the *histoire* and *discours* are uniquely his own, and uniquely contemporary, even if significantly informed by "past forms of expression." Although he recognizes the complexity of Seth's style, Grennan still fixes it to a particular past: "North America, pre-1959" (299). In this way, Grennan's sophisticated narratological approach may actually risk obscuring one of the fundamental aspects of Seth's style: that it reflects a longing for a past that never existed.

Especially in Seth's work, this kind of longing is always haunted by the specter of authenticity. When deployed as a critical term, "authenticity" often refers to a specifically modern literary articulation, a site where aesthetics and ethics tellingly overlap. Sontag asserts that the distinction between aesthetics and ethics is "a trap," the result of a Western misapprehension (*Against Interpretation* 23). Indeed, the inseparability of ethics and aesthetics seems to find its epitome in a stylistic quality like authenticity, which pretends to be not stylistic but natural, artless. What is at stake in a style that wants to efface itself? And what continues to make authenticity such an urgent concern in contemporary art and literature? "That the word has become part of the moral slang of our day," wrote Lionel Trilling in *Sincerity and Authenticity*, "points to our anxiety over the credibility of existence and of individual existences" (93). Seth's work reflects and engages with precisely this anxiety, which might be considered the kernel of his style, the most immediately apparent expression of which is an ambivalent nostalgia (what Svetlana Boym would call "reflective nostalgia").

Whether general or specific, reflective or restorative, nostalgia consistently entails a corresponding concern with what is natural and real, an inclination that becomes particularly visible in literature (and sometimes literally visible in comics). Nostalgic writers seem to strain toward a stable referent: in their texts, the past is "attached to other terms that make it a locus of authenticity" (Doane and Hodges 9). In this sense, Seth is not a nostalgic writer; he is too self-aware, constantly undercutting the credibility of nostalgic impulses. In *It's a Good Life, If You Don't Weaken*, Seth-as-protagonist explicitly voices anxiety about the material degradation he perceives in everyday life—"quality" becomes metonymically linked to authenticity, with the past as the locus of each—but he also second-guesses this nostalgic attitude (43). A more extreme instance of authorial disavowal is found in the satirical depiction of Jonah, Seth's hysterically nostalgic self-caricature from *Wimbledon Green*, who takes his longing for the past to absurd ends.

And yet, at a glance, a casual reader might still fairly remark that Seth's work looks "nostalgic" or "old-fashioned," or even "handmade," because to a significant extent it is the evident craft of his books that suggests something from a previous era. As much as Seth may discursively disavow nostalgia, the appearance of his work continues to make a case for the pleasures of longing and the value of an outmoded brand of authenticity. The ethical/aesthetic stakes of authenticity can seem implicit (if not explicit) in every brushstroke and background detail. Moreover, the very surface of the page seems charged with the tension between this authentic imperative and the artifice used to conjure it. Pervasive as it is, the appearance of authenticity is not always at the vanguard of the reader's attention, and the experienced reader can choose to "tune in" to it (or tune it out) to varying degrees. Nevertheless, this appearance, which is such a large part of Seth's style, is in many ways unavoidable.

The phrase "the appearance of authenticity" contains a number of closely related meanings, the most obvious being, plainly, "what authenticity looks like." In Seth's work, as noted above, authenticity often looks "handmade" or "nostalgic": muted colors, handwritten lettering, panel frames that are not perfectly straight, a drawing style that evokes the history of cartooning (more on this below). A second principal meaning might be paraphrased as "how authenticity discloses itself to the reader," the manner in which authenticity actively *becomes* legible. In comics, as in painting or sculpture, appearance is paradoxically a static becoming (or a network of static becomings) activated by the reader/viewer. This does not mean that the reader must be able to name the cartoonists who have influenced Seth's approach to the medium, or be intimately acquainted with the minutiae of comic book production. The visual literacy of the contemporary reader is sufficiently high to appreciate the tensions in Seth's work and be rewarded by his attention to detail.

Such a reader can immediately intuit, for instance, the difference between a mass-market superhero comic and Seth's work. It is not necessary to know that distribution of labor (into writer, artist, inker, letterer, etc.) is the norm for the mass market in order to appreciate the wager of authenticity made by the cartoonist working independently. To take a specific example: *It's a Good Life* operates within the genre of autobiography, one of the most familiar modes of expression in literary comics and likely the one most associated with authentic expression. As Bart Beaty observes in *Unpopular Culture*: "In the field of contemporary comic book production, autobiography holds a promise to elevate the legitimacy of both the medium and the artist" (144). A general sense of cultural context, even if only gleaned from peripheral exposure to comics, is all a reader needs to understand the tensions between art and pop culture that appear in an autobiographical comic.

The term "appearance" can also have an almost pejorative implication, as when it is set against "reality." In this sense, "the appearance of authenticity" may suggest a surface that is not credible or that seeks to conceal a decidedly inauthentic reality. Seth's work, in its ambivalent relation to authenticity, helps to dissolve this familiar hierarchy between appearance and reality. In *George Sprott*, for example, the credibility of the narration is constantly called into question. The narrator apologizes for gaps in information and, significantly, worries about conveying something "real" about George. The reality that does emerge is not entirely favorable: it gradually becomes apparent that George's entire career (television show, lecture series, his Institute of Polar Studies) is built around a handful of "expeditions" the actual cultural value of which is highly suspect.

However, this again is ambivalence expressed at the level of plot, and does not address the issues of authenticity and reliability that surround any other aspect of the narrative, namely its physical appearance. Seth's surface remains seemingly seamless—but does this necessarily mean that it has something to hide? Sontag may be useful here: "Even if one were to define style as the manner of our appearing"—a definition that suits the purposes of this chapter quite well—"this by no means necessarily entails an opposition between a style that one assumes and one's 'true' being. In fact, such a disjunction is extremely rare. In almost every case, our manner of appearing *is* our manner of being" (*Against Interpretation* 18). Under these circumstances, the critical aim should not be to peer "beyond" appearance, regarding it as a surface below which a more fundamental truth about the work lies hidden. Rather than assuming that appearance conceals or, at best, points toward meaning, it is necessary to recognize the potential for appearance in and of itself to contain meaning.

A great deal of meaning is contained in the surface of Seth's work, most notably its evocation of the early gag cartoons of the *New Yorker*—or, more specifically, the work of one of the *New Yorker*'s most renowned cartoonists: Peter Arno. In the glossary of *It's a Good Life*, Seth describes Arno as "possibly the *New Yorker*'s greatest stylist," and his sensibility has come to represent an entire era of magazine cartooning. The best scholarly introduction to Arno's work, and perhaps the best introduction to the cartoons of the *New Yorker*, is Iain Topliss's *The Comic Worlds of Peter Arno, William Steig, Charles Addams, and Saul Steinberg*. As the title suggests, the book is a study of four landmark American cartoonists and their relation to the *New Yorker*, which, Topliss contends, "might be described as the house organ of a key fraction of the American middle class" (4). Topliss ably balances explanations of both the context and content of the *New Yorker*'s cartoons, often demonstrating the inseparability of the two with careful analyses of individual gags. His approach is distinguished by attention to detail and an easy familiarity with the material, yielding a sturdy investigation that does not shy away from the significance of surfaces.

Topliss begins by situating the cartoon nearly at the center of the *New Yorker*'s distinctive style. "Cartoons have been a defining element in the *New Yorker* since Harold Ross founded it in 1925," Topliss argues, going on to say that "the cartoons, more than anything else in the early years of the magazine, set its tone, established its look, and offered anchorage for readers navigating the vast ocean of its text" (5). And more than any other cartoonist it was Arno, especially in these formative years, who exemplified the prevailing mood of the new magazine: "sophisticated, adult, and antisentimental" (21). Topliss looks closely at this by-now familiar attitude and finds that it is the product of conflicting impulses—to participate and to observe—which resolve themselves into the viewpoint delineated in Arno's work: "Disengaged intimacy, the hallmark of his humor, was the basis of the *New Yorker*'s famous sophistication" (22). In the cartoons of Peter Arno, Topliss traces the "emergence of a mood of rueful discontent with modern life" (15).

Seth reinterprets this mood in *It's a Good Life*, offering variations on the theme through his invented cartoonist Kalo, whose work is presented as contemporary with that of Arno.[1] Kalo is on the whole somewhat softer than Arno—lacking, perhaps, that insider's inclination to truly skewer his subject—but the similarities can be striking. In one of Arno's best-known cartoons, a long row of nearly indistinguishable Miss America contestants recedes into a vanishing point somewhere beyond the right edge of the panel. In the foreground, on the left side of the panel, are two men, likely contest judges, one of whom is saying: "Makes you kind of pleased to be an American, doesn't it?"

FIG 1.1 Seth, *It's a Good Life, If You Don't Weaken* (Montreal: Drawn and Quarterly, 1996), 169.

Compare this to a very similar Kalo panel from the collection at the back of *It's a Good Life* (fig. 1.1). Two stout, middle-aged, middle-class women stand face to face, offering the reader almost identical mirrored profiles. One of them says, "What a coincidence, I was Miss Oklahoma the year before you" (169).

The target of the gag in both cartoons is not just a certain kind of American homogeneity, but the superficial pride taken in a specifically sexualized homogeneity. The joke in both cases is illustrated by a pleasing repetition and similarity, which implicates the reader in the enjoyment and celebration of an idealized uniformity. In Kalo's far gentler cartoon, however, the lascivious male gaze is safely off panel and unvoiced, implicit rather than explicit. Nonetheless, Arno is a clear point of departure for the self-referential exploration of cartooning that Seth undertakes in *It's a Good Life*; Kalo allows Seth to experiment within the strict tonal and formal conventions of the single-panel gag, a cartooning practice that is in many ways very unlike the practice he has otherwise pursued in his books. Through the filter of metafiction, *It's a Good*

Life demonstrates that "rueful discontent" remains a benchmark for single-panel gag cartoons, a touchstone of authenticity for contemporary cartoonists. (Or, at least, for Seth; fellow Canadian cartoonist Chester Brown seems appreciative but not enthusiastic about old magazine cartoons [*It's a Good Life* 19].)

"In his best later work," Topliss writes, "Arno creates an alarmingly capacious comic world of disillusionment, failed purposes, and actuality's falling short of expectation" (24). The same might be said of much of Seth's work, not only in *It's a Good Life* but in his later books as well. Of course, where Arno compresses disillusionment into an ephemeral gag, Seth's capaciousness resides in allowing his characters' disappointments room to breathe in long-form narratives (see chapter 4). In Seth's work the reader finds thwarted expectations, but with consequences as opposed to punch lines. However, tempting as it is to suggest that Seth is heir to Arno, taking Arno's comic vision of modern discontent to its tragic conclusion, such a reading would likely overstate the similarity of the two cartoonists.

Seth's stories are not protracted Arno cartoons in which the humor has been turned inside out in an anxious effort to conceal the predecessor's influence. Rather, the influence is quite plainly visible, which is to say, visual. Seth's evident debt to Arno in creating Kalo reflects the broader importance of Arno in Seth's work. He explains:

> I can remember Arno being very influential for me for understanding how characters could be shapes, in a way. . . . He used the washes to make things solid, but he's really carving those figures out with a brush . . . that was something that really taught me how to approach drawing in a different way. Something I needed to learn at that point. (see page 216)

There is a definite family resemblance—not always reducible to specific details—between the drawing styles of Seth and Arno, and it is arguably more significant than any perceived correspondence in their temperaments. In his life and work, Arno epitomized a knowing dandyism, the particular energy and freedom of which is less apparent in Seth's drawing than is a reified visual trace of that Jazz Age esprit.

Flipping through *The Complete Cartoons of the New Yorker*,[2] it quickly becomes clear that the magazine accommodated a range of cartooning styles. (This is apparent even in the abbreviated spectrum that Topliss offers in his book, from the spotlit sensuality of Arno to the almost transparent linearity of Saul Steinberg.) To see the diverse work of a particular period juxtaposed is somewhat artificial—in the magazine, cartoons do not typically appear next to each other—but the anthology layout nevertheless provides an interesting sense of chronological context. Especially with Seth's work in mind, it is relatively easy to identify Arno amid a page of his contemporaries, set apart by (among other things) his theatrical lighting and a certain hard-to-quantify thickness and sureness of brushstroke. Seth puts it well when he says, simply, "Arno was pure modernity—bold lines, masterful compositions" (*IAGL* 180). In his own work, Seth seems to have domesticated these bold lines to some extent, perhaps deliberately, perhaps involuntarily. In his rare action-oriented sequences, in some of his people, and even in certain inanimate objects, there is a tendency toward this boldness—but it seems constantly held in reserve, never fully allowed to materialize.

"The line is always bold, confident, elegant, and stylish," Topliss says of Arno's work (34). (This last descriptor, "stylish," tellingly points to a fundamental elusiveness: What does it mean to describe someone's drawing style as stylish?) This list of adjectives could just as easily describe Seth's line, but with one significant addition: restrained. Particularly as his style matures, there is little that is splashy in Seth's line. At times, it seems almost tense in its restraint, the result of obvious labor and craft, full of carefully channeled energy. If Arno's authenticity is his boldness, Seth's is his restraint; Seth seems to make use of boldness as a counterpoint while remaining true to his more restrained inclinations. It may confuse matters to use the term "authenticity" in this way, although words like "essence" or "nature" are even more fraught and imprecise. At issue is the principal characteristic of a work, around which other characteristics seem to cohere, which is to say, *the structure of style*.

Seth offers a wonderfully practical explanation of the development and structure of style: "I think most drawing style is based on *how* you choose to simplify. And the stylizations you *build* out of those simplifications. Every cartoonist starts picking a series of noses they draw, for example. And they stylize that and a system develops" (see page 215, emphasis in original). Set side by side, it is the differences between Seth and Arno that are most apparent. Seth appears to have incorporated Arno's style at some deep level without copying his specific techniques. The difference is especially clear when a particular element is isolated from the whole—for instance, a nose. Ranging from elegantly aquiline to downright hawkish, Arno's noses are invariably sharp, whereas Seth's noses rarely, if ever, come to a point and certainly not in the same way that Arno's do.

Concretely identifiable resemblance is hard to locate—coherence nearly evaporates on close examination, as in a Seurat painting. The ghost of Arno remains, but it is in certain respects easier to *imagine* the stylistic similarities between his work and Seth's than to actually pick them out by sight. Topliss astutely observes that "Arno's drawings create their meaning first stylistically, in the way they are drawn, and only secondarily in their paraphrasable content (whether of drawing or caption)" (34). This is almost necessarily not the case with Seth's narratives, if only because he is not working within the single-panel format, in which the first impression is so paramount. Important as the first glance may be to the reader (especially the new reader) of Seth's work, it could not be said to really precede the content in its constitution of the work's meaning.

Although this last remark unapologetically distinguishes between form and content, it does so while still clinging to the critical orthodoxy that the two are not really separable. Both form and content contribute to meaning, and style emerges from an ongoing interaction between the two, mobilized by the attention of the reader. I have suggested that any reader is equipped to coordinate the interaction of form and content particular to the medium of comics, but who is Seth's *ideal* reader? Is it a style-literate comic book fan, attuned to the subtleties and history of the medium, who appreciates the array of techniques that Seth deploys? Arguably, Seth is not addressing himself to the segment of the middle class that Topliss identifies as the main audience for the *New Yorker*, but neither does he seek to exclude such an audience. It may be that Seth's books teach the reader how to read them, actively creating their audience; and perhaps this is the most credible sign of authorial authenticity.

The Polished Appearance

Seth holds up Robert Crumb as paragon of openness, to which he imagines future readers will respond: "Crumb's laying it all on the line and that works somehow for him, and I feel that that will continue to transmit as time goes on" (see page 214). By contrast, Seth describes himself as "uptight," lacking in precisely those qualities he admires in Crumb. "There's none of that freedom," he says, in his own work (see page 194). And yet, among cartoonists of his generation (which might fairly be labeled postpunk), Seth is by no means the most tightly controlled artist. Perhaps this is partly due to the lessons learned from Arno about how to carve out lively shapes with a brush. Describing Arno's line, Topliss says: "It has weight and presence and yet— when Arno is at his best—is never mechanical or dead" (34). The frontrunner for most mechanical contemporary cartoonist is Chris Ware, who has stated his deliberate intention to develop a cartooning style that is "cold and dead, like typography" (quoted in Juno 53); Adrian Tomine has also cultivated an extraordinarily neutral surface.

By contrast, Seth's surface could hardly be described as neutral. While it may be fairly seamless and restrained, it is sometimes too uncanny to fully recede into the background of the reader's awareness. Of his work, he admits: "It does have a mannered quality to it, and at its worst it becomes sort of fey in a way that I don't like" (see page 214). This may be another instance of Seth being his own harshest critic, but the observation is neither falsely modest nor imperceptive. This is not to say that his drawing is wooden or his compositions awkward, but the artifice of his craft is much in evidence. In terms of authenticity, this might be regarded as something of a double move: because it is not "natural" or effortless, artifice can seem to slide away from authenticity; at the same time, however, the evidence of craft and effort reveals the reality of the human hand that must work to create the polished appearance.

Seth's ability to draw "as Kalo" in a manner that is comparable to yet notably distinct from the rest of the drawing in *It's a Good Life* reveals not only his skill as a draftsman but also the fallacy behind the myth of "natural" or "authentic" style. As Seth observes:

> Artists are touchy about their drawing style. I've actually found that other cartoonists want to pretend that they didn't come up with it, that it just sort of happened by accident. I think cartoonists sort of look at it like it's a fashion statement or something. Picking a drawing style, developing a drawing style, is like wearing a fancy outfit, and they're a little ashamed that they've put that much effort into coming up with it. (see page 214)

As might be expected, Seth seems to be at his loosest, his least mannered, in his sketchbook, selections from which are collected in *Vernacular Drawings* and recent issues of *Palookaville*. This may help to account for the great appeal of *Wimbledon Green*, which offers the reader a winning balance of sketchbook looseness and narrative density. (Nowhere does Seth seem to resemble Arno more than in his sketchbook stories, *Wimbledon Green* and *The Great Northern Brotherhood of Canadian Cartoonists*.)

Seth reports that at the beginning of his cartooning career, when he was illustrating comics written and conceived by others, he still had much to learn about how to simplify his drawing: "I saw how many extraneous lines there were in every drawing and it was kind of a shock. There were little dots and fragments everywhere; I was just filling in space." This is in marked contrast to his drawing in *Palookaville*, even the very first issue, and especially his recent work, which is meticulous but decidedly unfussy. Seth has certainly succeeded in focusing his draftsmanship, now using, in his phrase, "only the absolutely necessary lines."

Of course, the notion of absolute necessity demands some attention. In all likelihood, this is an ideal toward which every mature cartoonist strives, though it will mean quite different things for different kinds of artists. For instance, it would be somewhat irrelevant to suggest that the obsessively drawn lines that make up Edward Gorey's densely textured interiors are unnecessary. Or, to take a less refined example, to dismiss Gary Panter's deceptively crude sketches as having extraneous lines. The question becomes: What conception of necessity has Seth developed for his work? Here it may be instructive to look at *Wimbledon Green*, ostensibly his most unpolished and least self-conscious book. Not only does this work feature a relaxed version of Seth's style, it also possesses that particular kind of economy that comes from working quickly and aiming for adequacy rather than perfection. Even this sketchbook story, however, is suffused with Seth's characteristic restraint, despite its energy and considerable looseness; as Matthew Screech says of another cartoonist's work, it is distinguished by "technical precision and tight graphic control," with nothing "arbitrary or left to chance" (27).

This is from Screech's discussion of the *ligne claire*, or "clear line," pioneered by *Tintin* creator George Remi, better known as Hergé. Seth identifies Hergé as one of "two big influences" (see page 190), the other being Arno; in some ways, Seth's drawing style might be considered a marriage of the two. Ann Miller, in her book *Reading Bande Dessinée*, describes the "clear line" as a technique that "eschews shading, gradation of colours and hatching, in favour of clear outlines, flat colours and geometrical precision," all of which contribute to a style that is not just appealingly clean but also, as a result, "implies narrative legibility" (18). She suggests that what makes the *ligne claire* so compelling is precisely this ideological corollary of its physical appearance, "the idea that the world is legible" (18).

For Seth, the legibility of the world is muddy at best, despite the clearness of his line. Indeed, this discrepancy is one of the driving tensions of his work, and one that sometimes works itself out on a purely visual plane. The most all-encompassing example of this may be Seth's muted palette, which is a crucial expression of his style. When *Tintin* first appeared in color, "Hergé selected fresh, pastel shades, sky blues, pale pinks and light greens, all of which conjured up an attractive, non-threatening and clean-looking world, where goodness triumphed" (Screech 28). Seth forgoes the vivid solidity of Hergé's colors in favor of subdued washes and subtle shading.

In fact, shading, in its ubiquity, may be the most inconspicuously insistent element in Seth's work, quietly setting the tone and giving the images added depth. This is particularly so in *It's a Good Life*, which is shaded with a single color—a delicate blue—that unifies the pages, offering the reader a reassuring,

FIG 1.2 Seth, *It's a Good Life, If You Don't Weaken* (Montreal: D&Q, 1996), 94.

consistent surface. (In this way it is not unlike Daniel Clowes's *Ghost World*, which is also shaded with an ever-present blue wash.) Everything depicted—a dream sequence, a card game in a diner, an incident from the past—has the same subdued appearance, becomes part of the same totality. Into this muted blue palette *Clyde Fans* introduces a range of grays, which further deepen the scenes and seem to reduce the distance between cartooning and illustration.

Related but in some ways quite distinct from Seth's shading is his depiction of shadows, which also highlight the tension between the simplicity of the drawing and its more illustrative tendencies. Here, "shadows" refer not to overlaid washes but to solid shapes rendered in the same bold black as Seth's line. Sometimes characters are subsumed within these solid black shadows, reduced to flattened profiles. This is not done for dramatic effect, to add suspense or unearned menace to the narrative, but as an environmental effect, so to speak, part of the mise-en-scène. Certain panels from *It's a Good Life* quite clearly demonstrate the distinction between shading and shadow, and the interaction of the two (fig. 1.2).

In *Clyde Fans*, this interaction is even more pronounced, particularly on the stairs and in the doorways of the Matchcard family home (fig. 1.3). As Simon Matchcard walks through the house, his face and shoulders frequently dip into the shadows, something of a signature technique for Seth (fig. 1.4). On the threshold of his office, framed by the entryway, Simon appears as a silhouetted bust, with a sliver of highlight to indicate an ear. Such deeply shadowed

FIG. 1.3 Seth, *Clyde Fans: Book 1* (Montreal: D&Q, 2004), 50.

images, with their suggestive, almost abstracted details, show Seth at his most gestural. He can also suggest the materials of his process: in the midst of an otherwise seamless surface, traces of the brush are occasionally visible, a technique used to add texture (fig. 1.5). Such techniques represent a break with the traditional *ligne claire* approach but are obviously not sloppy or careless; the rough edge of the brushstroke may be "left to chance," as Screech puts it, but it is by no means arbitrary.

Seth has always been quite deliberate, from the smallest detail to the overall design of a book. With *Wimbledon Green*, however, he reaches a new plateau: very much a book-object, it gives the stout impression of a collector's item, with rounded corners, a raised cover illustration and title lettering, and thick pages that evoke the materiality of a sketchbook (fig. 1.6). The sturdy cover is, appropriately, green, although the interior of the book is subtly autumnal, a limited but surprisingly rich palette of warm grays, faintly inflected with green, gold, and brown. There is the overall impression of yellowing newspaper, although some pages are cooler, devoid of color, offering a spectrum of pure grays that evoke black-and-white film or fresh newsprint. Rendered in Seth's distinctive strokes, these ink washes suggest an artifact from an early period of comic-book production. About his cartooning style in the book, Seth has little to say except that it is "sketchbook quality," insisting in his introduction that "the whole thing was drawn in the spirit of 'good enough'" (11). If

Style and the Appearance of Authenticity   33

FIG. 1.4 Seth, *Palookaville* 19 (Montreal: D&Q, 2008), 86.

FIG. 1.5 Seth, *Palookaville* 19 (Montreal: D&Q, 2008), 77.

Seth is to be taken at his word on this subject, then *Wimbledon Green* becomes all the more impressive an achievement, a true testament to his ability as a cartoonist. The book's apparently effortless layouts and illustrations—while occasionally more perfunctory than they might be in a polished work—are more than just readable. Many of the panels in the book are little more than one-inch-square thumbnail sketches, repetitive and single minded—and yet hardly insubstantial.

Seth's next book is a material triumph of a different sort: where *Wimbledon Green* is warm, compact, and "good enough," *George Sprott* is extremely polished, capacious, and often downright wintry. Part of its capacity can be attributed to its narrative structure, which (not unlike *Wimbledon Green*) comprises many disparate points of view, including that of an idiosyncratic narrator. However, "capacious" may not give an adequate impression of its sheer size—at 14¼ × 12 inches, the hardcover edition dwarfs most books and features full-page arctic tableaux that span nearly two feet. The imposing cover features simplified art deco detailing and a portrait of George. The

FIG. 1.6 Seth, *Wimbledon Green* (Montreal: D&Q, 2005), front cover.

modest subtitle, "A Picture Novella"—Seth's coinage, which appears on all his book-length, nonsketchbook narratives—here seems to ironically emphasize the outsize dimensions of the work. The back cover features the large raised logo of George's Institute of Polar Studies, complete with crest and solemn Latin motto. The book originated in a much different format, certain parts of it appearing serially—a page at a time—in the weekly *New York Times Magazine*. The version of the story serialized in the magazine is smaller not only in size but in scope as well, to such an extent that it seems in many ways incomplete when compared to the expanded book. (In addition to mute, two-page arctic spreads of icebergs and snowy landscapes, the full edition of *George Sprott* also contains unnarrated biographical interludes, photographs of cardboard models of Dominion City, and an inventive fold-out section. In many respects, the book is a tour de force, but in other ways it is so understated as to make such a phrase seem almost embarrassing.)

Palookaville, Seth's long-running comic book series, has also undergone a format change, but of a different and much more momentous kind. With

Palookaville 20, the series shifts from the traditional pamphlet-style comic books of numbers 1 through 19—typically sold only in alternative comics shops—to a more market-friendly, hardcover periodical that accommodates a range of material (sketchbook work, short articles, etc.) alongside the ongoing serialized story. The appearance of this story gradually evolves as Seth's style matures: by the time the Matchcard saga has begun to wind down, the appearance developed in earlier installments of *Clyde Fans* has become increasingly distilled, with bolder lines and high-contrast compositions. As ever, it is clean, reserved, and refined—but also full, with a certain cartoon sumptuousness. These qualities are on particular display in *Palookaville* 19 (discussed at length in subsequent chapters).

Seth's proficiency as a designer extends to page layout as well. In his work, as in all comics, graphic design is a significant code among other verbal and visual codes. As he astutely remarks, "comics are often compared to film or literature or a combination of the two, but I really think they're closer to poetry and graphic design" (see page 202–03).[3] Seth draws attention to an affinity among these forms that is based in economy and density of expression, as well as a shared sense of spatio-topia, to use Groensteen's terminology. Comics, Seth says, "are really about compression and about moving things around, like the way that you do when you design things. Moving images around, moving shapes around" (see page 203).

Gene Kannenberg Jr. discusses the innovative page designs of Chris Ware, which often press design elements to their narrative limit in the form of elaborate diagrams and inventive fusions of diverse visual registers. "For Ware," Kannenberg observes, "design thus becomes a crucial narrative element" (176). Ware's interventions at the level of graphic design are more apparently radical than those of most other cartoonists, more conspicuous—indeed, his genius is in bringing to the forefront of his work those potentialities of design inherent in any comics page. Seth's page design tends to be more low-key and, apparently, less premeditated. For the most part, Seth constructs his pages as a great many cartoonists do, using a network of rectangular panels of various sizes aligned into rows and columns. This sturdy structure accommodates a great range of variety and compositional possibilities.

According to Seth, he works more by instinct than intention when he begins to lay out the panels of a given sequence. His description of the process suggests that he is improvising on a latent grid, an as yet undetermined mental structure, which—in the act of drawing—is gradually actualized. In designing his pages, Seth notes that sometimes "there's an architecture to them that develops and you'll see that it needs to be a certain way" (see page 202). This approach is inductive rather than prescriptive but still allows for

Style and the Appearance of Authenticity 37

FIG. 1.7 Seth, *Wimbledon Green* (Montreal: D&Q, 2005), 18.

the development of carefully calculated sequences. Because the artist cannot fully visualize them in advance, comics sequences offer the reader a visible document of thinking on the page. For the cartoonist (even and especially a cartoonist like Ware), many conscious design ideas can surface only as the layout is being concretely rendered. As Seth says, "it just sort of happens as you're doodling it out" (see page 203).

The organization of page space *among* panels exists in tandem with another, equally significant element in comics: the organization of the fictive space *within* panels. Seth explains: "How you compose space within the panel is as big a part of your drawing style as what kind of faces you draw." He perceptively identifies the "deep space" of Chester Brown, the "blocky" genius of Ben Katchor, and the relative "picture box" flatness of Daniel Clowes. As much as line or shading, it is the creation of space that determines the feel of their work. "Feel" is more than just a metaphor here, because the representation of three-dimensional space, repeatedly perceived in panels from various angles, affords comics a strangely synesthetic quality; the sense of space shaped by a cartoonist is almost tactile.

What is the essential quality of Seth's spatial relations within the panel? It is surprisingly hard, in fact, to pin down—but perhaps it could be said that the reader will discern in his compositions a supple naturalism. Less stagy than Arno, but less naturalistic than Hergé, Seth is able to conjure a world that is unobtrusively realistic, even if it is rendered in a manner that is uniformly cartoonish. Seth's space has a softness, a malleability, but a definite presence: in earlier work, this presence feels lighter, the characters almost like paper cutouts in some panels. More recently, the space seems weightier, with a clay-like solidity. Seth's movement through this space, his point of view, is dynamic and flexible. Although it is not ostentatious in the manner of an artist like Jack Kirby (another favorite of Seth), it admits scenes of all kinds, for example: panels with a striking depth of field (fig. 1.5); the almost isometric views of urban and suburban environments that punctuate dream sequences (figs. 6.2, 7.5); and the countless talking heads of *Wimbledon Green* (fig. 1.7), a testimonial format that quickly takes on the feeling of a convention native to the medium (i.e., comic book characters in their natural milieu—the panel—speaking directly to the reader).

Style, according to Seth, is not accidental or inevitable but based on how an artist decides to simplify. Sontag makes clear the link between this process of simplification and the attention of the audience, which is focused by the artist: "Stylistic decisions, by focusing our attention on some things, are also a narrowing of our attention, a refusal to allow us to see others" (*Against

Interpretation 35). The most interesting works of art, Sontag maintains, are distinguished by "the intensity and authority and wisdom of that attention, however narrow its focus" (36). For comics—even literary, urbane comics—this focus can be quite narrow indeed, since simplification is the principal engine of the cartoon. "Every cartoonist," Topliss claims, "answers to some general category" (39). This general category, this space that the cartoonist constructs over time and comes to occupy, represents the distillation of an overall style to its most easily identified outlines. "Arno," Topliss says, "is the dandy." Hergé is the tidy adventurist. Clowes is the ironic anthropologist; Chris Ware is the cerebral technician.

What is Seth's general category? Could it be said that Seth is the ambivalent nostalgist? Not only is Seth openly skeptical of nostalgic impulses, but the artifice necessary to conjure his explorations of nostalgia and authenticity produces a certain tension on the page. In this chapter, I repeatedly describe the surface of Seth's work as "seamless"—but Seth himself uses a much different and potentially more fruitful word: mannered. It is possible that this mannered quality constitutes precisely the appearance of ambivalence that has been thus far obscured by the seamlessness of Seth's artifice.

The ultimate suggestion of this chapter is that Seth's work appears "mannered" because his style, in its role as a historicizing discourse, becomes a metadiscourse that comments on the concept of style itself. This claim signals a pause in the examination of Seth's style, which cannot fully conclude here; inclusive and elusive as it is, Seth's style will continue to be a subject of inquiry throughout the entirety of this investigation. However, for a final word on the relation between style and authenticity in Seth's work, there is likely no more apposite an observation than that of Oscar Wilde: "Truth is entirely and absolutely a matter of style" (788).

2

Return, Repetition, and Other Ambivalent Impulses

Seth's work is full of homecomings and homeward inclinations. This tendency repeatedly asserts itself over the course of his career, but is already fully formed in his earliest book-length stories: *It's a Good Life, If You Don't Weaken* is structured around several returns to several different homes; the Matchcard family home is the central space of *Clyde Fans*, to which the story always returns; when Wimbledon Green loses his memory, the reader discovers that he is most at home traveling on the open road, as he did in his youth. In one way or another, all of Seth's narratives are inflected with a nostalgia that brings to mind Svetlana Boym's description of the original seventeenth-century ailment: "nostalgia operated by an 'associationist magic,' by means of which all aspects of everyday life related to one single obsession" (4). However, although many of Seth's characters seem obsessed in this way, nostalgia is only one strand in a much larger network of impulses, which this chapter designates as "ambivalent"—following Freud's observation that obsessive neurosis is "derived from *ambivalent* impulses" (*Totem and Taboo* 35–36, emphasis in original).

Ambivalence, which Hayden White has called "the great discovery of Freud" ("Masterclass Lecture"), is in most cases not a self-evident concept. When Freud uses the term "ambivalence," he is typically making specific reference to "ambivalence in love-relationships." He lists it among the preconditions of melancholia (a close cousin to nostalgia)—for Freud, ambivalence is one of the principal features that distinguishes melancholia from ordinary mourning ("Mourning and Melancholia" 250–51). Although this investigation does not subscribe to psychoanalysis in any systematic way, it does find in Freud's writing a very rich vein of speculation that may be applied to the study of literature. This literary dimension is particularly strong in his essay

"The Uncanny," through which this chapter is ultimately able to propose some significant relations between ambivalent impulses.

Un-Disordering Ambivalence

Zygmunt Bauman opens *Modernity and Ambivalence* with this preliminary description: "Ambivalence, the possibility of assigning an object or an event to more than one category, is a language-specific disorder: a failure of the naming (segregating) function that language is meant to perform" (1). This definition may at first seem slightly too narrow to apply to comics, since Bauman uses the term "language" in the most familiar sense, to denote words, speech, and naming. The discussion of ambivalence undertaken in this chapter inclines toward a broader conception of language, such as that expressed by David Lodge when he states that "narrative is itself a kind of language that functions independently of specific verbal formulations" (4). However, Bauman's description of the naming function of language is not completely at odds with accounts that attempt to accommodate the nonverbal. His emphasis on segregating suggests that he is more concerned with what words *do* than what they *are* (a distinction that seems implicit in the Saussurean idea of the arbitrariness of signs). "To classify," Bauman says, "means to set apart, to segregate" (1). In this sense, it is possible to conceive of language as a system of segregations—a fairly permissive but also potentially fruitful understanding that extends beyond strictly verbal formulations.

Bauman goes on to say: "It is because of the anxiety that accompanies it and the indecision which follows that we experience ambivalence as a disorder." Is it possible to un-disorder ambivalence, to experience it without anxiety, but at the same time to retain something of its fundamental tension? Not, that is, to reorder or resolve ambivalence, but rather to preserve and even enjoy it in a sublimated form? In short: yes. One of the underlying claims of this chapter is that such sublimation is regularly achieved through narrative and literature, in which ambivalence expresses itself not as anxious disorder but as dramatic conflict and textual tension. There is a hint of Aristotelian catharsis in this notion, although that affinity does not take the analysis very far. This account of ambivalence in literature has more in common with the Freudian understanding that guides Francesco Orlando in *Obsolete Objects in the Literary Imagination*.

First published in 1993 and translated into English in 2006, Orlando's pioneering inquiry is an elaboration of what he refers to as a "general postulate, of Freudian derivation," which holds that literature is the imaginary site of a return of the repressed. In other words, it assumes that literature is either openly or secretly concessive, indulgent, partial, favorable, or complicit towards everything that encounters distancing, diffidence, repugnance, refusal, or condemnation outside the field of fiction. (5)

Sublimated ambivalence is not just comparable to but in fact directly related to the return of the repressed. "Constitutional ambivalence"—in Freudian terms, an ambivalent disposition that is not limited to a particular circumstance or love-relation—"belongs by its nature to the repressed" (Freud, "Mourning and Melancholia" 256–57). Ambivalence is often refused and condemned, diagnosed as disorder, but more than this it seems to govern the return of the repressed, which is to say, the fundamental inability of the repressed to remain so.

Originating in psychological literature, the terminology of ambivalence is only about a hundred years old. "Ambivalency," the *Oxford English Dictionary* notes, was first described as "a condition which gives to the same idea two contrary feeling-tones and invests the same thought simultaneously with both a positive and a negative character." In its emphasis on simultaneity, *ambivalency* provides a counterpart to Bauman's ambivalence, which is more concerned with language than with time. However, Bauman's apt pairing of modernity and ambivalence does call to mind the simultaneity of perspectives found in modernist art and literature—work that is contemporaneous with the flourishing of ambivalence as a recognized psychological condition. Etymology aside, this investigation does not find the definition of "ambivalency" particularly productive, and instead favors Linda Hutcheon's more recent account of ambivalence. In her engagement with modernism and postmodernism, Hutcheon cogently describes ambivalence as "the desire to be on both sides of any border, deriving energy from the continual crossing" (*Canadian Postmodern* 162). In this sense, ambivalence can be understood as a product of what Bauman calls "the master-opposition between the inside and the outside" (53).

This originary, subjectivity-forming tension between inside and outside significantly informs the structure of the comics page and the reader's perception of it. As Bauman compulsively points out: "The outside is what the inside is not" (53). To take this seemingly tautological statement to its conclusion: a boundary automatically springs up between inside and outside—there can be no division without a dividing line. The continual crossing of this line (which, in comics, takes a particularized form in the movement from panel to panel) is what makes ambivalence such a generative force.

Lodge is describing this generative capacity when he observes that "paradoxically, indeterminacy of meaning leads to an *increase* of meaning, because it demands more interpretative effort by the reader than does traditional narrative" (143, emphasis in original). This so-called paradox is ambivalence in action; as a general rule, this investigation names ambivalence as the logic of literature. Whether or not a narrative is "traditional"—Lodge uses the term as a measure of the interpretive burden placed on the reader—the fundamental ontology of the literary work of art remains the same. This is to say, literature always depends on the interpretation of the reader.

Marjorie Perloff offers a complementary account of indeterminacy in *The Poetics of Indeterminacy*. She draws a distinction between two "rival strains" of modernism, which she identifies as the symbolist or "High Modern" and the "Other Tradition" (33). This other modernist tradition includes poets like Gertrude Stein, William Carlos Williams, and Ezra Pound and is characterized by what Perloff calls "the mode of undecidability" (44).[1] Without attempting to clumsily map an account of poetry onto a discussion of comics, it may be useful to borrow Perloff's evocative concept and suggest that Seth's work sometimes operates within the mode of undecidability, a mode that entails a particular attitude toward images. As noted in the previous chapter, Seth observes that comics are "closer to poetry and graphic design" than to other forms. This surprising and perceptive pairing suggests that the poetry he has in mind is particularly modern (even modernist) in its approach to the image. In Perloff's description, undecidability challenges the reader to approach images on their own terms, as opposed to reading them for symbolic meanings. She quotes René Magritte on the inherent "mystery of the image" and the responses it evokes (Perloff 44). In Seth's work, dream sequences (some of which are discussed in the following section) avoid straightforward symbolism and provide perhaps the most obvious instances of the mode of undecidability.

Types of Ambiguity

Undecidability and indeterminacy are extremely useful terms, but the study of ambivalence in literature has been dominated by a far more familiar word: ambiguity. Although this chapter uses William Empson's *Seven Types of Ambiguity* mostly as a point of departure, it remains a significant touchstone. For Empson, ambiguity refers to "any verbal nuance, however slight, which gives room for alternative reactions to the same piece of language" (19). This description of *ambiguity* appears to align with Bauman's account of *ambivalence* as a disorder of language—but it would nevertheless be careless to conflate the terms. Although the two are very closely related, ambivalence and ambiguity are not quite interchangeable. How, then, do they relate? With regard to literature, perhaps the most precise statement would be that ambiguity arouses ambivalence in the reader.

Figuratively speaking, a literary work might be described as ambivalent; aspects of the work may appear to reveal some authorial ambivalence; within the world of the work, a character can behave in manner that seems to indicate ambivalence; but ultimately, a work cannot be ambivalent in and of itself. In her essay "Irony, Nostalgia, and the Postmodern," Hutcheon keenly observes that irony and nostalgia are not qualities that exist in objects, to be perceived, but rather are phenomena that observers "make happen" (chapter 7 contains a fuller discussion of this process). The same is true of ambivalence, which should be understood as something that happens rather than as a property of a work.

In a literary context, ambivalence is an impulse that I attribute to readers, a desire to make sense of perceived ambiguity, to master both sides of a border. Whether or not an author deliberately intends a literary detail to be ambiguous, the reader may read it as such. (One of the distinguishing features of the ontology of the literary work of art is the interweaving of countless spots of indeterminacy; in this way, the literary work is a fabric of potential ambiguity.) Nevertheless, Seth seems particularly adept at subtly fostering ambiguity and stoking the reader's ambivalence.

Each ambiguity constitutes an opening into which rushes the animating ambivalence of the reader. This is as true for a pun (a particularly distinct instance of Empson's third type of ambiguity) as it is for a complex arrangement of panels on a comics page. Needless to say, a comics page can easily accommodate both verbal and visual ambiguities, or even combine them in a meaningful way (this kind of combination sometimes appears in the foldout pages of *George Sprott*). No doubt, an exploration of the various types of ambiguity unique to comics could fill a book modeled after Empson's. This is not the place for a comprehensive new typology, but some suggestive types are examined below with examples from Seth's work.

If the panel is the base unit of the comics systems, then it is not surprising that one of the most common sources of ambiguity in comics is an ambiguous transition between panels. What Scott McCloud calls a non sequitur transition, "which offers no logical relationship between panels whatsoever" (72), is acutely ambiguous, but transitional ambiguity can occur in any of the transitions that he identifies in *Understanding Comics*. Every transition between panels holds the potential for ambiguity, but this is such a fundamental convention of the medium that it sometimes goes unnoticed. Throughout *George*

FIG. 2.1 Seth, *George Sprott: 1894–1975* (Montreal: Drawn and Quarterly, 2009), n.p.

Sprott, Seth massages conventions, quietly cultivating ambiguity, and the scenes often feel more fresh and immediate as a result. In one of the book's unnarrated sepia sequences, titled "July 10 1904," an unframed panel shows young George Sprott running in the empty space of the page; this image (the only unframed image on the page) is directly followed by one of Seth's heavy black text plates (fig. 2.1). It is soon revealed that this text is dialogue, the shouted taunt of another boy. The narrative pace and the context provided by the surrounding panels allow this moment to remain an unobtrusive part of an overall sequence, but this is in fact a rather ambiguous transition between atypical panels. The words—"Hey Smelly!"—appear abruptly at the end of a row of panels, followed at the beginning of the next row by an image of George braking on his heels. Even if only for a split second, the reader stops short along with the protagonist, caught off guard by a sudden verbal interruption. The row that this interruption completes seems to exemplify Seth's comparison of comics to poetry and graphic design, and the rhythmic progression of images inclines toward abstraction in a manner that could be described as modernist.

Rhythmic movement from panel to panel has a significant effect on the reader's perception of duration—how much time is represented within a panel—which is similarly loaded with potential ambiguity. Seth-as-protagonist spends much of *It's a Good Life* on the move, walking around one town or another, and to a great extent this steady walking pace informs the reader's sense of panel duration. The eye seems to follow Seth from panel to panel, even though it is the very movement of the eye that produces the apparent movement of the character across the page. As Thierry Groensteen observes,

"Each new panel hastens the story and, simultaneously, holds it back" (*System of Comics* 45). The reader responds to "this double maneuver of progression/retention" (45) and determines the cadence of the narrative, often unconsciously. When the protagonist is at rest, however, or absent entirely from the page (as in a sequence of *It's a Good Life* showing the changing seasons), the durational ambiguity of the panels increases considerably. With fewer rhythmic cues, the reader must decide how long to look at each panel. Both transitional and durational ambiguities are particular varieties of a more general type of ambiguity, unique to comics, which might be identified as spatio-topical ambiguities (following Groensteen's conception of "the spatio-topical system" of comics).

Another general type is diegetic ambiguity, in which the narrative implications of a convention of the medium are left open to interpretation. Seth's deployment of the speech bubble provides some specific examples. For instance, what is the status of speech issuing from a character who is alone in a scene? In the first part of *Clyde Fans*, Abe Matchcard seems to address the reader directly, but this could conceivably be read as a depiction of Abe talking to himself, thinking aloud. The speech bubbles in this sequence could also be understood as an engaging representation of Abe's purely interior life, externalized for the benefit of the reader (seventy pages of thought bubbles would strike a different tone entirely). The later parts of *Clyde Fans* contain even greater speech-related diegetic ambiguity, particularly those scenes in which Simon talks not only to himself but to inanimate objects—and they respond. What exactly is being represented when Simon's toys speak? Is Simon speaking aloud to himself, or is something else taking place? However the reader reads this ambiguity, Seth has eerily collapsed the distinction between Simon's interior and exterior worlds.

Simon is often portrayed as a bundle of ambivalent impulses—one evening brimming with optimism and determination, the next disgusted with himself for indulging in such feelings—and from moment to moment the outward manifestation of these impulses is hesitation and doubt. His uncertain, occasionally inexplicable conduct makes him one of Seth's most absorbing creations; there is ambivalence at the core of all of Seth's characters, but Simon is an extreme case, with an array of very conspicuous, eccentric behaviors. As the *Clyde Fans* story develops, Seth gradually overlays Simon's fairly typical reclusive tendencies with more specific traits, while at the same time portraying his idiosyncratic inner life with striking sequences that mingle dream, fantasy, and memory. This is one of Seth's great, understated achievements: in Simon Matchcard he has rendered an utterly convincing unconscious. There is much strangeness here, but none of it gives the impression

FIG. 2.2 Seth, *Palookaville* 17 (Montreal: D&Q, 2004), 25.

of being weird for weird's sake. Dream sequences are governed by a sturdy but elusive interior logic, conveyed with the same unsensational composure as the less remarkable aspects of Simon's life. His failure to relate normally to people is not made explicable but rather is compellingly contextualized. From behind his unassuming facade, Simon emerges as a singular figure, richer in some respects than Abe, inscrutable and a conduit for the uncanny.

One of Simon's more concrete behaviors is his rather obsessive, compulsive sketching habit, which is ambivalently productive in the sense of being prolific but creatively stagnant. Simon's odd drawings refract some of the reader's attention back onto the medium of comics, which often requires the cartoonist to repeatedly draw the same images over and over again. Simon's sketches are numerous (and numbered), but his subjects are few: trees, lighthouses, and beehives, each with their origin in Dominion City. The trees are based on those that Simon discovers at the end of *Clyde Fans: Book 1*; the lighthouse recalls a picture from Simon's room at the Dominion Arms; and the beehive is from a dream he had the night he spent there. The lighthouse and beehive in fact become linked fixtures of a recurring dream that is a maze of inside-outside relations, full of thresholds, windows, and doorways that open onto a version of Dominion (fig. 2.2). Although it is tempting to read Simon's sketching as an effort to make sense of the dream imagery, its purpose is ultimately unclear. In any case, the sketches constitute a return to Dominion and, in this sense, the actual act of sketching becomes as important to Simon as the repeated subject matter. (The reader is also able to observe the way that Simon's eccentricities bleed into each other—he sketches while arguing with his row of toys, beneath which are taped some of his drawings.)

The numbered sketches, drawn on the pages of a yellow legal pad, adorn the inside covers of *Palookaville* 16 (beehives) and 17 (lighthouses). These pages show not simply mindless repetition but rather ongoing variations on the forms (fig. 2.3). Through his sketches, Simon examines the images from multiple perspectives, experimenting and exhausting possibilities. Some sketches are more abstract than others, impenetrable cylinders or suggestive silhouettes. The beehive seems in some way to be a double of the lighthouse—both are conical forms that typically have an opening at the base and sometimes give off light. The possible significance of these shapes and their relation to each other remain obscure, operating, like Simon's dreams, within the mode of undecidability. Numbering is the only apparent organizing principle that Simon imposes, but it is enough to turn his compulsion into an ordered collection. (Simon's various collections are examined in more detail in chapter 5.)

George Sprott repeats himself in a different manner—he becomes a public figure—but his fame nevertheless derives almost entirely from return and

FIG. 2.3 Seth, *Palookaville* 17 (Montreal: D&Q, 2004), inside front cover.

repetition, the endless rehearsal of trips he made to the Canadian arctic. From a detached (and perhaps ungenerous) vantage point, George's long-running lecture series and television show seem to offer more than anything else a demonstration of redundancy. Seth, however, tells the story from a decidedly generous perspective: the distinctive narrator of *George Sprott* is not at all aloof or typically omniscient, recounting events with affection for the protagonist and unmistakable ambivalence with regard to the actual task of storytelling. As a result, the narration itself is occasionally redundant: on the page titled "A Fresh Start" (fig. 3.7), which contains mostly perfunctory biographical details and dates, the narrator refers to George's death in 1975—and then almost immediately mentions the date of his death again in a subsequent caption. Here Seth's playful approach provides an exaggerated illustration of the common observation that "redundancy is a principle of the vast majority of comics" (Groensteen, *System of Comics* 115).

Some of the characters "interviewed" in *George Sprott* are not as charitable as the narrator. A television colleague, who identifies himself as a good friend, warmly recalls that "George was a crashing bore." Far less warm is the damning testimony of Jimmie Freeze, a cartoonist who accompanied George on his first expedition in 1930.[2] His recollections of the trip are not fond, and he does not care to return to them by means of George's TV show. "He tried to bring me on air a few times, but I always brushed him off," Freeze says. "I had no desire to rehash all that hogwash."

Developing in the Direction of Ambivalence

Ambivalence features significantly in Seth's account of the creative process, especially his revealing description of

> that strange thing that happens when you're working which is that you start to develop an idea that this is really good, what you're working on, that it's really great, that it's the best thing you've ever done . . . and then you take the mood swing to where it's the worst. 'It's terrible, how can I even release this?' And I think that kind of combination between the two is important, to keep the work in balance. (see page 209)

Ambivalence toward one's work—which is not critical objectivity but rather the competition between two polarized subjective responses—becomes a defining part of building stories. However, in addition to this general, productive ambivalence, Seth also betrays a more focused ambivalence toward particular aspects of his work. Troubled by the possibility that over time his books will seem wanting in ways he can't foresee, he admits, "I'm already aware of certain elements in my own work that I can't control" (see page 214). One of these elements is what he refers to as a "mannered quality," which in the previous chapter was considered as a "double move" with regard to authenticity/artifice, the very appearance of ambivalence in Seth's work. Obviously, this investigation does not regard the mannered tendencies of Seth's work as defects; indeed, in some instances they may even be thought of as peculiar strengths, and certainly as points of interest.

For instance, *George Sprott*, despite the unpredictability of its narrator, has a stately quality that is attributable to more than just its sheer physical size. Like its title character, it exhibits a kind of grandeur that borders on grandiosity (in fact, the book often fares better than the man in this regard). The composite narrative proceeds at a measured pace, with lots of still intervals and page titles like "And So, Here We Are" and "Merrily We Roll Along." There is much to consider for the detail-oriented reader as well, moments in which the eccentricity of the narration recedes and what remains is a distilled, distinctive voice. After describing the gradual decline of a once successful restaurant, the Melody Grill, the narrator offers a closing speculation: "In a few years, you may notice that it has been boarded up. And even if you pause to consider it, you will be hard-pressed to pinpoint just when it passed from the living to the dead." There is something in this preemptive epitaph that is slightly ponderous but quite compelling, something perhaps in the deliberate phrasing and use of second-person narration. Moments like this demonstrate that the term "mannered" can describe not only the material appearance of Seth's work but other aspects of the storytelling as well.

To be clear, this is not to suggest that Seth's storytelling is overwhelmingly mannered, that this is the prevailing tone of his work. But at times there is an almost cumbersome, vaguely anachronistic quality that simultaneously captivates and holds the reader at a distance. This uncanny tension is also present in the cartooning shorthand of comics (e.g., onomatopoeia, action lines, sweat beads), although most of these techniques have become so familiar that their distancing effect seems much diminished. *George Sprott* is something of technical laboratory, in which Seth continually experiments with the conventions of the medium. The book's elaborate foldout section abandons naturalism entirely in favor of a somewhat modernist narrative approach in which the repetition of images and phrases creates a hypnotic approximation of the rhythms of memory. Seth's forays into more experimental territory offer a clearer view of the mannered quality of his work, which is less noticeable against the background of more straightforward sequences. (Both his experimental storytelling and his mannered storytelling might be contrasted with the naturalistic "realism" of works like Daniel Clowes's *Ghost World* or Adrian Tomine's *Shortcomings*.) The word "mannered" generally indicates some stylistic affectation, but Seth's remarks suggest that his mannerisms are involuntary, almost compulsive.

Compulsion, like its frequent companion obsession, is an ambivalent impulse often entangled with nostalgia in Seth's work. This chapter began with references to the nostalgic tendencies of his stories, and also invoked Boym's account of the obsessive logic of association by which nostalgia operates. Under the influence of its subject matter, this investigation itself proceeds by association to some extent, but a formalized, deliberate association that attempts to map a network of conceptual connections. Having marked out the parameters of ambivalence—its generative capacity, its distinction from ambiguity, its relation to the return of the repressed—it is now possible to revisit nostalgia with a fuller understanding of similar impulses. In the previous chapter, Seth's style was identified as ambivalently nostalgic, a mode of longing that was explored in the context of authenticity; what follows explores nostalgia by means of its unexpected neighbor, the uncanny (or *Das Unheimliche*, as Freud terms it).

Both nostalgia and the uncanny orbit the home (*Heim*), and both as well concern that which is familiar. Or, more specifically, that which is *heimlich*, ambivalently familiar and private (Freud, "The Uncanny" 222–23). Freud observes that "*heimlich* is a word the meaning of which develops in the direction of ambivalence, until finally it coincides with its opposite, *unheimlich*. *Unheimlich* is in some way or other a sub-species of *heimlich*" (226). Nostalgia is a similar subspecies, a longing for that which is *heimlich*. Nostalgia and the uncanny are each mobilized by a return, but where nostalgia mourns the impossibility of returning *to* the past (Boym), the uncanny comprises an unexpected return *of* the past (Freud). In both cases, the past is *heimlich*; like nostalgia, the uncanny "leads back to what is known of old and long familiar" (Freud, "The Uncanny" 220). In this way, the uncanny is never just strange or foreign, but rather "a peculiar commingling of the familiar and unfamiliar" (Royle 1). This combination of familiar and unfamiliar, this continual crossing of the boundary between the two, is a defining feature of the uncanny, but it does not constitute a full definition. One of the keys to Freud's account of the uncanny is his explanation that "everything is *unheimlich* that ought to have remained secret and hidden but has come to light" (225). Boym characterizes nostalgia in very similar terms when she notes that "*nostos* is connected to the Indo-European root *nes*, meaning return to light" (7). It would not seem to be an overstatement to suggest, as Susan Linville does, that the uncanny is "a double of nostalgia" (Linville 27).

In the same way that nostalgia exceeds its original medical diagnosis, reproducing itself and extending across history and geography, the uncanny "overflows psychoanalysis" (Royle 24). Even Freud's essay begins with an apologetic acknowledgment that the uncanny is not quite within the purview of a psychoanalyst (219). He classifies it as an aesthetic phenomenon, "undoubtedly related to what is frightening—to what arouses dread and horror" (219), to what in literature is often identified as Gothic. According to Orlando's general postulate, Gothic literature might be understood as a field of repressed impulses related to death. In his work on the genre, Robert Mighall argues that the Gothic is in a broader sense "about history and geography" (xiv), that it is "an attitude to the past and the present" (xxv). In these respects it is well within sight of nostalgia.

The generic category Gothic serves as a useful point of departure, and it is probably fair to classify *Clyde Fans* as "Southern Ontario Gothic" (more on

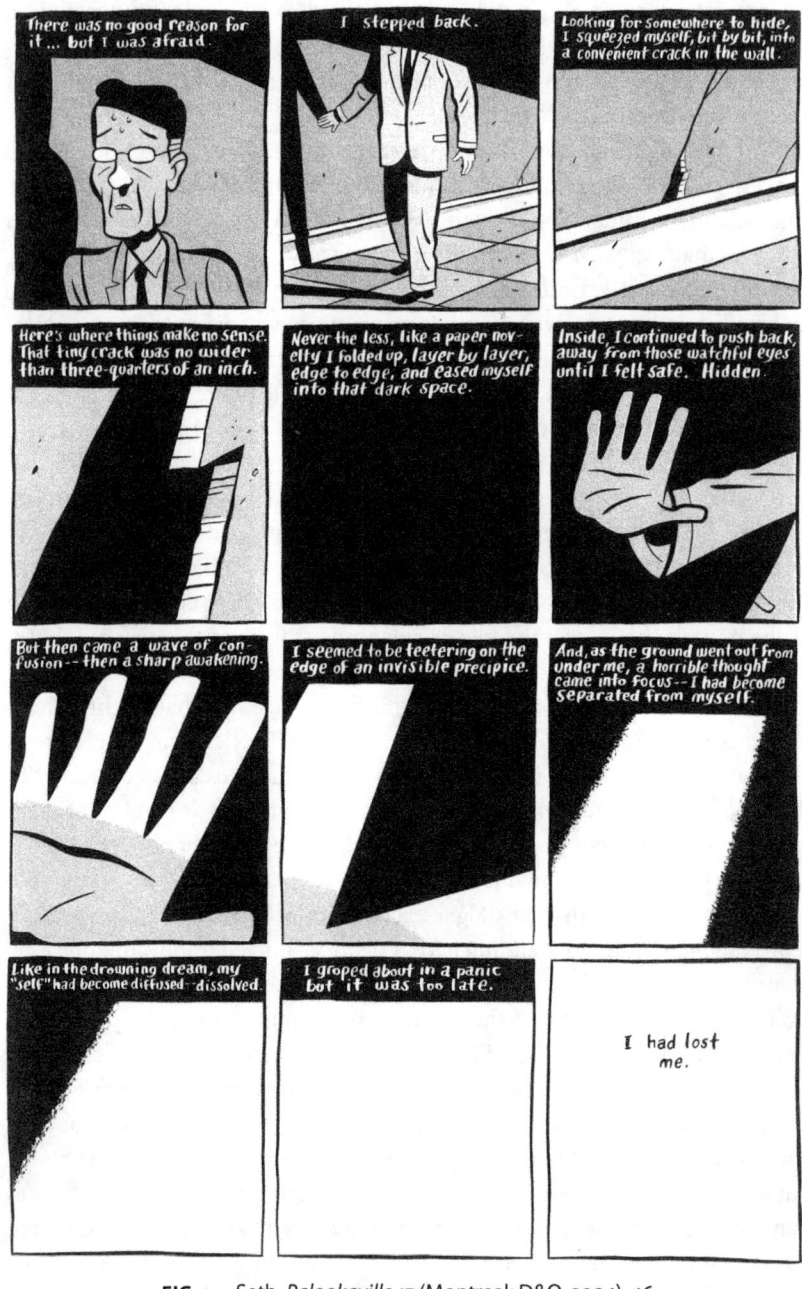

FIG. 2.4 Seth, *Palookaville* 17 (Montreal: D&Q, 2004), 46.

this in chapter 7, which engages explicitly with the national/regional dimensions of Seth's work). Simon Matchcard comes to personify the Gothic tendencies of *Clyde Fans*. A brief, extraordinary sequence at the end of *Palookaville* 17 (roughly the midpoint of part 3 of *Clyde Fans*) finds him descending into a paranoid nightmare that seems to grow exponentially stranger with each panel. There is an existential undercurrent to the scenario, something almost Kafkaesque, but that comparison does not quite convey the unique tone of the episode, in which Simon becomes convinced that he is being watched and hides in a crack in the wall (fig. 2.4). "Here's where things make no sense," Simon says. "That tiny crack was no wider than three-quarters of an inch. Nevertheless, like a paper novelty I folded up, layer by layer, edge to edge, and eased myself into that dark space" (*Palookaville* 17, 46). This episode is told from Simon's point of view and is not presented as a dream sequence or hallucination. The plainspoken, almost quaint language—"a convenient crack in the wall"—is perfectly pitched for mingling the everyday with creeping dread to achieve a positively uncanny effect. The very logic of the incident follows the ambivalent trajectory that Freud describes, as Simon seeks to make himself *heimlich*, concealed, out of sight. "Inside, I continued to push back, away from those watchful eyes until I felt safe. Hidden" (*PV* 17, 46). This is a rare incident; for the most part, even the most conspicuous expressions of Simon's ambivalence do not take such an overtly uncanny form.

A far more subtly ambiguous sequence appears at the very end of part 2 of *Clyde Fans*, just after Simon discovers his "enchanted place," a hilltop stand of trees (155–56). He touches one of the trees and then sits beneath it, his back against its trunk. What happens next is something of a puzzle: the last two panels of the page are visually very similar and yet at odds in their evocation of Simon's emotional state (fig. 2.5). In the penultimate panel, Simon looks content and relaxed, almost beatific, his head slightly raised, the thin line of his mouth tracing a mild, unforced smile. In the following, final panel, his head is bowed, his shoulders hunched, his mouth now a nervous squiggle (which is mirrored by his fluttering tie and a loose lock of hair on his forehead). Perhaps most significantly, his glasses have slipped down his nose to reveal that his eyes are closed. This panel raises a number of questions, both on its own and in relation to the preceding panel and the interceding gap between the two. How much time has passed between the two panels? What accounts for the shift in Simon's expression? Is he conscious in the final image, or has he slipped into an anxious sleep? What, ultimately, is Simon thinking? Some inscrutable change appears to have taken place between these two frozen moments, and it is left entirely to the reader to determine what has not

FIG. 2.5 Seth, *Clyde Fans: Book 1* (Montreal: D&Q, 2004), 156.

been shown. Most gaps between panels ask tacit questions that the reader answers instinctively, but this transition, emphasized by its position at the end of *Clyde Fans: Book 1*, urges a more attentive approach.

The inscription of borders and boundaries necessitated by the presence of panels on the comics page can be understood as a very particular, concrete, visual expression of Bauman's master-opposition between inside and outside. The comics reader continually shuttles between the inside and outside of the panel in an ambivalent maneuver that both advances and suspends the narrative. This generative ambivalence entails what may be the defining semiotic operation of comics, but it is nevertheless only one specific way in which the medium accommodates ambivalence. Like all literature, according to Orlando's general postulate, comics narratives house a return of the repressed and are consequently suffused with ambivalent impulses.

Such impulses are at the heart of a distinctly modern family of phenomena that includes nostalgia, which as Boym observes is a longing for the repetition of the unrepeatable, and the uncanny, in which the repressed returns in a form that is at once strange and familiar. Behind the repetitions and backward-looking preoccupations of Simon Matchcard, George Sprott, and other characters is an ambivalent impulse to return. Seth's own ambivalent impulses as an author also reveal themselves, especially in those moments when the storytelling takes a mannered turn. Like the other ambiguities that make up Seth's work, these mannered elements tend to have a mildly alienating effect that at once attracts and repels, ensnaring the reader in an ambivalent impulse. Whether unique to the medium of comics (transitional, durational, etc.) or observable across a range of literary forms (the mode of undecidability), ambiguity mobilizes the ambivalence of the reader, which in turn reciprocally animates the text.

3

Pictures at a Remove:
Seth's Drawn Photographs

> The metapicture is not a subgenre within the fine arts but a fundamental potentiality inherent in pictorial representation as such: it is the place where pictures reveal and "know" themselves, where they reflect on the intersections of visuality, language, and similitude, where they engage in speculation and theorizing on their own nature and history.
> —W. J. T. Mitchell, *Picture Theory*

To begin, a metapicture from the history of photography: a framed picture, which hangs unassumingly in the center of Louis Daguerre's early photograph *Still Life (Interior of a Cabinet of Curiosities)*. The picture is too small to clearly make out—although a figure is visible—and the top of its beveled frame is obscured by the hazy edge of the daguerreotype. The lower left corner of the frame meets the rounded contour of a wicker-wrapped flask, also suspended and taking up a central position, serving as a counterpoint to the rectangular picture. Arrayed below is a collection of plaster casts, one of which—a bas relief panel angled against a wall—has its own built-in frame. The objects, presumably arranged by Daguerre, draw the eye around the cramped cabinet in several passes, from one image to another. In this way, one of the oldest surviving photographs (circa 1837) offers the viewer a series of contiguous, copresent representations, the largest and most prominent of which are isolated by frames and panels.

Photographs of pictures—of paintings, drawings, illustrations—remain extremely familiar to readers in any number of contexts (newspapers, magazines, websites, textbooks, advertisements, etc.). The inverse, which is to say nonphotographic representations of photography, is far less common. A photograph of a picture is rarely even acknowledged as such; in many cases, it is simply considered a "reproduction" of the original. A drawn photograph, however, is first and foremost a drawing.

Photography is still commonly regarded as objective, mechanical, scientific, democratic, and on the whole quite public and accessible—in other words, the ideal medium of history. Cartooning, by this imperfect logic, can seem subjective, manual, intuitive, insular, and, overall, comparatively private—with regard to the past, much more a medium of memory. Of course, in practice, photographs pervade private and domestic spaces and have always functioned as souvenirs and mementos. By the same token, although comics do not quite constitute a truly popular culture (in the same way as, for instance, television), they are hardly exclusive and by no means exclusively used to tell personal stories. Nonetheless, notions of photographic objectivity and cartoon subjectivity persist. Nancy Pedri summarizes in this way: "The distinction between photography and painting as theorized along the axis of reference, where photography is unmediated and painting is authored, has been extended to cartooning." Pedri notes that, according to this distinction, the cartoon "cannot be further removed from the photographic image." Seth's drawn photographs exploit this perceived difference between the two modes, allowing the ambivalence of the reader to animate them.

This ambivalence envelops the ambivalence that photography on its own arouses in the viewer (but does not strictly compound it, as in the case of a photo of a photo). The inherent indeterminacy of the photographic image is rooted in its relationship to the past, which in certain respects corresponds to the relationship of Seth's comics to the past.[1] This chapter reviews some considered observations about photography in an effort to illuminate these similarities. As ever, Susan Sontag's remarks—despite their occasionally vexing aphoristic quality—ring too true to be ignored. Although certainly not an infallible sourcebook, *On Photography* does serve as a useful point of reference. For instance, Sontag writes, "photographs actively promote nostalgia. Photography is an elegiac art, a twilight art" (15). As John Tagg notes, such statements are "neither supported historically nor developed theoretically" (204), but they are nevertheless suggestive and may be productively aligned with the observations of other critics. Sontag's identification of photography as a nostalgic medium is bolstered by Siegfried Kracauer's comparable reflections on Proust and "the possible role of melancholy in photographic vision" (Kracauer 16). One of the broad concerns of this investigation is the role of melancholy in Seth's cartoon vision of the world, a twilight quality that is particularly apparent in his drawn photographs.

Framing Different Immobilities

Seth's drawn photographs are patent meta-images, representations of representations. They give the impression of being twice mediated, and in rare instances this is actually the case (as in the yearbook sketch from *Palookaville* 20 and the drawing of the snapshot of "Kalo" in *It's a Good Life*, discussed below). Many of these drawings, however, presumably have no photographic referent, and yet they carry on representing nonetheless—what is it that they mediate? C. S. Peirce's semiotic typology (index, icon, symbol) still proves useful in attempting to untangle such representational knots. Christian Metz notes that "Peirce considered photography as an index *and* an icon" (82). In Peircian terms, the cartoon operates principally in iconic and symbolic modes. A cartoon rendering of a photograph may be read as a photographic index of the fictional world—it *symbolically* and *iconically* represents an *indexical* perspective.

Sontag draws attention to some of the distinguishing features of this photographic perspective: "The camera makes reality atomic, manageable, and opaque. It is a view of the world that denies interconnectedness, continuity, but which confers on each moment the character of a mystery" (*On Photography* 23). In many of these respects, the photograph is fundamentally different from the comics panel, which exists in a network and depends on interconnectedness and continuity for much of its legibility. Each panel remains somewhat opaque by virtue of its relative separateness—the typical comics page is atomized—but the panel's co-operation with adjacent panels lends the images a narrative transparency, because the reader must consolidate them to generate meaning. Here, film may provide a helpful point of comparison: cinematic images are so automatically consolidated for the viewer as to be totally transparent; there is no need for cinematic frames to be adjacent in space because the sequence of images is so rapidly adjacent in time.

These observations almost necessarily lead the discussion toward the issue of duration, which may aid in the comparison of media because each medium has a distinct relation to time and temporal perception. Between photography and film, Metz addresses a fundamental difference in

> the spatio-temporal size of the *lexis*, according to that term's definition by the Danish semiotician Louis Hjelmslev. The lexis is the socialized unit of reading, of reception: in sculpture, the statue; in music, the "piece." Obviously the photographic lexis, a silent rectangle of paper, is much smaller than the cinematic lexis. (81)

In comics, as in traditional literature, the lexis is the book, or for shorter works a certain number of pages. Metz goes on to explain that "the photographic lexis has no fixed duration (= temporal size): it depends, rather, on the spectator, who is the master of the look, whereas the timing of the cinematic lexis is determined in advance by the filmmaker" (81). Like the photograph, the comics panel has no fixed duration; however, the story within which the panel operates has a duration that is both guided by the author and mobilized by the reader (who is in this context the "master of the look"). In these durational terms, if in no other terms, it may be fair to situate comics somewhere between photography and cinema.

The frame plays a very significant role in the determination of these lexes, especially in photography, where it essentially constitutes the entirety of the lexis: not only does the photographic frame instantly establish spatial parameters, it is also the symbol of the photographic image's temporal isolation. For the comics panel, the frame similarly serves "to enclose a fragment of space-time belonging to the diegesis" (Groensteen, *System of Comics* 40); the panel, however, is rarely a self-sufficient totality. The standard photograph pictures a discrete moment and as such suggests the moments not pictured, somewhere beyond the frame. Metz compares photography and film in this regard, and suggests that the cinematic "off-frame space is étoffé, let us say 'substantial,' whereas the photographic off-frame space is 'subtle.' In film there is a plurality of successive frames . . . so that a person or an object which is off-frame may appear inside the frame the moment after, then disappear again, and so on" (86).

In comics, "frames" are not successive but rather consecutive, adjacent in space. For the purpose of narrative progression, they are also typically arranged in a sequence that approximates the passage of time—but it is the copresence of images that defines the comics page. For the reader, this means that a person or object may appear in several places at once, or even doubled, side by side in adjacent panels. In comics, there is no photographic or cinematic "off-frame" space, because this space is usually swarming with other panels (this is of course not the case for the single-panel gag). The off-frame space—or, rather, off-panel space—is the gutter between panels, which accommodates (some might say demands) readerly interpolation.

About framing in photography, Sontag says that "the point is precisely to see the whole by means of a part—an arresting detail, a striking way of cropping" (*On Photography* 170). On the comics page, by contrast, the whole is seen by means of many different parts, an array of arresting details. Comics share with film what Metz calls "the plurality of images" (83), a plurality that implies the passage of time. At one point, he imagines a hypothetical film in which each shot is a still image, a film composed of "successive and different immobilities"—this phrase might be adapted to describe the comics page as a network of sequential and simultaneous immobilities, sometimes different, sometimes quite similar.

Immobility is the quality that comics and photography have most in common: both offer static images to the reader (most critics insist that photographs are not simply viewed but read). The stillness of the image appears more pronounced in photography than in comics, even and especially in blurry "action" shots that indicate objects in motion, primarily because of the photograph's uniquely mechanical, vestigial relation to what it represents. The photographic image is frozen in time—"a neat slice of time," as Sontag puts it (*On Photography* 17)—in a way that has no real parallel in other media. In comics, the temporal interval of an image is never so tidy and definite as it is in a photograph, even a long-exposure photograph of unknown duration. Frozen, isolated from the flow of time, the photograph is always, as a result, invoking time more insistently than other image-based media. "Precisely by slicing out this moment and freezing it," Sontag says, "all photographs testify to time's relentless melt" (15).

The stillness epitomized by the photograph is characteristic of many contemporary literary comics (which to some extent are reacting against action-oriented comics). Photography lingers in the background of Seth's comics, fortifying the stillness of his pages, occasionally coming to the foreground in moments that emphasize the affinity between the two media but at the same time muddle the reader's perception. The first part of *Clyde Fans* ends with six panels that alternate between Abe and a drawn photograph of Simon (fig. 3.1). It is a simple but dense sequence that plays various kinds of stillness off each other. Just as stillness is a notable feature of Seth's drawing, here it becomes clear that it is also a significant component of his storytelling. As part of this complex of narrative and visual stillnesses, the sequence also invokes *motion* pictures: there is the sense of a cinematic "zooming in" until the portrait of Simon fills the last panel, and this magnification is "intercut" with a "shot" of Abe sitting. Although this sequence strongly suggests film, it highlights an absence of motion and could only be achieved on a comics page.

In the opening pages of part 2 of *Clyde Fans*, the reader encounters a panel that is very similar to the drawn photo that closes part 1: a frontal view of Simon on a train, reading in his seat. By all accounts, the two panels are almost identically rendered, but through sheer force of context, and subtle differences in lighting and posture, the drawn photograph presents itself as especially static. In the sequence described above, the drawn photograph of Simon has already appeared twice on the page, with increasing prominence,

FIG. 3.1 Seth, *Clyde Fans: Book 1* (Montreal: Drawn and Quarterly, 2004), 77.

reinforcing its stillness, before it fills its own panel completely. By contrast, the image of Simon reading appears in the center of its page, surrounded by panels that depict passing scenery outside the train as well as the train itself. Part of a symmetrical two-page spread, this central image of Simon mirrors a corresponding panel on the opposing page that shows him looking out the train window. The change between these mirror images of Simon (each emphasized in the center of their respective, opposing pages) gives the impression of movement and activity, however minimal.

Both the photograph and the panel are autonomous units, isolated by frames that are so similar they may be seamlessly superimposed. Even though the panel typically exists within a network of panels, it remains an isolated fragment of the narrative, just as the photograph appears as an isolated fragment of time. The relation between narrative and time may be more than just analogous: as Peter Wollen observes, with reference to photography, "it is impossible to extract our concept of time completely from the grasp of narrative" (77). In freezing time, photography necessarily fragments it and in this way affects its narrativization; a comics page offers a sequence of copresent narrative fragments that are understood by the reader in temporal terms. Seth's drawn photographs synthesize these complicated temporal relations in metapictures that silently invite the reader to consider the nature of visual mediation.

Absence and Pseudopresence

This silent invitation does not overtake the story. Even when the similarity between photographic image and comics panel is emphasized, the coherence of the represented world is not really compromised in any way. In fact, Seth's drawn photographs are as common and apparently neutral as any actual photos the reader might encounter in day-to-day life. Their appearance seems perfectly natural, shoring up the credibility of his characters' shared, documented histories. So it is not particularly jarring when an actual photograph appears in one of his books: the final page of *It's a Good Life, If You Don't Weaken*—just before Seth's author photo—features an actual snapshot of "Kalo." The reader has already seen a version of this picture, drawn by Seth, earlier in the book. No doubt this snapshot went a long way toward encouraging early readers to believe that the story was true, made up of events actually experienced by Seth. "Since its inception," Pedri notes, "the photographic medium is considered to be closely associated with the real through the referent." The photograph of the man labeled "Kalo" is not real in the way that a

FIG. 3.2 Seth, *Palookaville* 20 (Montreal: D&Q, 2010), 10.

credulous reader might suppose, because Kalo is of course a fabrication, but it is still a real photograph, an undeniable fragment of the past repurposed by Seth to substantiate a narrative.

Sontag asserts that "a photograph is not only an image (as a painting is an image), an interpretation of the real; it is also a trace, something directly stencilled off the real, like a footprint or a death mask" (*On Photography* 154). Comics are by no means traces of the real in this sense, but at the same time

FIG. 3.3 Seth, *Palookaville* 20 (Montreal: D&Q, 2010), 30.

the panel is not "only" an image as a painting or drawing is, especially when read in sequence with other panels. In fact, even when a panel is alone on a page, a relatively isolated cartoon image, it does not behave like a painting or a drawing. Part 4 of *Clyde Fans* features two such full-page panels, framed only by the physical edge of the page.

The first offers a cross-section perspective of Abe Matchcard's office and the surrounding structure, and in this way the scene *is* visually framed by the spaces beyond the floor and ceiling, which mimic the linear grid of panels and gutters (fig. 3.2). There is the distinct suggestion in this image of a stage, with the peaked rafters standing in for a proscenium arch, or even an elaborate movie set, but in its immobility, its cartoon iconicity, and its playful understanding of the medium's conventions, it is quintessentially a comics page.

The same can be said of the second full-page image, even though it is in many ways the polar opposite of the transparent, framed cross-section view: an imposing picture of Clyde Matchcard as seen from behind (fig. 3.3). Monumental in more ways than one, it reveals almost nothing. Unlike the more typical paneled pages that precede it, and unlike the previous single-panel page, this page is closed, cryptic, opaque—and in this sense almost photographic. Speaking in terms of "shots" and "close-ups," Seth addresses the seemingly inevitable influence of the camera perspective on comics production:

> You can't avoid it. I think that that has great power. To be inside a character's head, to see that head blown up large, it implies that you're ... how do I put this? ... you get that sort of sensory experience of being the character's head. And that is something that can only be done by presenting a large, iconic image on the page. (see page 199)

The large panel showing the back of Clyde Matchcard's head is uniquely cartoonish, decidedly not one of Seth's drawn photographs, and yet at the same time it has a recognizably photographic resonance.

This particular resonance is quite aptly described by Sontag when she states that a photograph is "both a pseudo-presence and a token of absence" (*On Photography* 16), a definition that is as evocative as it is ambivalent. Do Seth's drawings of photographs rehabilitate the presence of the images, or amplify their implied absences? In fact, the two qualities are so closely related that it is effectively impossible to emphasize one and not the other. Sitting with Chester Brown at a deli counter in *It's a Good Life*, Seth's gaze wanders to a nearby collection of wedding photos. Three panels, which correspond to his point of view in the scene, drift from Chet's profile to increasingly detailed depictions of the assorted photographs. The reader may gloss quickly over this sequence, propelled by the dialogue toward the next part of the conversation, but the deliberate progression of panels encourages a slower, more attentive reading that considers the presence of the photographs and the absences they suggest.

In part 4 of *Clyde Fans*, Seth draws attention to photographs in an even more emphatic sequence—although it is not a sequence of panels in the usual sense. More of a photographic caesura, it features two Matchcard family

FIG. 3.4 Seth, *Palookaville* 20 (Montreal: D&Q, 2010), 17–18.

pictures, on facing pages, both of which bear crude alterations (fig. 3.4). In the first, a child stands facing the camera but looking up at the man behind him, who has been cut out of the photo at the shoulders so that the upper portion of the image is missing. The photograph on the opposing page is similarly arranged, with two children standing in front of a parental figure, whose head has been excised from the picture with a noose-like incision. This striking pair of images is part of the extended campaign of visual absence that surrounds Clyde Matchcard, epitomized by the full-page posterior portrait discussed above (fig. 3.3). Of course, neither photograph has a caption and there is no explicit indication that these are Matchcard family photos or that the removed figure is Clyde Matchcard. It is left to the reader to substantiate these hollowed-out traces of the past, an interpolation that occurs almost effortlessly as a result of the accumulated narrative context of *Clyde Fans*. In the same way that the comics reader fills the gaps between panels and imbues simplified cartoon drawings with life, so does the viewer (or reader) turn the photograph's absence into a pseudopresence.

Seth's drawn photographs make a double appeal, soliciting both kinds of readerly interpolation, although they do not all have an equal effect. The

FIG. 3.5 Seth, *Palookaville* 20 (Montreal: D&Q, 2010), 62.

inside covers of *Clyde Fans: Book 1* feature rows of drawn photographs, portraits with names beneath them in the standard yearbook format. This very familiar method of arranging images of people is conspicuously similar to the grid of the comics page, which more often than not comprises rows (strips) of panels and incorporates text to make the images more intelligible. Seth also uses yearbook pages as the basis for a marvelous sketchbook exercise included in *Palookaville* 20 (fig. 3.5). In comparison to the deliberately staid and uniform images that bookend *Clyde Fans: Book 1*, these sketchbook pages seem to thrum with life. In some ways, it is difficult to imagine more evocative images of people in any other medium: not quite caricatures, but certainly not straight illustrations, these cartoon portraits are uncanny in their ability to convey distinct personalities and suggest entire lives with a few deft brushstrokes. Although obviously drawn from photographs, these sketches seem to surpass the lifelike capacity of the mechanical medium even as they evoke it—there are few better examples in Seth's work of what his drawn photographs can communicate. Pedri's remarks about the drawings in a work of comics journalism, *Le Photographe*, could just as easily describe the effect of Seth's drawn photos: "The drawings trouble the security of the photographic image, producing a differentiated space of representation that opens up a more complex articulation of the way in which photography cannot fulfill its promise to make the 'real' or the 'true' visible." The real always remains somehow absent.

Abbreviating History

Le Photographe does not feature drawn photographs in the way that Seth's work does, but it does extensively combine cartooning and photography. Comics, in their fundamental heterogeneity and mode of organization, have a great capacity to accommodate signs. Nearly anything (photography, painting, long passages of text, etc.) may be admitted without compromising the category "comics." The surface of a photograph, however, can only admit so much before it seems to become something else (a photo collage, for instance). Victor Burgin maintains that photography draws on "a heterogeneous complex of codes" and that each specific photograph "signifies on the basis of a plurality of these codes, the number and type of which varies from one image to another" (131). This is undoubtedly true, but the photograph is still a closed and sleek totality, a classical body, whereas comics are by nature open and fragmented, grotesque bodies (this useful distinction is borrowed from Mary Russo).

FIG. 3.6 Seth, *Clyde Fans: Book 1* (Montreal: D&Q, 2004), 57.

A *collection* of photographs, however, takes on the qualities of a grotesque body and as noted above has clear structural similarities with a page of comics panels. Seth takes advantage of this resemblance when presenting a group of drawn photographs, which offers the reader an open and fragmented history. "Any collection of photographs," Sontag asserts, "is an exercise in Surrealist montage and the Surrealist abbreviation of history" (*On Photography* 68). Simon Matchcard's collection of novelty postcards exemplifies a domesticated surrealism: "folksy photographic manipulations," as Abe calls them, they feature farmers and fisherman dwarfed by outsize crops and catches (fig. 3.6). It may, however, be somewhat redundant to say "domesticated surrealism"— Sontag defines surrealism as "the art of generalizing the grotesque" (74). Perhaps the photo collections in Seth's work simply underline the unexpectedly domestic qualities of the grotesque body and the surreal point of view. Sontag goes on to say: "No activity is better equipped to exercise the Surrealist way of looking than photography, and eventually we look at all photographs surrealistically" (74).

The reader does not ultimately look at all comics panels surrealistically, but comics do certainly permit this type of reading. Metz refers to the "timelessness of photography," which he claims is "comparable to the timelessness of the unconscious and of memory" (83). Comics as well possess a certain amount of this timelessness, and Seth's work in particular is concerned with the memories and unconscious goings-on of its characters. The timelessness of photography is most apparent in Seth's work when he emphasizes it by making the frame of a panel congruent with that of a drawn photograph (fig. 3.1). In such instances, the reader has the sense of an invisible double frame, or rather a metaframe, which is not quite the same as a *visible* frame within in a frame. The inherent stillness of the panel is amplified by that of the drawn photo that occupies it entirely.

Both Seth's frame and the frame of the photograph tend to historicize whatever is pictured. Sontag claims that the photographer is engaged in

> the enterprise of antiquing reality, and photographs are instant antiques. The photograph offers a modern counterpart of that characteristically romantic architectural genre, the artificial ruin: the ruin which is created in order to deepen the historical character of a landscape, to make nature suggestive—suggestive of the past. (*On Photography* 80)

In this sense, Seth's comics relate to the past in much the same ways as photographs: like Sontag's photographer, Seth also seems to be in the process of "antiquing reality" by means of his drawing style, which similarly produces instant antiques.

"In all photographs," Metz notes, "we have this same act of cutting off a piece of space and time, of keeping it unchanged while the world around continues to change, of making a compromise between conservation and death" (85). This subtle observation has much in common with one of Sontag's far blunter, aphoristic statements: "All photographs are *memento mori*" (*On Photography* 15). Seth, meanwhile, maintains that "the whole process of cartooning is dealing with memory" (Taylor 15). It is impossible to proceed by axioms alone, but taken together these three related claims form the powerful suggestion that Seth's drawn photographs are densely, doubly mnemonic, cryptic reminders of reminders that, ultimately, do not point to any specific remembered experience. Rather, they are like death masks of the process of cartooning.

FIG. 3.7 Seth, *George Sprott: 1894–1975* (Montreal: D&Q, 2009), n.p.

The page in *George Sprott* titled "A Fresh Start" mimics a scrapbook, every panel a drawn photograph with visible (even dog-eared) borders, some of which overlap each other (fig. 3.7). Whereas most comics panels appear as ideal shapes, windows through which the reader sees the represented world of the narrative, these panels are emphatically objects—they look pasted onto the background, giving the entire page a rather photographic opacity. Although arranged in a roughly chronological sequence, the self-contained drawn photographs do not represent a sequential narrative, and the page has about it the photographic timelessness that Metz identifies as well as the attendant timelessness of memory. Precisely whose memory, however, is not clear: it is not George's memory—he has not assembled these photos—but neither does it seem to be the memory of another character, or even the narrator (who provides assorted biographical details in captions). It is a kind of atmospheric memory apparently untethered to any particular subjectivity. In this sense, it approaches history, but a history so germinal, domestic, and as yet opaque as to frustrate conventional notions of the historical. This scrapbook page leaves the reader somewhere between history and memory, and it is the reader's own interpolations between panels/photographs that determine the ultimate meaning of the images.

The reader must exercise even more autonomy, although of a slightly different sort, when perusing *George Sprott*'s remarkable foldout section, six large pages from which the narrator is entirely absent. Neither chronological nor even particularly sequential, this section is composed of drawn photographs mingled with clusters of panels that depict disjointed scenes from a first-person perspective—unmistakably George's memories. Notably, the recollections and the photographs are treated almost synonymously, and the connection between "the timelessness of the unconscious and of memory" is reinforced not only by the overall feeling of liminality that the pages engender but also by the specific moments they inscribe. For instance, many of the memory clusters begin or end with austere text plates that contain a single word, "WAKE" (or, occasionally, some similar variation, such as "WAKE UP, GEORGE").

Not surprisingly, death as well becomes a significant point of articulation between the photographs and memories, as in the case of the car accident that kills George's wife, which is depicted both as memory and as drawn police photograph. An odd cemetery snapshot of a Sprott family obelisk—both a mini-monument and a meta-memento—impresses a sense of mortal finality that seems impassively overdetermined. It is perhaps also worth noting that in these examples where death is made present, it is in relation to family, another important point of intersection between photography and memory.

Family photographs have always been a fixture of Seth's longer works, beginning with the Kalloway family album featured in *It's a Good Life, If You Don't Weaken*. As the book builds to its quiet climax, there is a brief pause in the home of Kalo's daughter, Susan, in which she and Seth exchange traces of her father's past: a silent panel shows Seth looking at photographs of Kalo in a family scrapbook while Susan sees her father's cartoons for the first time in the dossier that Seth has assembled (151). In *Clyde Fans*, family snapshots are joined by their corporate counterpart, the company photo. "Through photographs," Sontag writes, "each family constructs a portrait-chronicle of itself—a portable kit of images that bears witness to its connectedness" (*On Photography* 8). Company photographs appropriate precisely this domestic practice, staging portraits that are meant to show a familial cohesion. In the fourth part of *Clyde Fans*, these artifacts of manufactured togetherness ironically punctuate the conversation in which Abe Matchcard and his lawyer finalize the dissolution of Borealis Business Machines (*PV* 20, 13–16). (Between the family portrait and the company portrait is the club portrait: the most prominent drawn photograph in *Wimbledon Green* shows the founding members of the Coverloose Club, a group of comic book collectors from which Wimbledon Green was pointedly excluded.)

At the beginning of *George Sprott*, before the title page, a two-page spread features a large group portrait, "The Stars of CKCK, 1966"—and in the background of this drawn photograph, looming behind the assembled TV personalities, is a large, framed picture of the queen of England! This odd portrait within a portrait is full of ambivalences. Easy to overlook, once noticed it becomes a point of focus, seeming to radiate a benign equanimity that sets the tone for the larger image in which it appears. It at first seems out of place, something of a non sequitur, but is in fact evocatively period-specific and of course perfectly Canadian (royal imagery remains commonplace in Canada, for instance on currency). It is also strangely positioned, both in the drawn photograph (the top of its frame cropped off by the border) and on the physical page, or rather pages, almost perfectly bisected by the center seam of the book. Altogether it is a peculiar, dense image, both unassuming and regnant—and, unexpectedly, it has these qualities in common with a drawn photograph featured at the end of the book, a tattered snapshot of the Inuit woman George impregnated and promptly abandoned on one of his expeditions.

This neglected memento is hidden out of sight at the very back of *George Sprott*, preceded by the CKCK station sign-off, a sequence of familiar Canadian images (a silhouetted moose, an ice-breaking boat, a coastal lighthouse) that is afforded two full pages. This chapter has occasionally turned to film as a point of comparison, but in *George Sprott* it is television that provides the primary counterpoint to photography. "Television," Sontag writes, "is a stream of underselected images, each of which cancels its predecessor. Each still photograph is a privileged moment, turned into a slim object that one can keep and look at again" (*On Photography* 18). George's long-running TV show, *Northern Hi-Lights*, revisits the same familiar territory for more than twenty years, a profusion of images but hardly a progression: each is cancelled by a subsequent image that is more or less identical. In a sense, the show takes on the monolithic, unchanging, frozen qualities of the northern landscape to which it continually returns (the same qualities generally attributed to photography). George is not exactly a media visionary; he uses the medium of television more or less as he would still photography, as a means of repeatedly privileging long-past moments.

In the same way that George's show is not "good" television, Seth's drawn photographs are not examples of "good" photography. Kracauer identifies certain "affinities" of photography—qualities to which the medium seems formally inclined—for instance, an "affinity for unstaged reality" (18) and chance occurrences. "Random events," Kracauer says, "are the very meat of snapshots" (19). Like most family snapshots and company photos, Seth's drawn photographs do not take advantage of the medium, they are not of particular aesthetic interest, they do not capture surprising moments; in short, they are not art.[2] Indeed, as photographs they are almost invariably mundane, perfunctory, sterile—and yet this seems to be part of the reason that they are such superb, even pioneering, examples of drawn photography.

This is not to say that photographs and drawn photographs are essentially at odds. Here is another of Kracauer's photographic affinities, which holds for comics as well: "Photography tends to suggest endlessness . . . it precludes the notion of completeness" (19). This preclusion of completeness (Sontag uses the terms "absence" and "pseudo-presence") makes demands on the reader not at all unlike those made by comics, which are likewise "founded on reticence" (Groensteen, *System of Comics* 10). Seth's comics in particular seem to share with photography the affinity for melancholy ambivalence that Kracauer associates with Proust. In their remoteness from any real or represented past, Seth's drawn photographs abbreviate history in a way that provokes an ambivalent longing for that past.

Mitchell suggests that, ultimately, what the metapicture most calls into question is "the structure of 'inside and outside,' first- and second-order representation, on which the whole concept of 'meta' is based" (42). Mitchell's understanding of the concept of "meta" helps to illuminate the *inside-outside* structure of metafiction or autocritique, which chapter 7 addresses in more detail. As noted in the previous chapter, this ambivalent structure is also central to the reader's actualization of a fragmented narrative in the movement between the inside and outside of panels on the comics page.

A final maxim from Sontag: "To possess the world in the form of images is, precisely, to reexperience the unreality and remoteness of the real" (*On Photography* 164). Above all, it may be this alienated reapprehension of the real that Seth's drawn photographs, at such a distinct remove, most facilitate. These metapictures trade in ambivalences, apparently caught between (among other things) the subjective and objective, the atomized and continuous, the opaque and transparent, the classical and grotesque, the absent and present. At the seat of these tensions is an ambivalent relationship to the (historical) referent, inherent in the photographic perspective and amplified by Seth's drawing. In their extreme reticence—an uncommon synthesis of photographic and cartoon stillnesses—Seth's drawn photographs exemplify his method of compelling the reader to take a position between history and memory in order to make sense of images.

4

The Rhetoric of Failure

This chapter considers a wide range of fairly familiar failures—financial, interpersonal, narrative, material—but what is meant by the term "rhetoric"? For the most part, it is not used here in the most everyday sense of the word, which denotes contrived or persuasive speech (and which implies the possibility of more transparent or neutral language that is free of rhetoric). As Jennifer Richards writes in her compact survey of the subject, "language is essentially and inescapably rhetorical" (11). There is little contemporary resistance to this observation—that "rhetoric permeates all language" (11), that language is inherently figurative no matter how plain and seemingly unadorned—but can this insight be extended to other kinds of communication? For instance, there is a tradition of allegory in painting: does this bluntly metaphorical mode of representation constitute a wrenching of the visual into the realm of language, or does it indicate a rhetorical potential in even those forms that do not explicitly contain words? Perhaps every interaction between artist and audience is invested with the sort of rhetorical significance most easily discerned in speech. It might even be argued that, in nonrepresentational art, abstraction attempts to free the work from precisely this burden of language.

Before this line of inquiry leads too far afield, however, or haphazardly revisits material better explored by others,[1] it may be prudent to return the focus to comics. Although the medium is fundamentally visual, it is also decidedly narrative[2] and open to a range of familiar critical approaches rooted in the study of rhetoric. It is clear that even a lengthy sequence of "silent," wordless panels can be read for its rhetorical significance; what may be less immediately apparent is the rhetorical significance inherent in the form itself, the cartoon, apart from the connotations of the narrative (although still linked to them). Cartooning works in much the same way as metaphor, with an iconic element standing in for some part of the represented reality of the work, and the distance between the two provoking the reader to a new awareness of that reality. It may be the case that cartooning is a particularly figurative (i.e., not literal) or even rhetorically charged mode of drawing, in contrast to more realistic forms of draftsmanship. Of course, cartoonists frequently combine modes of representation that have varying degrees of realism. For example, Hergé is known for his naturalistic environments populated with relatively cartoonish characters (a combination of styles the rhetorical implications of which would certainly be worth investigating).

By comparison, Seth's cartooning is more or less of a piece: his environments and the people who move through them are all rendered in the same evocative style. His accomplished brush strokes and ink washes form an almost seamless appearance, matched by his storytelling, which tends toward the deliberate and the contemplative. But just below this palatable and unassuming surface lies the disorder of his characters' various failures and disappointments. This ironic contrast reflects the realization of a certain narrative balance: neither polished to the point of superficiality nor choked with bleak plot points, Seth's storytelling draws a quiet energy (and a certain slow-building momentum) from the tension among its various elements.

The Irony of Unfulfillment

Deliberately or not, Seth is working in a Chekhovian tradition of literary fiction. Radislav Lapushin's work on Chekhov helps to establish some parameters for what this specifically means: Lapushin argues that "the fundamental trait of Chekhov's poetics" is "inbetweenness" (3). This corresponds with the observations of Ruth Davies, who addresses some more particularized aspects of what Lapushin calls "a permanent dynamic vacillation" (3). Davies notes that among "the most pervasive elements in the writing of Chekhov is irony, especially the irony of unfulfillment" (328).

Seth's work is subsumed by the irony of unfulfillment; nearly every one of his characters deals with thwarted expectations.[3] This far-reaching disappointment is neither monotonous nor melodramatic but matter of fact, part of the texture of the stories. There does not seem to be any attempt to overwhelm, manipulate, or even necessarily move the reader to pity—only to provide a fuller understanding of the characters by illuminating the particular dimensions of their regret. Unfulfillment accrues organically, without much regard for any timetable of anticipated character development that the reader might have in mind. The rhythm of narrative dips and disappointments is not predictable, especially in a long story such as *Clyde Fans*, published in ongoing serial installments for over ten years. As the stories progress, they acquire an unforced depth and substance, a kind of naturalism that both offsets and plays off their distinctly unnaturalistic qualities (most notably Seth's iconic drawing style). As in much of Chekhov's work, it is the irony of unfulfillment that gives weight to events and makes the characters so recognizably lifelike. Seth's work is imbued with a sense of day-to-day authenticity that is anchored by its depiction of the way that little failures accumulate into substantial disappointments.

One of the more compact and linear examples of this accumulation can be observed in part 2 of *Clyde Fans*, which introduces the reader to Simon Matchcard through his ill-fated business trip to the town of Dominion. His first and last excursion as a sales representative for Clyde Fans begins on an optimistic, even redemptive note: he sees it as an opportunity to alter the course of his life and make up for decades of torpor. "I mustn't underestimate the importance of these next few days," Simon writes in his journal on his first night in Dominion. "Perhaps by exercising some self-will I can erase the fruitless years I've spent hiding" (*Clyde Fans* 94). It is also a chance to prove to his brother that he can overcome his agoraphobia and make a significant contribution to the family business beyond the walls of their home. "This small, sad effort," he writes, "is the largest thing I've done in more than a decade." It soon becomes clear, however, that Simon is in no way suited to the task of making cold calls: introverted, apprehensive, and apologetic, his natural instinct is to flee even the most vaguely confrontational situation. Case by case, Simon's failure to make a sale is understandable, a combination of his own inapt temperament and the airtight deflections offered by his unwilling customers. On his first two attempts, he is promptly dismissed—gently, by a man who insists that he has all the fans he needs, and then rather indignantly by a stubborn store owner who refuses to see salespeople on any day but Friday (*Clyde Fans* 101, 111). With each failed attempt, the circumstances seem more and more discouraging, and, as the failure mounts, resignation begins to set in. Eventually, Simon cannot even bring himself to speak to potential buyers, let alone offer a compelling sales pitch.

Years later, mulling over the details of the trip, he recalls having taken a book of poetry with him. "Poetry. No surprise I'm a failure. What sort of man brings poetry on a sales trip?" (*PV* 16, 16). The book in question is a Penguin edition of work by the nineteenth-century American writer Stephen Crane, known for his concentrated, often allegorical poems. On the night that he arrives in Dominion, Simon reads in his hotel room (*Clyde Fans* 96), and Seth offers the reader a fragment of one of Crane's untitled poems, reproduced below in full:

> A man saw a ball of gold in the sky;
> He climbed for it,
> And eventually he achieved it—
> It was clay.
>
> Now this is the strange part:
> When the man went to the earth
> And looked again,
> Lo, there was the ball of gold.
> Now this is the strange part:
> It was a ball of gold.
> Aye, by the heavens, it was a ball of gold. (Crane 37)

Crane's vivid yet ultimately ambiguous parable of striving and disappointment, perception and reality, is indeed the last thing one would expect a salesman to read in preparation for a long day of selling. Someone of Simon's temperament, however, might be reassured by this compact meditation on perspective and the way in which success seems sometimes to flicker into a semblance of its opposite.

Part of Seth's accomplishment in *Clyde Fans* is to dramatize—without any anticonsumerist interludes or overwrought Miller-esque dialogue—the desperation of sales, a desperation acutely felt by Simon and, by extension, the reader. We see Simon's failure through his eyes, from the inside out, and this small-scale view can be achingly clear because Simon understands so well his weaknesses but is still, ultimately, unable to overcome them. His pathos is not that of Willy Loman: it does not signify the failure of a national dream to come true, but is rather an entirely private, insular failure—in many ways, a failure to connect with anything as vast and communal as a national dream. Simon's failure should not be understood as the concluding point on a trajectory of disillusionment but as a circle of dread and self-doubt.

Not all failure is so fraught with centripetal anxiety. Toward the end of *It's a Good Life*, Seth tracks down Ken Tremblay, one of Kalo's closest friends. Ken admits at once that he doesn't know a great deal about John Kalloway's cartooning career, but Seth is eager to find out what he can and asks a number of questions, the most pointed of which concerns Kalloway's feelings about his decision to stop drawing professionally. In many ways, Ken's answer exemplifies the attitude toward unfulfillment that is particular to *It's a Good Life*: "Life isn't a series of good or bad choices. It's harder to steer it one way or the other than most people think" (fig. 4.1). This might be read as a kind of fatalism or resignation, but Kalo's apparent contentment in spite of his relative failure as

The Rhetoric of Failure 83

FIG. 4.1 Seth, *It's a Good Life, If You Don't Weaken* (Montreal: Drawn and Quarterly, 1996), 155.

FIG. 4.2 Seth, *George Sprott: 1894–1975* (Montreal: D&Q, 2009), n.p.

a cartoonist (especially as framed by the title of the book) makes it clear that Ken's sentiment is about fortitude in the face of disappointment. Much of Seth's work is characterized by this stoic disenchantment, what Davies identifies in Chekhov as "a gentle melancholy which is marked by peace as well as pain—the peace that comes from not expecting much from life. This is the twilight tone in Chekhov's writings" (330). (In Seth's books, this twilit quality is not limited to the writing: the brushwork, lettering, and color palette all contribute significantly to the overall tone of the work.)

Another of Davies's observations is that "Chekhov was not concerned with salvation, but he was acutely aware of frustration" (328); Seth as well seems intimately familiar with frustration. *It's a Good Life*, for instance, chronicles a search the only constant of which seems to be the searcher's frustration, while *Wimbledon Green* teems with tales of resentful collectors who were unable to secure a particular item. More than these somewhat superficial examples, however, there is the deeper frustration experienced by those characters who are jolted into a fresh awareness of their present circumstances—often by a fragment of their past—and are startled to find that their lives have not proceeded as they had expected. For George Sprott, it is the obituary of a girlfriend from his youth that provides the jolt: "George felt as if he had woken up from a long sleep. As if, in 1916, he had forgotten who he was ... and then, one day, unexpectedly remembered who he was and where he was supposed to be" (fig. 4.2).

Although *George Sprott* is as saturated with regret as any of Seth's works, the figure most mired in the rhetoric of failure is not the book's eponymous protagonist but rather its contrite narrator. The narrating voice of *George*

Sprott is unmistakably distinct from that of Seth-as-author, although it could be read as a parody of his characteristic modesty, familiar to readers from other works (for instance, his introduction to *Wimbledon Green*). Where Seth typically comes across as humble and serene, *George Sprott*'s narrator compulsively apologizes for lapses in omniscience, emphasizing the unreliability of the narration, which is characterized by false starts and amendments. The idiosyncratic prelude to the book—a somewhat dreamy rumination on time and narrative sequence, discussed in chapter 6—is presented as a demonstration of "how little your narrator really knows."

Soon after, on the page titled "A Fresh Start" comprising drawn photographs (fig. 3.7), the narrator seeks to begin again: "I must admit I have done a rather poor job of 'setting things up.'" The page is peppered with such remarks, which, along with sketchy biographical details, appear as captions for the photos. Nearly half the images bear annotations that refer in some way to their own inadequacy. "As an omniscient narrator," one caption reads, "I realize I leave much to be desired. Again, I apologize." At the bottom of the page, after scattered highlights from George's life have been related, the narrator decides that the present scrapbook introduction is not succeeding: "Damn! This is no good! I've entirely failed to give you any of the flavour of these events. I'm sorry. And once again, I've imparted nothing 'real' about the man himself." The final photo shows George Sprott's headstone, which affords the narrator's apologetic caption—"I'm so terribly sorry"—the suggestion of condolence.

Despite such conventional unreliability, the narrator is elsewhere articulate and insightful, as when describing George's reflections on the death of his

FIG. 4.3 Seth, *George Sprott: 1894–1975* (Montreal: D&Q, 2009), n.p.

mother (fig. 4.3). The perspective is extremely flexible; the reader can never predict what the narrator will and will not know, which allows for genuine anticipation and surprise. In many ways, it is the narrator's very fallibility, the failure to be omniscient in the usual sense, that gives the narration its unique strength and momentum. Often, this is accompanied by a certain sentimental attachment to George. Particularly in the depiction of George's final moments, the narrator betrays an aversion to the sensational, and a curious sense of decorum: "Now that the moment has come . . . I find that I can't show it to you. It's too awful." These kinds of remarks seem to both maintain and obscure the distinction between the narrator and Seth, who as author also speaks through other characters. Daisy Sprott confesses, "I was the one who found Uncle George when he died," before adding, "I won't talk about that." The reader is shown the moment that precedes Daisy's discovery, but the final panel of the page detailing the minutes of George's death is unillustrated, white text on a black background: "I will spare you this scene as well." In such instances, the narrator emerges as a distinct personality, one who has an undetached affection and esteem for George and his family.

Many of Seth's other characters would benefit from such a benevolent presence, especially the Matchcard brothers, who are left to tell their own stories and tend to be rather critical of themselves (and each other). One of the tragic through lines of *Clyde Fans* is that the family business manufactures a product that is in many ways obsolete: by the 1950s, Abe tells the reader, air conditioners were on the rise, but he "never foresaw the day when little offices or private homes would be able to afford such a machine" (*Clyde Fans* 47). He attributes this lack of foresight to a certain "wrongheadedness" that he and Simon share. Reminiscing about earlier years in the business, Abe says, "Something of the flavour of those times and those people . . . has been lost. I say this with a kind of sadness—and that is my great failing" (29). Abe sees

his tendency to mourn for the lost past as a distinct failure, especially for a businessman who must always be looking ahead in order to succeed.

Often in Seth's work it is the characters' livelihoods that come to seem obsolete. In *It's a Good Life*, *Wimbledon Green*, and *The Great Northern Brotherhood*, cartoonists are cast as an obsolescent breed. Those who don't give up cartooning for a more lucrative trade frequently die broke or unacknowledged, their once popular work now widely dismissed as old-fashioned and insignificant. In these books, it is collection that redeems these obsolete objects by assigning historical and monetary value to them (although countless stacks of comics are nevertheless consigned to the landfill). Collections surface in *George Sprott* as well, some kept by attentive collectors and fans of George, others seen as worthless and callously discarded (like the CKCK video library, which comprised tapes of *Northern Hi-Lights* and other local programs).

Francesco Orlando offers a convincing account of obsolescence in *Obsolete Objects in the Literary Imagination*. This substantial, systematic work of literary analysis is built around a highly elaborated, symmetrical semantic tree that diagrams possible contexts for and tensions among literary instances of "nonfunctional corporality." This tree yields twelve categories of nonfunctional corporality, such as "the threadbare-grotesque," "the sinister-terrifying," and "the prestigious-ornamental," illustrated by Orlando with examples spanning the full range of Western literature in works both familiar and obscure. His system is perhaps too schematic to be usefully adopted in its entirety, but the governing principals of his analysis may serve as reliable points of reference. Literature, like dream-life, is understood as a field of repressed impulses, a repository of the irrational and immoral. Orlando suggests that literature is also particularly suited to accommodating a return of the "antifunctional" repressed (7), which is to say the obsolete.

As his term "nonfunctional corporality" suggests, the failure of the obsolete body is the failure to function, a failure that is directly related to the passage of time. Many of Seth's characters value objects precisely because of their age or clumsy corporality. Orlando explains:

> What is called into question is an ambivalence intrinsic to the relationship—for human beings—between things and time. Time uses up and destroys things, breaks them and reduces them to uselessness, renders them unfashionable and makes people abandon them; time makes things become cherished by force of habit and ease of handling, endows them with tenderness as memories and with authority as models, marks them with the virtue of rarity and the prestige of age. (11)

In Seth's work, a counterpart to obsolescence is the seeming degradation or vulgarization of the present; this degraded present can appear to characters as a failed version of the past, which leaves them longing for those earlier times. The personification (or, rather, caricature) of this longing is Jonah, the ultra-nostalgic egomaniac collector from *Wimbledon Green*, who refuses, even in his daily life, to admit objects that do not conform to his pre-1950 collection. Here, and in less extreme instances, the failure of obsolete objects to remain relevant becomes a virtue—but a virtue that is always marked by ambivalence.

An Honest Sort of Failure

Financial failure hangs over nearly all of Seth's work, occasionally coming to the fore and almost always looming somewhere in the background. In *George Sprott*, the various successes of the protagonist are rimmed by the hard times faced by many of the peripheral characters. There is the relative poverty of the small, northern town where George left his unacknowledged daughter and her young Inuit mother, having visited briefly during one of the "expeditions" on which he built his fame; there is the near bankruptcy of Daisy Sprott's arctic-themed literary journal, *Northwinds*; but most of all there is the general decline of Dominion City, where George lived and worked for much of his life. The Dominion of George's prime has been largely eroded by the gradual, and seemingly inevitable, financial collapse of some its most distinctive landmarks: the local television station (where George was one of a gallery of personalities), the Coronet Lecture Hall (where George gave weekly talks for thirty-five years), and the Melody Grill (once a high-end spot for the "entertainment crowd" where George often held court). In time, each place becomes a husk of its former self, usually in a futile attempt to stay solvent.

Only the TV station remains, but in an unrecognizable form, while the lecture hall and restaurant all but disappear from local memory.

Failed ventures are at the heart of *Clyde Fans* as well. In part 4 of the story, Borealis Business Machines—the parts manufacturer acquired by Clyde Matchcard in his years at the helm of Clyde Fans—sinks into utter bankruptcy despite the efforts of Abe Matchcard to keep it afloat (*PV* 20). On the eve of a public announcement to the plant's middle-aged employees, who are picketing in vain for a living wage, Abe tells his lawyer, "I have been running this place, Walter, since I was 29 years old . . . This bankruptcy represents complete personal failure for me" (13). Taken out of context, this quotation may seem expository, even heavy handed, but it succinctly illustrates the significant link between individual and economic failure in Seth's work. The reader senses this link in Kalo's apparently practical decision to give up cartooning—"he just wasn't making any money on it" (*IAGL* 154)—and even more acutely in Seth's depiction of the popular cartoonists of *Wimbledon Green*, almost all of whom end up penniless.

If this recurring circumstance in *Wimbledon Green* does not alert the reader to Seth's anxiety about the value of his chosen vocation, his introduction to the book certainly will. He sets out to lower expectations: "The drawing is poor, the lettering shoddy, the page compositions and storytelling perfunctory. . . . The character designs are gross and rubbery. . . . Even I find some of the characters ugly. My apologies for all of this" (11). To say the least, this apology elicits an ambivalent response from the reader, who is not inclined to doubt its sincerity but is nevertheless faced with a book that abounds in Seth's trademark elegance and gentle wit, buoyed by a sketchbook energy. Is this simply an instance of polite modesty, or does the author hold himself to unrealistically high standards? Perhaps both. David M. Ball identifies a comparable tendency in the work of Chris Ware, a "characteristic self-abnegation" (45), particularly when the cartoonist addresses his own work or comics as a medium. Ball places Ware in a literary tradition that stretches back to Melville: "American authors have long cultivated a self-conscious rhetoric of failure as a watchword for literary success, effectively transvaluing the meanings of success and failure in reference to their own writing" (46).

This specific type of rhetoric constitutes a deliberate strategy intended to sway the reader.[4] Especially in extraliterary contexts, Ware is certainly the foremost practitioner of this mode of heightened deficiency, but it is fairly common in contemporary comics. When, for instance, Daniel Clowes names a character "David Boring," it could be considered a rhetorical ploy in this same vein, one that rewards an expectation of irony and cements the reader's interest. The back page of *Palookaville* 16 features columns of miniadvertisements and notices, one of which announces the availability of part 2 of *Clyde Fans* (collecting numbers 13 through 15). The ad copy is characteristically ironic: "This time a middle-aged man (filled with dread) walks about silently for 70 more pages. The excitement knows no bounds!" (23).

Ware's deployment of the rhetoric of failure, Ball argues, is a central component of his broader project: "not only to write comics with the texture and sophistication of literary fiction, but to have them treated as such" (46). The introduction to *Wimbledon Green* reads as an extension of this rhetoric, or even a playful homage to Ware's persona. After all, Seth is not merely acquainted with Ware; *Wimbledon Green* is dedicated to him, and the title character "came together on a trip to London taken with Mr. Ware" (11). When examined together, Ware's and Seth's campaigns of self-disparagement take on the appearance of an inadvertent humility contest. Not surprisingly, Seth has anticipated this most basic of critical acts, the comparison, and preemptively deflected it with another humble aside: "Certainly no one would mistake this gentle poking of the comics world with Mr. Ware's profound and moving work" (11). (It is true that Seth does not strain toward the profound in *Wimbledon Green*, but the book is nonetheless quite poignant at times.)

With all this in mind, it will come as little surprise that Seth's introduction to the 2001 reissue of *Palooka-ville* no. 1 is disproportionately scathing. It begins: "If there's one thing I've learned from my career as a commercial illustrator it's that you don't bad-mouth your own work.... I wish I could follow my own advice here—but this comic book is truly awful." This is an unnecessarily harsh assessment, and it is hardly the only one; what follows reads more like a retraction than an introduction, filled with amusingly acid condemnations. "This work is not old enough to simply dis-own as youthful ineptitude. It clearly shows that only ten years ago I was an idiot." Much of Seth's bile is reserved for his younger self's choice of story: an occasionally alarming anecdote about being the victim of a vicious homophobic assault. (Seth is not gay, but—seemingly on principle—lets his attackers believe he is.) While Seth's later, fictional narratives are certainly more subtle and sophisticated, this early story is compelling in its own way, and the illustration is already quite accomplished, with line work that is light, confident, and distinctive (fig. 4.4). Of course, this is not something that Seth would be likely to concede: "When I pulled out the artwork to ready it for this edition," he writes, "I was unprepared for the depth of hatred and shame I would feel toward it."

Shame and self-loathing are minor hallmarks of Seth's output, especially his autobiographical work, and can be found in comical abundance in a sketchbook account of his 2001 trip to an author's festival in Calgary, included in *Palookaville* 20. Full of loneliness, feigned cheer, and awkward encounters,

FIG. 4.4 Seth, *Palooka-ville* 1: Special Reissue (Montreal: D&Q, 2001), 9.

these unpolished journal entries—not quite a series of anecdotes, certainly not a fleshed-out story—seem to provide a window into Seth's actual day-to-day life, free of the conventions of fiction. The trip ends on an appropriately hopeless note that somehow manages to sound like a punch line: Seth examines his reflection in a bus window and thinks, with certainty, "I hate myself ... much more than anyone else in the world" (89). This was evidently a somewhat grim episode in Seth's life, and yet his perceived shortcomings read like high comedy. In contemporary literary comics, nothing succeeds like failure.

Self-loathing is a familiar attribute of Seth's characters as well, particularly the Matchcard brothers. It seems closely tied to the desire to hide, a "family trait" according to Abe (*Clyde Fans* 52). Unlike Simon, Abe has the ability to suppress this trait. "That was the central dilemma of my life—the sin of sociability. I could push down my fears, my hatred, my disgust. I could play the game." He goes on to say that such performances were inevitably followed by self-loathing, his "penance" for going against his instincts (53). In a rare moment of esteem for his brother, Abe remarks that he "couldn't help but admire Simon's sheer inability to cope" (52), even as he resented him for it. Here, failure becomes almost a principle, a refusal to "play the game" or engage with life on any terms but one's own.

Of all Seth's variously compromised characters, failure seems to cling to no one so steadfastly as it does to Simon. He appears as a finely wrought archetype, something of a loner, whose occasionally paralyzing inability to relate to people is familiar but by no means formulaic. As Abe suggests, his brother is colored by an honest sort of failure, a failure that, once admitted, serves to

FIG. 4.5 Seth, *Clyde Fans: Book 1* (Montreal: D&Q, 2004), 150.

FIG. 4.6 Seth, *Clyde Fans: Book 1* (Montreal: D&Q, 2004), 124.

shield and in certain respects even embolden Simon. After two unproductive days in an unfamiliar town, unable to bring himself to speak to his overbearing brother by phone, Simon reaches out to a stranger, the owner of a general store on the outskirts of Dominion. He examines some penny postcards before asking, almost involuntarily, "Sir—did you ever feel that your every action, your every thought, was being scrutinized? As if an intense light was focused on you" (*Clyde Fans* 150). The man's response is dishearteningly obtuse but hardly surprising (fig. 4.5). Rebuffed in such unmistakable terms, Simon displays his bulky Clyde Fans sample case on the store's front counter and halfheartedly makes a sales pitch, which is promptly declined. It is at this point that Simon's failure seems to coalesce into a form of integrity—in a moment of quiet, apathetic triumph, he curtly pays for the postcards and leaves, abandoning the open sample case with the perplexed store manager.

Simon not only fails to make any sales of his own but he also fails to resist the transparent pitch of a fellow salesman and hotel neighbor, Whitey, who explains that he arrives in a town with trunks full of wares and works out of his hotel room. In conspicuous contrast to Simon—who has spent a demoralizing day making entirely unsuccessful cold calls on foot—Whitey phones potential clients and they visit him in his room, just as he has invited Simon to do. Gregarious and verbose, Whitey displays his "procession of the trivial," as he refers to it, with a carnival barker's relish (fig. 4.6). His catalog includes all manner of "novelties, souvenirs, knick-knacks, small housewares and related inexpensive goods" (124). Of this vast inventory of cultural detritus, Simon selects perhaps the most loathsome item on offer: a cheap toy distinguished

FIG. 4.7 Seth, *Clyde Fans: Book 1* (Montreal: D&Q, 2004), 129.

only by its casual racism. Several pages before the reader discovers that Simon has given into this base consumer impulse (fig. 4.7), Whitey aptly describes the item as "a revolting trifle. When you open this celluloid watermelon—out pops a little pickaninny" (125). The reader may be quite shocked to see the thing in Simon's possession, but only briefly, for it also seems all too appropriate a souvenir of his trip.

Why is this grotesque, cheap caricature at once so shocking and so at home in this story? Perhaps because, surprising as it initially is, it encapsulates so much failure. A failure of restraint and of taste on Simon's part, in many ways a characteristic failure of will; in a broader sense, a sudden failure of repression, a strangely cathartic instance in which repression is broken through. Simon's decision to buy the toy constitutes a distinctly uncanny moment, when "beliefs which have been surmounted"—in this case, a warped, sentimental attachment to racial difference—"seem once more to be confirmed" (Freud, "The Uncanny" 249). As Whitey says of the toy watermelon, "to men of our intelligence this is a tawdry thing" (*Clyde Fans* 125)—and yet Simon feels compelled to have it.

This is consistent with Simon's other compulsive habits, such as repeatedly sketching the same group of abstract objects and obsessing over events from his past. Undergirding much of Seth's work is this other species of failure, a Freudian-inflected failure to resolve inner conflicts, which often shows itself in fixed patterns of behavior. The characters' compulsive tendencies frequently find expression in the act of collecting, although a wide range of fixation is evident. In *It's a Good Life*, for instance, Seth describes "two very mundane and potent childhood memories"—witnessing a lackluster Christmas parade, reading on a couch in front of the TV—which he repeatedly returns to, especially when depressed (11–12). Throughout the book, the reader sees evidence of Seth's habit of placing himself in familiar or reassuring circumstances. Later in the story, he encounters Annie, a nervous hoarder who lives amid accumulated detritus in a motel room; she compulsively stutters over the pronoun "I" and has a weak grasp of conventional social boundaries. Seth is initially unsettled by Annie, but he ultimately seems to recognize something of himself in her and leaves a kind note on her door when he checks out of his own room at the same motel.

On the other end of the spectrum are the very social habits and routines of George Sprott, many of which span decades: his weekly TV show, as well as his weekly talk at the Coronet Lecture Hall, both of which revisit ad infinitum the series of trips he took north. Like Simon Matchcard, George Sprott spends much of his life reliving a set of early experiences; unlike Simon, George has managed to parlay these rehearsals into a livelihood. Nevertheless, even George inevitably loses momentum, and the reader finds that his interior life is characterized by regret. Here, the fundamental ambivalence again discloses itself: the past is lamented even as it is fervently recalled. The repeated thoughts and actions of Seth's obsessive collectors, compulsive nostalgics, and introspective neurotics reveal the ultimate impossibility of actual repetition, of redoing, of redressing past failures.

In Seth's work, character is delineated as much by failure as by accomplishment—or, more precisely, by the distance between the two, by the sobering irony of unfulfillment. This irony reflects a Chekhovian attitude to failure that is both ambivalent and fundamentally humane. Chris Ware's extraliterary rhetoric of failure, as Ball observes, "maps his characteristic ambivalence toward the very notion of 'graphic literature'" (47); Ware deploys this rhetoric to great effect in reference to his own work as a means of addressing the low expectations associated with comics. By comparison, Seth's rhetoric of failure seems less tactical. It is similarly bound up with an overarching ambivalence, but it has less to do with his own literary status than with broader notions of worth and what constitutes a good life. It is part of an aesthetic tendency in his work toward attentiveness, second looks, and reevaluation. Davies claims that Chekhov is not interested in salvation—if so, it is here that Seth breaks with Chekhovian tradition. There is a sense of "inbetweenness," of constant vacillation, in Seth's work, but also a strong impulse to save. Despite his unmistakable "twilight tone," Seth is, ultimately, concerned with salvation, with "the redemption through artistic euphoria of the painful or the ugly" (Orlando 11). In Seth's work, the reader repeatedly witnesses an ambivalent transmutation of clay into gold: failure develops in the direction of ambivalence, until finally it coincides with its opposite. Although such inversions are not stable, the antifunctional repressed briefly becomes the antifunctional redeemed.

5

Collection and Recollection

Memory, recollection, remembrance—these words are not quite identical or interchangeable, but little is gained from rigidly differentiating between them. To narrow the meaning of each, to try to reduce the overlap among them in an effort to render their usage more technical, is an exercise in almost arbitrary definition. The empirical impulse to build a stable of terms with reliable, distinct denotations is continually frustrated by the fluidity of the concepts and their rough equivalence in everyday speech. Etymological inquiry can only take an investigation so far: in the case of "memory" (circa 1225), "recollection" (1576), and "remembrance" (circa 1330), the *Oxford English Dictionary* reveals a centuries-old nest of intersecting connotations. Memory, from the Old French and Anglo-Norman *memorie, memore, memoire*, rooted in the classical Latin *memor*, "mindful, remembering"; and remembrance, from the Old French for "awareness, consciousness," which at the same time (early twelfth century) had the more familiar meaning of "memory, recollection."[1] Recollect comes from the Latin *recolligere*: "to gather up again, reassemble, to repossess oneself" and "in post-classical Latin also to recall, remember." Ultimately, the lineage of these words does not especially illuminate their contemporary significance, although it does demonstrate that they have always been closely related and also foregrounds the long-standing association between recollection and an aware, attentive frame of mind.

It may be more productive to revisit the Aristotelian classification, which understands "recollection" as an activity and "memory" as an affection or pathos. W. J. T. Mitchell observes a shift from ancient to modern conceptions of memory that seems to mirror precisely this distinction. "The ancient memory systems," Mitchell notes, "are artificial, cultivated techniques designed as aids to public verbal performance; the modern sense of memory treats it as something more like a natural faculty, an aspect of private consciousness"

(193). Mitchell challenges these categories, arguing that memory/recollection—as an imagetext—permeates the borders between ancient and modern, public and private, artificial and natural: "the composite imagetext structure of memory seems to be a deep feature that endures all the way from Cicero to Lacan to the organization of computer memory" (193). The imagetext structure of Seth's work likewise blurs the boundary between the natural process of memory and the cultivated process of recollection.

As for the process of collection, perhaps the best way to begin to conceive of it is as a product of Zygmunt Bauman's master-opposition between inside and outside. This opposition is in many ways the root of all those behaviors related to boundaries, containment, and compartmentalization; the comics page is the result of such behavior carried out within a visual plane, in most cases with the aim of conveying a narrative. The panel is a representation of a bounded narrative interval, "a fragment of space-time belonging to the diegesis" (Groensteen, *System of Comics* 40). Beyond this fragment (which can exist even without an explicit frame) is the gutter, the gap that is visually and otherwise interdependent with the panel. Together, the panels and the gaps between them define the inside/outside relations that establish the narrative integrity of the page. Many of Seth's more recent works employ a narrative method that has become fairly common in contemporary literary comics, which he explains in his introduction to *Wimbledon Green*: "It's an approach wherein you tell a longer story through a variety of shorter, unconnected comic strips. Cumulatively they add up to a bigger picture" (11). It will be apparent to even the casual reader of comics that this technique mimics not only the process of serial publication—which remains a distinguishing feature of many comics—but also the very structure the medium itself. As Jared Gardner suggests, the comic book collector is driven by "the compulsive need to fill in the gaps, to make connections between issues (the serial gap inherent to comic production, mirroring and complicating the gaps between the frames themselves)" (800). A comic book is accumulative by nature, a collection of panels, moments, images.

This chapter focuses on *Wimbledon Green* and *Clyde Fans*: the former is explicitly about collectors and collecting in a way that exceeds any of Seth's other books, even *It's a Good Life, If You Don't Weaken*; the latter features Simon Matchcard, a consummate collector and one of Seth's most distinctive, fully conceived characters. Reading Seth's introduction to *Wimbledon Green*, the reader suspects that the integrity of that narrative world owes much to *A Gentle Madness*, Nicholas A. Basbanes's first book on bibliomania, which Seth cites as a source of "great character material" (*Wimbledon Green* 11). The aim here will not be to trace didactic lines between the books but, knowing the extent to which Basbanes's work informed Seth's sketchbook creation, to allow *A Gentle Madness* to enrich a reading of *Wimbledon Green*. Basbanes undeniably captures something of the texture of book collecting, and though he is not a source of paradigmatic theories or keen historical reconsiderations, he does offer this useful definition in a later book, *Among the Gently Mad*: "Book collecting is synonymous with book hunting" (23).

Indeed, a lengthy book-hunting adventure, "The Green Ghost," is granted a central position in *Wimbledon Green*, a lively justification of the title character's passion. The incidents that constitute this adventure—memory lost, acts of self-reliance, memory regained, keen detective work—suggest that a collection is a more than anything else a story that the collector tells himself about his identity. Stuart Hall argues that "identities are the names we give to the different ways we are positioned by, and position ourselves within, the narratives of the past" (225). Collecting is a means of not only positioning oneself within existing narratives of the past but also forging new narratives.

In *Patience and Fortitude*, Basbanes drily asks Umberto Eco for "a painless definition of semiotics" (225). With some reluctance, Eco quite helpfully replies that it concerns "the activities by which we use something present—a word, an image, an object—in order to tell you something which is not there" (225). In many instances, the collected object is a stand-in for something more elusive. Susan Pearce offers this subtle, suggestive point of departure in *Collecting in Contemporary Practice*: "Collecting as a process works in the shadowland, making its meaning on the edge where the practices of the past, the politics of present power, and the poetic capacity of each human being blur together" (1). It is in this shadowland that both Wimbledon Green and Simon Matchcard seem to collect themselves, although in very different ways.

Collecting Comics, Collecting the Self

In the museum, that familiar institutional extension of the collection, where visitors are invited to have a personal interaction with history in a public setting, the boundary between inside and outside is in some ways collapsed. Part 3 of *It's a Good Life* finds Seth at Toronto's Royal Ontario Museum: the opening panels depict the skeletons of prehistoric sea creatures, suspended, as though in water, by not-quite-invisible wires. Seth estimates that the exhibits "must've been put together in the 50's . . . or maybe the early 60's. The fake plants, the plaster-of-Paris rocks . . . those faded background paintings. Those paintings are so primitive, so naively beautiful" (61). Here, the distant past is conveyed by outdated techniques from a past that is just distant enough to elicit pangs of longing from the observer. Unsurprisingly, there is anxiety lurking behind his nostalgic appreciation: "I'm afraid one of these days I'm gonna walk in there and find it all renovated and hi-tech. I couldn't stand that" (61). The unsophisticated artifice of the museum colors its collection and creates a space for various engagements with the past. Notably, these engagements with the past take place while wandering around a public space, sometimes in the company of strangers.

It is in *It's a Good Life* that collecting first comes to the fore of Seth's work: he casts himself as a collector of gag cartoons drawn by an obscure Canadian artist, John Kalloway. Seth closes the book with "reproductions" of these cartoons, "Kalo's Famous Eleven," as he ironically calls them. With great skill and affection, this fabricated collection tangibly recalls the gag cartoons that appeared in the late 1940s and 1950s (figs. 1.1, 6.6). With these invented artifacts, Seth is not presenting a set of historical documents that trigger memory or contribute to an objective conception of the past. Rather, he is offering the reader something approaching memory itself—a highly subjective and fully imagined conception of the past.

Were Kalo not a fictional character, a collection of his cartoons might simply be a site of mediation between the reader and an ultimately inaccessible past. In the case of a conventional collection, such mediation mingles imagination, memory, and history, lending imagination and memory some of history's substance and authority. Kalo's "Famous Eleven" lack historical substance and authority, although they brilliantly imitate both. Not quite memory, either, the collection is instead Seth's impression (in nearly every sense of the word) of a particular moment in the history of cartooning. Kalo's cartoons confuse the distinction between an imagined past and a historical past—or, in cruder terms, fiction and nonfiction—both of which are only accessible through artifacts.

Wimbledon Green is in this respect far less confusing, although Seth's deployment of (fictional) collections persists, most explicitly in full-page selections "from the Library of Wimbledon Green" (fig. 5.1). On these pages, Seth abandons framed panels and presents a three-by-three grid of nine exemplary items from Wimbledon Green's comic book collection, each accompanied by a detailed catalog entry that includes issue number, condition, date of publication, a brief descriptive note, availability, and value. Each object in a collection recalls a world, a narrative, and this is particularly so when the objects are books. Although *Wimbledon Green* does very occasionally overlap with the real world, each of the comic books is a metafictional invention, as is the vast collection that they represent. Poring over the evocative details of these catalog selections, the reader may struggle to parse the various degrees

FIG. 5.1 Seth, *Wimbledon Green* (Montreal: Drawn and Quarterly, 2005), 19.

of literary collection: Wimbledon Green's comic book collection is a collection of stories, which exists within the collection of stories that constitutes the comic book *Wimbledon Green*. Is this dense and inverted concatenation significant, or just striking? In attempting to pin down this invented collection, the reader is obliged to consider the invented component of both collection and recollection.

If the fictional auction catalog can be considered not only a device but a distinct literary genre, one of its most notable examples, discussed by Basbanes, is a fourteen-page item widely distributed in the summer of 1840 that announced "the forthcoming dispersal of a private library gathered over four decades" by a collector identified as Count Fortsas (*Gentle Madness* 116). The auction was "canceled" one day before it was scheduled to occur and was not publicly acknowledged as a hoax until much later. More recently, and with no intent to deceive, Leanne Shapton published *Important Artifacts and Personal Property from the Collection of Lenore Doolan and Harold Morris, Including Books, Street Fashion, and Jewelry* (2009), a novel in the form of an auction catalog. In these two works—as in the selections from Wimbledon Green's collection, and Simon Matchcard's catalog-like tour of his mother's bedroom in *Clyde Fans*—the actual (non)existence of the items catalogued does not detract from their charm. Many suspected that the collection of Count Fortsas may have been a fabrication, but its very possibility remained enticing (Basbanes, *Gentle Madness* 118). The effect of Shapton's book, which includes many photos and "reproductions," depends on its fictitious status. The invented catalog acts as an index of a larger, unseen collection: *Palookaville* 20 literally features a catalog page, namely a page with twenty different fans from the May 1975 Borealis Business Machines catalog (fig. 5.2). Part of the pleasure derived from peeking into Wimbledon Green's library is the knowledge that it is an invention, that the books it contains can never be read. In certain contexts, the unread text is more appealing than the book that has been completely realized—a popular maxim holds that a book collector is someone who buys books with little intention of reading them. The unread (or unreadable) book always holds the spark of potential.

Although this chapter is less concerned with direct correspondence between *A Gentle Madness* and *Wimbledon Green* than with a shared (or, perhaps, borrowed) sensibility, certain explicit parallels are too striking to be omitted. This is not to say that Seth's protagonist is a mere composite of real-life figures—what makes Wimbledon Green so successful as a character is that his behavior is not only recognizable but also unexpected. But in his occasional posturing and obscure origins, and given the funds at his disposal, he unmistakably recalls one of the collectors depicted in *A Gentle Madness*:

FIG. 5.2 Seth, *Palookaville* 20 (Montreal: D&Q, 2010), 6.

Haven O'More. Basbanes describes this American collector as noteworthy but with a disproportionately high regard for his accomplishments. In one instance related by Basbanes, O'More hectors a bookseller into giving him a 10 percent discount on a number of fifteenth-century editions of Aristotle's works (after first insisting on 40 percent). "I am the greatest book collector in the world," he is quoted as saying by way of justification (*Gentle Madness* 253). *Wimbledon Green* opens with a similar, though somewhat less off-putting incident, in which the eponymous hero insists on seeing a rare comic that is to be auctioned. When an underling at the auction house refuses, he erupts in pompous frustration, declaring himself "the greatest comic book collector in the world" (14). The phrase is given an authoritative twist because the reader has already encountered it on the cover of the book (fig. 1.6). Although this subtitle cannot be taken at face value, neither can it be considered plainly sarcastic. The status of the claim, like the status of the character to whom it refers, remains productively ambiguous.

Wimbledon Green's name-making break came, as he tells it, in 1974, when he discovered the notorious Wilbur R. Webb collection, to which many pages of *Wimbledon Green* are devoted.[2] The nine-hundred-odd mint-condition items that ultimately sold at auction represented only a fraction of Webb's original collection, the vast remainder of which vanished at his death. Wimbledon Green admits: "I had been trying to keep him [Webb] for myself. When I did return he was gone and the apartment was empty. Of course, he had died" (*WG* 32). In these scenarios, it is always knowledge that the collector hoards and cunningly deploys in order to steal these bits of the past, although not always with the same success. About the unrecovered bulk of the Webb collection, Wimbledon Green ruefully tells the reader, "I was never able to determine the fate of the remaining comics. The city dump, no doubt!" (32). His regret is less for the potential loss of money than for the loss of the objects themselves. Here, collecting coincides with preservation—for Wimbledon Green, what the collection seems to preserve is memory.

Collecting, to return to Eco's definition of semiotics, is one of "those devices we use in our everyday life to make something present which is not there" (quoted in Basbanes, *Patience and Fortitude* 225). What is being made present by the collections of Wimbledon Green and his fellow collectors is the past, and often a past that is almost completely conflated with childhood. The collectors portrayed in *Wimbledon Green* often collect children's comics: the title character closes the book with a reminiscent, meandering tale, in which he fondly recalls, among other things, Pete's Corner Store, "the glorious site where all the comics of my youth were purchased" (119). He plainly asserts that "these childhood images rest at the very core of who I am"; they constitute a "stockpile so potent—so meaningful that I can't help but return to them again and again" (119). It is tempting to assume that he speaks on behalf of Seth.

Seth is given an opportunity to speak for himself (in a certain sense) in Joe Matt's collection of autobiographical vignettes, *Spent* (2007), which features Seth as one of the main characters. In fact, Seth appears on the first page, which opens in a very familiar location, a secondhand bookstore. As Matt and Seth bicker and browse, Matt discovers a rare volume of *Birdseye Center* strips by the much-forgotten Canadian cartoonist Jimmy Frise. Seth pleads with Matt to let him have the book, noting its poor condition; Matt purchases it for himself for ten dollars. "You wouldn't even know about it," Seth rails, "if I hadn't shown you my old newspaper clippings!" (Matt 10) The scene has the archetypal heft of a vaudeville routine: two collectors, arguing over the right to own a rare book. Later, as they sit in a diner with Chester Brown, Matt haggles with Seth and sells him *Birdseye Center* at seven times its original price.

As a collector, Matt exhibits the typical signs of a completist. Although he goes to extreme lengths to save money and is often frustratingly parsimonious, he admits his willingness "to spend whatever it takes to complete my collection of 'Gasoline Alley' newspaper strips" (Matt 118). However, it is Matt's other, more sordid collection—which seems to overshadow even his interest in comics—that illuminates the intersection of his completism with a kind of purism. He has amassed hundreds of hours of video pornography, painstakingly copied and edited into dozens of dense compilation tapes. This collection reveals that Matt is concerned not just with quantity or quality, but with a sense of necessity, distillation, and consolidation. These tapes, highly "edited and refined" (55), have been cleansed of any footage deemed extraneous or substandard (for instance, images of male performers' faces). In the diner scene, Brown jokes that he and Seth should nominate Matt in the category of "Best Editor" for an upcoming cartoonists' award (79). The quip plays on the pervasiveness of editing as a cultural practice, from the esteemed revision of a collection of literary work to the maintenance of Matt's less publicly recognized collection.[3]

The collector's compulsion to edit is closely tied to the pursuit of new acquisitions, which is an integral part of the collecting process. Matt explains that "to find and excavate the rare gems" that constitute his collection, he "had to wade and sift through" an abundance of low-grade material from the collection of an acquaintance (55). Editing is always preceded by accumulation, and the two practices seem almost to overlap in the form of a third practice: selection. In fact, it is tempting to identify selection as the germ of collection, the most fundamental element of the process; to a large extent, the act of selection is what distinguishes the collection from the archive.

Whereas the collection is a carefully selected group of items, the archive often overflows with unsystematically accumulated material, more a source for history than a spur to memory. Like comics narratives, both the collection and the archive are necessarily fragmented, structured around gaps. Jared Gardner convincingly compares comics to the archive, arguing that "the comics form retains that which cannot be reconciled to linear narrative—the excess that refuses cause-and-effect argument, the trace that threatens to unsettle the present's narrative of its own past (and thereby of itself)" (801). The accumulating excess of the archive is certainly a part of Seth's work, but on the whole his narratives remain highly edited and deliberately assembled.

Accumulating, selecting, editing: these necessary components of collecting form a hazy continuum of at times indistinguishable behavior. The familiar tension at work in such behavior is between inside and outside: every act of collection is a revision of the boundary that determines what is interior and what exterior. It is not uncommon for this preoccupation with inclusion and exclusion to reveal itself in the social life of the collector; for Joe Matt (as for Simon Matchcard) it frequently takes the form of self-exclusion. Much of *Spent* finds Matt either alone in his bedroom or alienating those closest to him with a range of stubbornly antisocial habits. At the same time, however, throughout *Spent* Matt positions himself within an exclusive clique of acclaimed contemporary cartoonists (and collectors).

It is perhaps this sort of group that Seth had in mind when he conceived *The Great Northern Brotherhood of Canadian Cartoonists*, which shares with *Spent* and *Wimbledon Green* a largely unexamined and apparently inevitable homosociality. This atmosphere seems to cling to any appreciation of the comic book medium and recalls the old-fashioned notion that bibliomania is related to castration anxiety and "applies strictly to men" (Basbanes, *Gentle Madness* 28). Basbanes ably deflates this theory with examples of well-known female collectors, but the stereotype persists, particularly when the books collected are comic books, as evidenced by the dearth of female characters in *Wimbledon Green* and *The Great Northern Brotherhood* (it is not insignificant that the club is a brotherhood). Meanwhile, the most notable link between women and collecting in *It's a Good Life* and *George Sprott* is that the respective protagonists—Seth and George—seem to collect women in a series of short-lived relationships. (The same might be said of Chester Brown in his autobiographical work *Paying for It*, which details his experiences with prostitutes.) The female characters given the most reverent attention in Seth's work tend to be mothers, particularly in the case of Simon's treatment of his mother.

Seth's collectors seem to be loyal to their own personal pasts above all else. "At first glance," the character Ashcan Kemp explains, "all comic collectors might seem like backward looking sorts. And to some degree, that's true. But most collectors are merely reaching back to their own childhoods" (*WG* 65). Why do comic books, collecting, and a "sense of loss connected to childhood" (11) correspond so effortlessly? I have already suggested that the collection is a narrative of the collector's identity, and in much of Seth's work this identity is presupposed by the collector to reside in a lost childhood. Perhaps it could be said that the comic book collector in particular is someone for whom this sense of loss, this void signified by childhood, is the seat of identity. To put this in Eco's straightforward terminology, identity is the absent thing being made present by the collection.

Wimbledon Green is a collection of fractional recollections, each from a distinct perspective. Taken together, these fragments—some as short as a single strip, others spanning multiple pages—provide a portrait that is stable but never static. (The same can be said of *George Sprott*.) Seth employs a wide range of storytelling techniques, primarily personal recollections related by characters but also tales told from a more detached narrative perspective, as well as historical documents, an index of eminent collectors, and items from collections—all fabricated. The individual details are credible and, more than this, they cohere into a whole that is too compelling to be doubted.

Interlude: Forgetting

In *Palookaville* 16, Simon Matchcard muses on the coherence of identity over time and the role memory plays in the continuity of the self. However, the idea of the self as a stable bundle of memories moving through time is quickly complicated: "Are the memories even the same," he wonders, "or have they changed too?" (18). When Wimbledon Green loses his memory, what remains is very revealing. The reader is introduced to a more essential Wimbledon Green, who—stripped of wealth, sense of status, and even the urge to collect—delights in the carefree isolation of lonely highways and open roads. "It seems I've lucked into a grand situation! Freed of self and past, I am left to revel in the moment" (54). (Incidentally, the immobility of comics permits such appreciation of the moment in a way that other media cannot, allowing the reader to linger over images in panels without disrupting the narrative.) The extent to which collection and recollection are attempts to forestall loss—not only of the objects preserved in the collection but also of the self—is cast in sharp relief by the circumstance of an amnesiac collector.

The collection can serve as a reminder of that which might otherwise be forgotten, but more than this it focuses recollection, fortifying particular memories in particular ways while allowing others to mutate, recede, and fade away. The shuffle of recollection leaves nothing completely intact, there is no remembering without forgetting, and forgetting seems to perform a deeper, more cryptic function in the ongoing process of collecting. On the subject of personal libraries, Eco has said that sometimes "the forgotten book is the most important book you can have" (quoted in Basbanes, *Among the Gently Mad* 19). What is to be made of this murky statement? Is it merely a prescription for unconditional accumulation, the indiscriminate collection of even those items whose significance is not immediately apparent? Or is it about blind spots, gaps, and the often unacknowledged value of forgetting? Or, perhaps, it is a more subtle comment on the relation between collecting and memory, the ultimately strange and unpredictable ways in which the two reproduce each other. Waiting to be rediscovered, the forgotten book—not unlike the unread book—is full of potential, but an entirely invisible, abstract potential that is not part of the collector's awareness.

By contrast, the collector is sometimes fully aware of forgetting and may consequently overvalue the blank potential of the things forgotten, as Simon does when he attempts to recall the contents of his childhood treasure box. "Sometimes," he says, "I imagine that if I could just remember those objects, find them again, and place them back in the box in just the right order, then (like a magic recipe) it would open up that time barrier and I'd be on the other side ... in a better moment" (*PV* 16, 20). Perfect recollection, for Simon, becomes nearly equivalent to the impossible reconstruction of the lost past.

Simon Matchcard's Cabinet of Curiosities

In the third part of *Clyde Fans*, Simon and Abraham Matchcard take their mother, Lily, to a nursing home. For years Simon has been caring for her by himself, attempting to manage her escalating dementia; now, for the first time in his life, he will be alone in the family home. His somewhat daunting return home leads to an extended rumination on his mother by way of her just vacated bedroom. Although she has not died, her absence from the house is palpable, and Simon—like many of Seth's other characters—instinctively turns to reminiscence to alleviate feelings of loss. For nearly five pages at the end of part 3 (*PV* 19), he methodically (obsessively?) describes the contents of the room, which are for the most part unremarkable. The sequence is made up of over one hundred square panels, most of which contain a single item or detail of an item, accompanied by running narration that contextualizes the objects with observations and memories (fig. 5.3). Seth's deceptively simple

FIG. 5.3 Seth, *Palookaville* 19 (Montreal: D&Q, 2008), 93.

approach is to imbue these mundane objects with lifelike significance simply by focusing on them, using Simon as a lens.

This sequence is in fact one of the clearest instances in Seth's work of a character exploring the familiar recesses of recollection by way of a bounded collection of objects. Despite the explicitness of the scenario, Simon's reminiscences seem unforced and understated, perhaps because the items in his mother's room constitute an inadvertent collection. In this sense, it is unlike the collections of the characters in *Wimbledon Green* and very unlike Simon's own vast, meticulously organized collection of novelty postcards. But the objects are by no means less meaningful to Simon for being less deliberately collected: to a collector, almost any group of familiar items may warrant the same consideration as a calculated collection. For many of Seth's characters, and certainly for Simon, collecting is a way of thinking.

Of course, to conceive of collecting as an abstract mental process in this way is to abbreviate the distance between collection and recollection—a maneuver that may be facile or, worse, imprecise. Collection and recollection remain quite distinct, even as modes of thought, although there is significant overlap between the two. The similarities are made especially apparent by some of the techniques deployed by Seth. The expansive foldout section toward the end of *George Sprott*—six generous pages of moments and photographs from George's life—resembles nothing so much as a scrapbook. Unlike a standard album, however, which consists of physical items that may act as prompts to the collector's memory, this scrapbook is composed primarily of memories themselves, loosely organized fragments of experience that are interspersed with drawn photographs. Seth's intuitive and innovative approach to the spatio-topia in this section demonstrates the fundamental flexibility not only of the medium of comics but also of the medium, so to speak, of collection.

At a glance, the reader can appreciate the extent to which a collection often contains other collections: one of the sequences within the six-page spread wordlessly displays the items in an old cardboard box; another shows a series of memories from extramarital affairs; a third classifies flora (goldenrod, Canadian thistle) on the hill behind George's childhood home. As a whole, the foldout scrapbook is a self-contained unit in the much larger collection that makes up *George Sprott*. Nested collections are also a hallmark of *Clyde Fans*: Simon remarks that the vanity desk in his mother's bedroom "has always been something of a cabinet of curiosities for me" (*PV* 19, 90). The pages showing her everyday items resemble a very orderly display case, each uniform panel a compartment, in which these extremely private items take on some of the public, scientific mien of a museum collection. Here, as

Collection and Recollection 111

FIG. 5.4 Seth, *Palookaville* 19 (Montreal: D&Q, 2008), 90.

much as anywhere else in Seth's work, the reader is encouraged to browse with the protagonist, an act that is highly compatible with collection and does not necessarily require a public space. The sequence recalls Svetlana Boym's account of the museification of the home in the nineteenth century, the rise of "armchair nostalgia" aided by "a multitude of archival drawers, display cases and curio cabinets" (15).

What Simon offers the reader in this sequence amounts to a kind of guided museum tour. His commentary is meandering but not haphazard, tending to follow the layout of the room ("Next to the vanity is a bookcase"). He is affectionate but not uncritical: describing, for instance, a diamond-encrusted gold engagement ring hidden within the folds of a souvenir scarf, Simon frankly admits that "it is a rather ungraceful object" (*PV* 19, 92). By all accounts he is the ideal guide, perceptive, invested, with an intimate knowledge of what his mother's things say about her. Looking at the titles on a shelf of the bookcase,

FIG. 5.5 Seth, *Palookaville* 19 (Montreal: D&Q, 2008), 94.

Simon notes that they reflect "the tastes of an early 20th century woman of intelligence and middle-class breeding" (92). In these ways, Simon turns his mother's bedroom into a genuine collection, not an absent space but a memorial suffused by her presence.

The recollection of each item provides a multilayered perspective: Simon's view of his mother's self-perception. The process of browsing is sustained by his attention to detail, which exemplifies the alert, mindful aspect of recollection. Seth gives Simon ample room to attend closely to objects, devoting four panels to a pair of flared black gloves with zigzag cuff stitching and another six to a green plastic radio from the late 1940s (fig. 5.5). This sense of capaciousness is augmented by the occasional appearance of empty panels, devoid even of text, solid black squares that sit at the beginning of some strips. These blank black panels operate as brief caesuras that punctuate the regular rhythm of the grid, adding another kind of porousness to the page: the readerly interpolation provoked by a filled black panel is of a different order than that invited by the familiar gaps *between* panels. Both types of gaps, however, work to accommodate the reader within the structure of the comics page.

Seth's techniques are not merely structural. One of the more engaging ways in which Seth draws the reader into the fictional world is by describing invented products, which evoke entire company histories in a single panel. The top drawer of Lily Matchcard's vanity is a trove of beauty products that possess, in Simon's phrase, "names and packages recalling a time gone by" (90). Among the many items are an enameled tin of "Morning Glow Face Powder #15" (90) and a package of "Lady Frost Melting Face Cream," which is "Trademarked to the Milksoft Company of Montreal" (91). These products, in their detail and specificity, assume an unexpected tangibility, an impression that is enhanced by their narrative and visual isolation from each other in discrete panels (fig. 5.4).

"Collectors," Basbanes states, "are tactile people" (*Among the Gently Mad* 69). Simon describes many of his mother's things from memory, his facility with the objects a result of regular handling: "Each object—its form impressed upon me by years of contact. I think I would recognize anything here even if I were to encounter it in a darkened room" (*PV* 19, 90). Some items (the perfume bottles atop the vanity, the volumes on the bookcase) are initially presented in groups, before appearing individually in their own panels. Seth's cartoon rendering of the items—restrained but elastic—gives them a distinctive weight, and substantiates the tactility so crucial to this collection. Simon's familiarity with the objects, however, is accompanied by occasional obscurity. One of the pictured beauty products is a peculiar applicator, the function of which remains "an utter mystery" (91).

The contents of a box in the vanity's top drawer appear only as a fragmentary image. Simon's treatment of this "variety of odd rubber hoses, bulbs, bottles and pads" clearly indicates that the utter mystery is not any specific artifact but rather maternal femininity in general. In sharp contrast to painstakingly described hairbrushes, jewelry, and other relatively neutral possessions, these intimate objects receive very little attention. In a sequence (and story) that is otherwise characterized by an excess of detail, this is no accident. Simon's narration glosses quickly over the items, "which I have tried not to look too closely upon for fear of discovering their purposes" (91). Here more than anywhere else it becomes apparent that Simon is actively preserving his own naïve innocence along with his mother's memory.

The final strip of the sequence illustrates a cardboard box and its contents, the remains of a vase, which stands intact in one panel and lies broken in shards in the next (fig. 5.5). Both panels are imagined by Simon—the box remains beneath his mother's bed—but the first demonstrates the great capacity of individual memory to "make its way to objects from the past that are physically intact in their distance" (Orlando 115). Simon succinctly describes the vase as "a thing so precious, that even though ruined, it could not be tossed away" (*PV* 19, 94). For Simon, it is the ruin that reveals the object as precious. Unbroken, the value of the vase might remain hidden; broken but stubbornly preserved, it takes on a new significance and more powerfully evokes the memory of his mother.

Collection always entails various related forms of preservation, often the preservation of an artifact with an attendant set of memories. The binding of object to past experience is one of the collection's primary operations, in some respects its driving mnemonic, but the vagaries of preservation are not always guided by such a straightforward correlation. Simon's collection of novelty postcards, for instance, appears at first to have little to do with recollection or the maintenance of personal memories evoked by specific items. Meticulous nearly to the point of being clinical, this collection becomes an outlet for Simon's obsessive and compulsive inclinations, with the significance of individual postcards subordinate to the much broader logic of a planned book on the subject—a "grand history," as his brother Abe says (*Clyde Fans* 61). "He spent years collecting, researching," Abe tells the reader, "filing them away. All these little boxes are filled with carefully sorted and ordered postcards" (56). It is difficult to determine which is ultimately more important to Simon, the book for which he has prepared hundreds of "carefully typed notes" or the actual process of researching and collecting, assembling those notes. In any case, there is little to doubt in Abe's account of Simon's quiet devastation "when someone beat him to the punch in the mid-'70's and published a book on the same subject" (61).

What Abe does not know, however, and what the reader does not learn until the end of *Clyde Fans*' second part, is that Simon's preoccupation with the postcards began by chance during his fateful trip to Dominion, every detail of which gradually becomes a fixture of his psyche. Even the mere name of the place, Simon admits, "has a deep power over me" (*PV* 16, 15). Like some of his other collections (namely, his repetitive sketches), the collection of postcards becomes far more legible in the broader context of Simon's lifelong fixation on his experiences in Dominion. That this unsuccessful sales trip should prove so indelible is hardly surprising: it is one of the few events in Simon's life to occur outside the reassuring routines of the Matchcard home. Even far less momentous occurrences seem to stand out against the great, uniform interior Simon has created for himself. Of the people he has briefly encountered throughout his life, he says: "In their thoughts I have grown smaller and smaller . . . or ceased to exist entirely. However, for me, they live on, carrying on some sort of continuing daily relationship. They only grow larger" (*PV* 16, 17). The postcards, as well, grow over the years, in both volume and significance. Abe suspects that Simon's collection and the extensive research surrounding it is simply "busy work" (*Clyde Fans* 57), and to a certain extent this may be so, but it is not quite arbitrary in the way that he suggests.

It is possible to understand Simon's extension and elaboration of this trivial subject as an expression of his desire to fix himself in a moment in time. Not necessarily a particular moment—not, that is to say, the moment in Dominion when he first discovered the postcards—but any moment. He describes an adolescent preoccupation with trying to reconcile the various incarnations of a self that is separated, "cut apart by time" (*PV* 16, 18). Although he dismisses this as "a meaningless mental exercise" (19), it is clear that he still retains something of that childhood wish to halt the terrible, identity-splintering flow of time. On the comics page, of course, this splintering is made explicit: multiple moments in time, and the multiple Simons that inhabit them, are visible at once. For many of Seth's characters, collection is much more than simply the physical preservation of plastic-sleeved comic books kept in pristine condition; it is more, even, than the preservation of a particular experience associated with an object. Through collection, what is being recollected is the self. Simon's collection of postcards is one of the means by which he preserves his identity.

Various other means include: the objects in his mother's bedroom, his numbered sketches of beehives, trees, and lighthouses, the childhood "treasure box" once filled with now-forgotten artifacts, and, perhaps most striking of all, a relatively recent collection of toys kept on a shelf above the desk in his study. In one of the most overtly uncanny sequences in the *Clyde Fans* story, the toys talk to Simon and bicker with each other in a manner that suggests familiarity and long acquaintance. They are, however, an antagonistic presence whose critical, nagging remarks are largely unwelcome. The most outspoken toy—a wide-eyed figure with a large spherical head, long peg nose, and frozen grimace—is also the harshest and the most self-aware, responding to Simon's complaints about their temperament with the question, "Are you even capable of imagining a pleasant conversation between two people?" The toy goes on to remind Simon that "you're speaking for both of us" (*PV* 17, 35). The strange collection of anthropomorphic objects both splits Simon's personality and reveals this splitting as a centripetal swirl of self-talk.

The house in which Simon spends so much time alone, attending to his various collections, eventually becomes the site of a final, less insular collection. Abe observes: "I've come to see that Simon prepared this place for me" (*Clyde Fans* 54). This preparation is somewhat ominous but also considerate, an outward-looking, communicative gesture from Simon. In contrast to the unintentional collection left by Lily Matchcard in her bedroom, what Simon leaves for his brother is almost a bequest. Part exhibition, part missive from beyond, Simon's collection is more or less imbricate with the Matchcard home. "Only by infusing this whole place with the spirit of his lonely struggle," Abe says, "could I ever come here and understand him" (54). The "piles of books he left," for instance, are not merely a bunch of diverting volumes but a synecdochic record of his interior life. Likewise the other items: "Somehow he put some of himself into every object in here." Simon seems to have intuited that his brother would eventually retreat, like he did, into the house, and so he organized a private collection with the hope, expectation, or foresight that Abe would one day need it. As Abe says, he has found in the interior of the family home "the contentment that the outside world never gave me" (54).

It is this kind of contentment—or, at least, solace—that Simon seems to find in his mother's bedroom. It is the comfort of an inherited collection, intimate but still surprising, at once familiar and unfamiliar. Describing a group of items, Simon notes that "this is just a small sampling of a much larger assortment" (*PV* 19, 91), a statement that underscores the rhetorical method of the entire bedroom sequence. The final page of Simon's recollections begins with two rows of panels containing only white text on a black background (fig. 5.6). Simon suggests various ways in which his reflections could be deeper and more nuanced, exploring the minutest contours of objects or the hidden

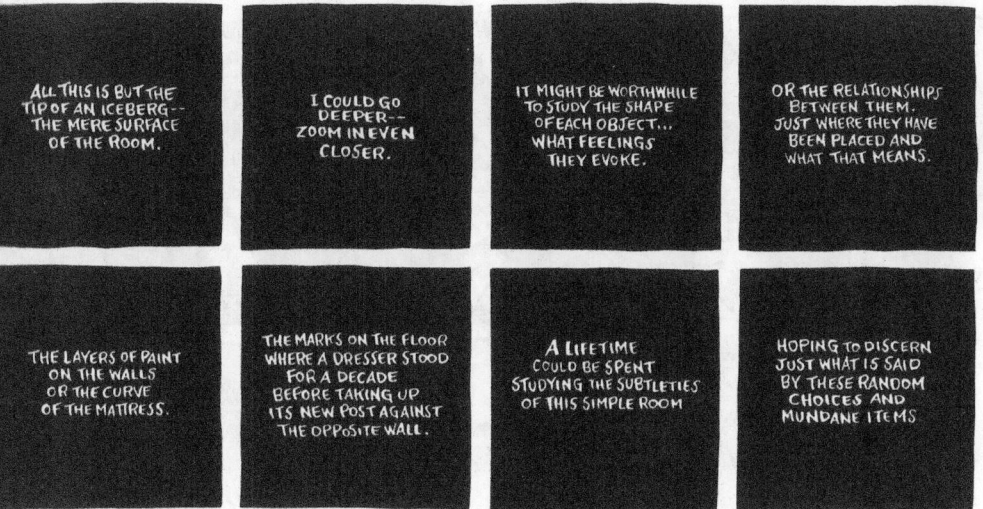

FIG. 5.6 Seth, *Palookaville* 19 (Montreal: D&Q, 2008), 95.

meaning of their position in relation to one another. For Simon, the collection is almost necessarily cryptic, something to be deciphered.

The collection can also be considered cryptic in another sense—as resembling a crypt, using the word in much the same way that Jacques Derrida has used it, to describe the manner in which traumatic experience consolidates itself. In his foreword to Nicolas Abraham and Maria Torok's *The Wolf Man's Magic Word*—a dizzying reanalysis of Freud's famous patient—Derrida considers the process by which a kind of interior tomb is constructed as a "monument" to trauma (xxii). He repeatedly asks, "What is a crypt?" It might be said that, for Derrida, a crypt is a structure that keeps a secret safe (from the self) within the self. "The inhabitant of a crypt," he writes, "is always a living dead, a dead entity we are perfectly willing to keep alive, but *as* dead" (xxi).

Although Derrida goes into greater detail about interiority/exteriority and the formation of the self, this abridged description of the crypt is enough to reveal a fundamental correspondence to the process of collection. Collection similarly forms a monument to house the past, to keep it alive and present, but always as something absent. At the root of this structural similarity is an ambivalent impulse—like the collection, the crypt manifests and mediates the boundary between inside and outside.[4]

The Matchcard home is like a collection of crypts, a mausoleum in which ever more interior spaces adjoin and intersect (and as the brothers move through the house, they appear, by virtue of the copresence of images on the

FIG. 5.7 Seth, *Palookaville* 16 (Montreal: D&Q, 2002), 12.

page, to occupy multiple spaces at once). The innermost of these interiors is a crawl space, most easily accessible through Simon's mother's bedroom by way of a small door in a slightly recessed part of the wall. The reader also sees Simon, as a young child, enter the space through an even smaller door in an upstairs hallway (fig. 5.7). What is the secret he keeps safe in the crawl space? In this liminal domestic area, behind and between the walls of the home, reside the predecessors of Simon's talkative toys: a group of stuffed and mounted animals. Taxidermy serves as an unexpectedly apt literalization of Derrida's description of the inhabitant of a crypt—an entity that is kept alive as dead—but it is not an owl or a beaver that Simon keeps hidden from himself. As his grimacing toy perceptively suggests, for Simon the stuffed animals operate as a metonym for the person who stuffed them: his long-absent father, Clyde Matchcard.

Clyde Matchcard is the absent presence at the center of *Clyde Fans*, the living dead that gives the story many of its crypt-like qualities, the fragment of identity that Simon most conceals from himself. Through his collection of bad-tempered toys, Simon seems to have neutralized the traumatic memory of Clyde in ways that his mother and brother have not; this is a somewhat inverted circumstance in which the process of collection actually appears to inhibit recollection, but with the same ultimate consequence: the preservation of identity.

If identities, as Hall suggests, are positions within narratives of the past, then it should come as no surprise when these positions change, multiply, or otherwise fail to remain fixed in response to those ever-shifting narratives. This is nevertheless a threatening prospect, to which the collector responds by attempting to fix a relation to the past. Seth's characters are so often on the cusp of anachronism, slightly out of step with the times, because they are continually attempting to fix their positions within narratives of the past. The collection helps to fortify identity by arbitrating between inside and outside, what is part of identity and what is not. Out of the chaos of the past, something specific, stable, and representative emerges.

A similar operation is at work in the medium of comics, which is structurally very similar to the "medium" of collection. Particularly in their immobility, comics give the reader every opportunity to master the narrative—to recall earlier moments, to re-collect disparate parts—and yet in their fragmented presentation they simultaneously demand constant repositioning in relation to the narrative. Through collection and recollection, the collector means to keep loss at bay—Seth reveals the fragility of these processes, the ultimate failure to forestall loss, but at the same time the potential for meaning that resides in this loss.

6

Dense and Porous: Browsing, Parataxis, and the Texture of Comics

The medium of comics is structured around narrative absences, which frequently take the form of observable spaces on the page: gaps, gutters, and margins. The corollary of this basic structural principle is an acknowledgment of the reader's significant role in filling these absences, actualizing the interdependence of panels and gaps. As was briefly noted in the previous chapter on collecting, the story structure of Seth's recent books reflects the fractured yet unified surface of a comics page. This approach mimics, on the scale of a sustained narrative, the operation that occurs in the spaces between comics panels, what Scott McCloud calls "closure," which depends on the reader's capacity to "mentally construct a continuous, unified reality" out of fragmentary images. Seth often offers the reader a variety of discrete moments, images, and ministories without making explicit the connection between them—this highly ambiguous juxtaposition of fragments can fairly be labeled parataxis.

Parataxis is frequently associated with modernist literature, especially certain strains of poetry.[1] In the introduction to her complex study *The Zukofsky Era*, Ruth Jennison plainly states: "Paratactical construction is the signature strategy of Objectivism" (3), a branch of modernist poetry strongly influenced by the Imagism of Ezra Pound and William Carlos Williams. Jennison goes on to explain that "paratactical form throws into relief the historical and material specificity of each particular against that of its neighbor" (3). In Seth's work, this technique reaches a particularly patent manifestation in the scores of items collected in Lily Matchcard's bedroom; each object, although isolated in its own panel, provides contrast and context for its neighboring objects. The final section of this chapter addresses the effect of this technique in a discussion of framing, which leads into a reflection on pacing and Seth's notion of sublime boredom. The foregoing sections similarly attend to some of Seth's most unassuming formal innovations, many of which prompt a particularly measured and/or nonlinear reading practice and all of which reveal something about the formal operations of comics as a narrative medium. As part of its effort to describe the surfaces and liminal spaces of comics, this chapter contains an exercise in suspended perception, which deliberately resists familiar reading practices, as well as an extended consideration of the single-panel gag.

These and other related lines of inquiry often aim to provide an account of *texture*, a term that this chapter favors because it evocatively designates the "feel" of a *text*. As in chapter 1's account of spatial composition within a panel, even "feel" becomes a useful word (occasionally deployed here without quotation marks) despite its terminological imprecision. Open and heterogeneous, the comics text has a unique capacity to "feel" at once dense and porous. With juxtaposition as its foremost feature, the simultaneously fragmented and coherent page of comics panels holds enormous potential for parataxis. Inventive as Seth's approach to storytelling can be, it is important to note that even his most highly paratactic sequences operate according to the same fundamental principles that structure more conventional comics narratives.

Reading Like a Flaneur

Encounters with strangers are a recurring feature in Seth's earlier work and serve as an instructive instance in the development of his approach to panel composition and marginality. For the most part, these encounters are either incidental or accidental, but they also seem somehow inevitable, a result of the urban setting of the stories. Seth's very first story, in *Palookaville* 1, revolves around a particularly ugly run-in with strangers, sparked by the forced intimacy of public transit. It begins in a subway car and ends violently in front of a crowd of commuters. In *It's a Good Life, If You Don't Weaken*, Seth-as-protagonist continues to cross paths with strangers, although these encounters are far less dramatic and far more one-sided, often consisting entirely of Seth's interior reactions to (and projections onto) the strangers he observes in fleeting moments around the city.

Significantly, these passing encounters are not exactly ephemeral for the reader, who can linger and return to them in a way the protagonist cannot. Even those background characters who elicit no verbal reaction from the protagonist remain permanently inscribed on the page, open to readerly scrutiny.

Indeed, it is these characters in particular who are most open to the reader's own reactions and projections because they fall outside the zone of verbalized authorial attention. The reader who pays attention to these peripheral characters almost automatically enlivens them with even a brief look. As is often the case in comics, it seems to require more effort *not* to read the simplified images, *not* to imbue them with life. The panels of Seth's early urban scenes are full of such strangers, too many for the main character to describe (or in most cases even notice). Seth's drawings, however, are sufficiently descriptive in and of themselves; the occasional caption commentary simply refocuses the reader's attention, bringing these ubiquitous "extras" briefly to the foreground. The reader's engagement with Seth's background characters (sometimes deliberate, often largely involuntary) serves as an example of McCloud's contention that the cartoon engenders a specific "way of seeing," and that it operates as "a vacuum into which our identity and awareness are pulled" (31, 36). The absence of explicit authorial comment produces precisely this type of vacuum, a site for readerly interpolation.

In more literal terms, these urban characters are often already in the shadowy foreground of panels (*IAGL* 44). In such urban scenes, the composition of space within the panel—which significantly affects the feel of the represented space—is often defined by the ambivalent tension between foreground and background. Seth uses shading and compositional conventions to draw the reader's eye to the protagonist in most panels; nevertheless, his work consistently emphasizes moments of meandering and lingering in which the protagonist becomes a vehicle for the kind of nonlinear narrative pleasures that are specific to the medium of comics. The third part of *It's a Good Life* opens with a wordless sequence in which Seth wanders around the Royal Ontario Museum, alone but in close proximity to strangers. Here, the comics page invites a combination of reading and looking that might best be described as "browsing" (with that term's connotations of leisure and consumerism left largely intact). In such sequences, the main action of the plot recedes. Or, more precisely, the negligible action reveals that the imperative of plot progression is not more important to the story than contemplative moments in which the reader and protagonist look around.

In this way, Seth's books offer a spectacular, peripatetic experience that attunes the reader to what Walter Benjamin calls "the tempo of flânerie" (*Arcades Project* 422)—and it is the very structure of the medium of comics that encourages the reader to act as a flaneur. One of the peculiarities of the comics page (peculiar, that is, for a page of literature) is that the reader can choose to focus on those aspects of the narrative that remain unwritten. The visual density of the comics page offers a great deal of nonverbal narrative information and affords the reader greater freedom in processing this information and filling narrative gaps. Having become accustomed to browsing by the regular appearance of certain kinds of sequences, the reader of Seth's work remains alert to unwritten details even when the story proceeds at a more conventional pace.

It is not really possible to "read around" a traditional narrative text in this fashion. The reader of prose fiction—say, a novel by Zola that contains a vivid crowd scene—does not have access to a minor character's wardrobe unless it is explicitly described, in which case it has been given a particular emphasis and exists on the same narrative plane as the rest of the book. By contrast, the viewer of a film—for instance, the opening of Charlie Chaplin's *City Lights*—can easily perceive the hat of an extra, but the image is likely to be fleeting and irrelevant to the narrative. The strangers who populate Seth's panels are often marginal, but at the same time they are available for prolonged examination, as explicitly depicted as the main characters.

In certain cases, peripheral characters are not relegated to the margins. A diner scene in *It's a Good Life* features an older man who seems to be listening to Seth and Chester (fig. 6.1). The sequence is very deliberate: after his profile appears, framing a scene in one panel, this character is subsequently shown at a neighboring table and is then afforded his own panel, with Seth's dialogue in a speech bubble above him. This eavesdropper does not hold any enigmatic significance and never makes another appearance; he is simply part of the mise-en-scène on this particular page, and this seems to be the only reason that Seth has emphasized his presence. The unusual attention given to this apparently trivial character challenges the expectation that central and peripheral aspects of the story will literally correspond to the center and periphery of the panel. In disrupting this standard visual hierarchy, Seth gently pushes against conventional notions of narrative significance and further encourages the reader to browse.

Browsing is by no means the only reading experience that puts the reader in the position of a flaneur. Another distinguishing feature of Seth's earlier work is the continuous scene, which he sometimes describes as an element of "naturalistic storytelling" (see page 197), storytelling that closely follows a character from moment to moment. The most languid of these continuous scenes, which takes up almost the entire first part of *Clyde Fans*, consists of a single, uninterrupted, sixty-five-page sequence in which Abraham Matchcard wakes, dresses, eats, smokes, reads, bathes, and more than anything else wanders from room to room in the Matchcard home, all the while talking to the reader. Seth suggests that this sense of continuity is one of the great assets of comics: "I think that's what initially interested me in cartooning, was natural

FIG. 6.1 Seth, *It's a Good Life, If You Don't Weaken* (Montreal: Drawn and Quarterly, 1996), 71.

storytelling, where you follow someone walking around and you see it as if you're a ghost walking with them" (see page 197). This approach does cultivate a very smooth, intimate reading experience and also lends itself to the portrayal of urban perambulation, which in turn reinforces the testudine tempo of *flânerie*.

In comics, even the smoothest reading experience almost necessarily appears as a series of disconnected images. On those occasions that Seth dispenses with panels, the result is monumental and/or instantaneous—narrative suspension as opposed to narrative continuity (figs. 3.3, 7.9). Curiously, an image that spans a full comics page is much easier to read when it has been divided into panels, submitted to the narrative logic of the multiframe. This eye-catching partition, in which a single image is at once coherent and

126 Browsing, Parataxis, and the Texture of Comics

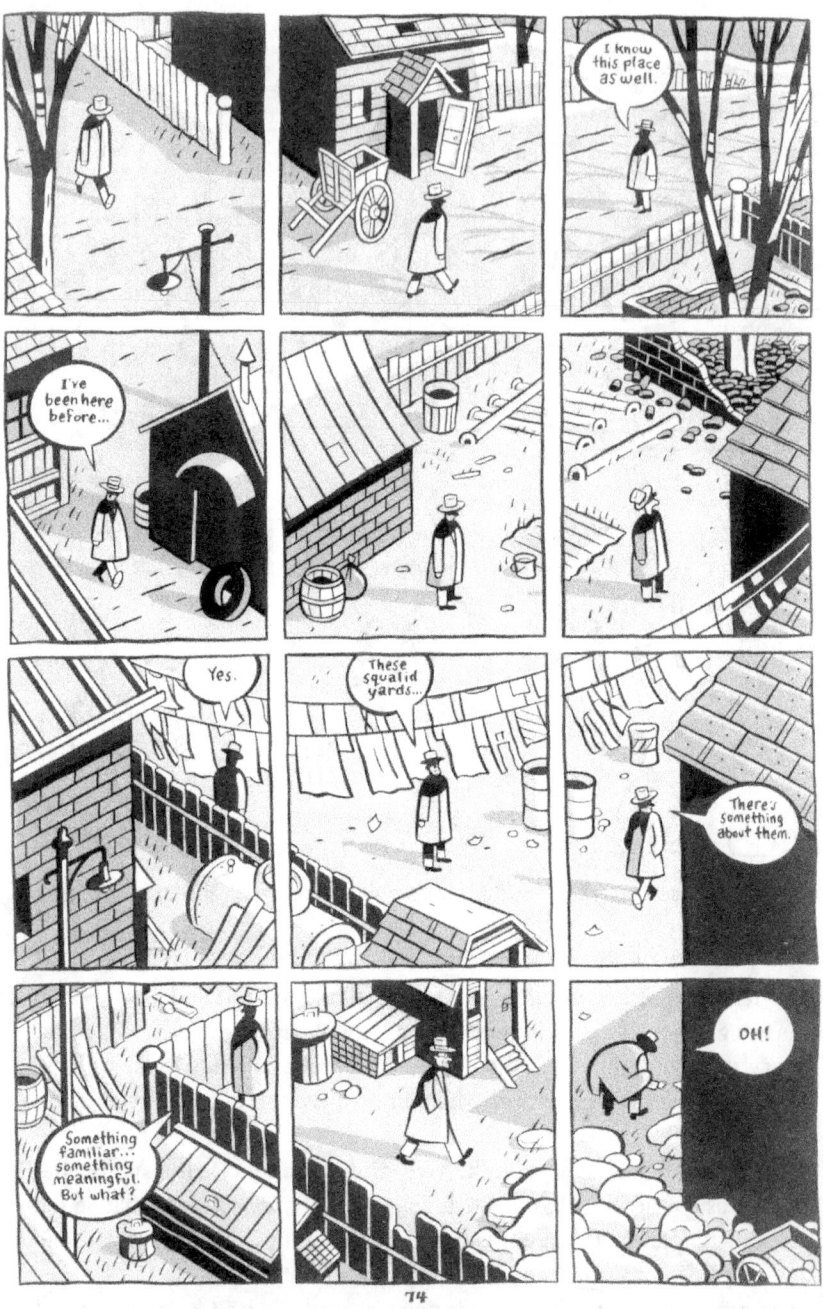

FIG. 6.2 Seth, *Palookaville* 19 (Montreal: D&Q, 2008), 74.

fragmented, demonstrates the unique capabilities of the medium. A page near the end of *George Sprott* divides a nighttime tableau into a grid of twenty-five panels, many of which contain running caption narration. Even more striking is a dream sequence in *Palookaville* 19 that shows Simon wandering around "squalid yards"—a single image is divided into twelve panels, each of which contains a representation of Simon (fig. 6.2). This page updates a paratactic mode of pictorial storytelling that has a long history, a mode in which multiple representations of a central figure appear in different areas of a single image.[2] As Peter Quartermain observes, parataxis has the capacity to create an open field in which the reader is free to "wander at will" (54). This wandering—or, as this investigation sometimes terms it, browsing—is precisely the kind of reading experience that Seth is so adept at providing.

Seth's elegant, transparent page design very effectively underscores the manner in which repetition and juxtaposition permit narrative continuity in comics. It is not unusual for a character to appear in every panel of a comics page, but the visual connection between time, space, and narrative in comics becomes particularly clear when each of these panels is part of a single image. Through Simon's almost zoetropic progress across a unified background, Seth arrestingly illustrates one of the structuring principals of comics storytelling. The dozen Simons also produce a somewhat uncanny doubling effect, which is well suited to the logic of this particular dreamscape. In such sequences, which draw special attention to the particularities of the medium, Seth's work reveals that unified and coherent narratives are necessarily composed of fragments.

The Materiality of Surfaces and Liminal Spaces

In the overtly metafictional narratives of *It's a Good Life*, *Wimbledon Green*, and *The Great Northern Brotherhood of Canadian Cartoonists*, Seth foregrounds his deep understanding and appreciation of comics, often to ironic effect. Even a work like *George Sprott*, however, offers musings on the medium: Seth explicitly addresses the way that time behaves on a comics page in a sequence titled "George Is Born." Before the prologue, before even the title page of the book, this unusual preface offers the reader two pages of panels in which floats George Sprott, both as a newborn and in old age. Many panels depict only a disembodied head with captions that contemplate the unknowable void beyond time-bound life. "Is it even relevant to discuss time in such circumstances?" the narrator asks. "Or are the before and after realms two different places? Two voids separated by a brief spurt of time?"

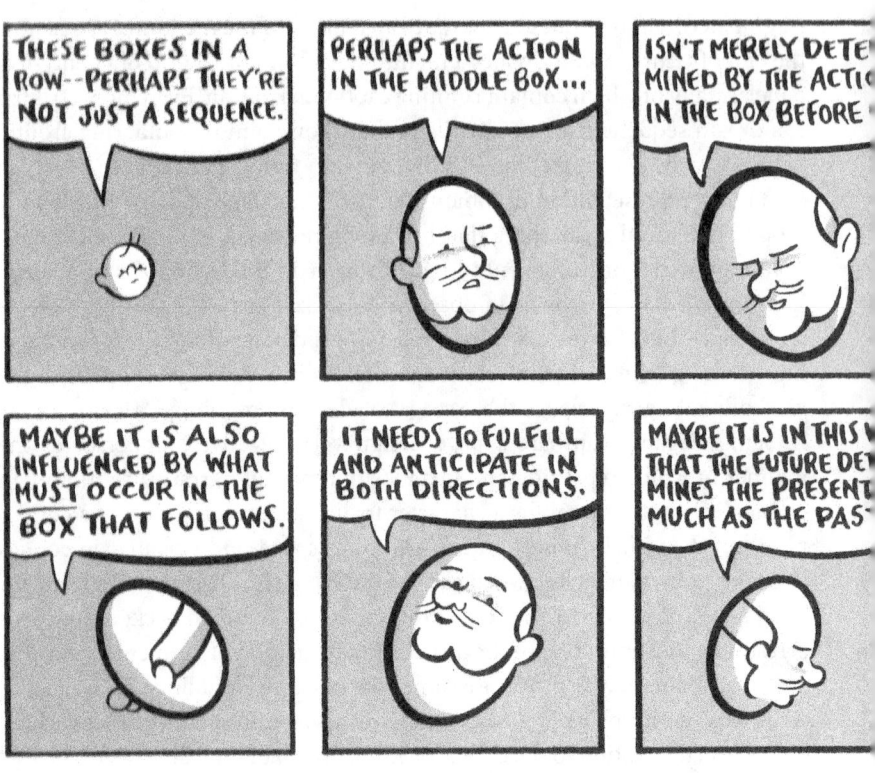

FIG. 6.3 Seth, *George Sprott: 1894–1975* (Montreal: D&Q, 2009), n.p.

The narrator ultimately acknowledges that "these are very naive questions"—but first describes a moment of insight that George experiences while reading a comics page (fig. 6.3). Perhaps action, George muses, "needs to anticipate and fulfill in both directions. Maybe in this way the future determines the present as much as the past." This account of the linear coherence of time—although its philosophical rigor may be questionable—straightforwardly explains the sophisticated interdependence of fragments on the comics page. The reader anticipates and fulfills the temporal and narrative potential of these fragments, almost involuntarily generating the continuity of the sequence.

It is an uncommon practice to simply look at the pages of a book without reading them, one that requires either great distraction or great concentration. As an exercise in perception, however, it can be revealing to suspend the operations of the page—and, like many of Seth's more idiosyncratic sequences, "George Is Born" actually encourages this kind of suspension.

If the discontinuity of the images is allowed to remain intact, it is their homogeneity that becomes most immediately striking. The panels offer the same images again and again, with only slight variations and an extremely restrained color palette. The images are motionless, of course, but even taking this into account there is very little in the way of action: the characters float and occasionally speak; the blue void that surrounds them remains solid, flat, inconspicuous; the floating heads, tilted at various angles, evoke a sketchbook character study or the perspectives depicted on an animator's model sheet.

"Read" in this way, the pages reveal themselves as quite airy, the images of George marked out in thick but not heavy brushstrokes, while the captions and balloons give the layout a sense of balanced uniformity. Still, the sequence appears as a stuttering, almost compulsively repetitive utterance in which a very limited number of elements are insistently reinscribed. Much of the stuttering quality can be attributed to the gutter, which is far more apparent as an element on the page when one does not grant it its basic function of propelling the narrative in the customary way. This investigation often emphasizes the role of the reader's interpolation into the gutters and gaps of a comics narrative—but this emphasis can actually obscure the materiality of these liminal spaces. Refusing to read, the reader finds that the spaces between panels have nowhere to hide. Like a mild optical illusion, they appear at once as window frames through which the panels can be seen and, receding, as a single continuous background on top of which the panels sit. Even when all else is rendered immobile by this concentrated nonreading, the gutter remains restless, caught ambivalently between foreground and background, continuing to fluctuate.

Since the reader is not generally understood to be filling narrative gaps by physically inscribing the page with new images, the visual properties of the gaps are easy to ignore. Particularly in his recent work, Seth occasionally embellishes the standard format, and the normally overlooked gutters become sites of experimentation and play. The earliest examples can be found in *Wimbledon Green*, where Seth sometimes disrupts the continuity of a page's negative space by extending the lines of panel frames *through* the gutter, fully realizing the grid-like nature of the layout, creating a system of small squares and slim bars held between the panels. This has the effect of flattening the page somewhat; as opposed to the appearance of more conventional layouts, these panels neither look like they are "floating" before the single background plane of the page nor like they are slightly recessed. In certain layouts, this playful manipulation of gutter conventions is accentuated with color. In a section titled "Rivals of Wimbledon Green"—a kind of dramatis personae in which other major collectors are described in terms of their relation to the title character—the intervals between panels are shaded to match the background of the panels themselves, which transforms the grid of the layout into a kind of warped checkerboard. The light ink washes that Seth favors give the impression of diffused light originating from behind a flat plane, as in a stained-glass window (fig. 6.4).

The Great Northern Brotherhood of Canadian Cartoonists also features playful violations of the gutter. On several occasions, two panels are connected through the gutter by an element from the drawn world of the story. The impression is simple but effective: objects appear to be breaching the frame, leaping up out of the panels in an instance of cartoon trompe l'oeil. The most striking example shows a pod launching from a space station, piloted by the Inuit astronaut Kao-Kuk, the trail of the pod's trajectory sweeping across the gutter from one panel to the other (fig. 6.5). In a subtler, more droll instance, separate panels that share a background image are linked together by a fishing rod (34).

FIG. 6.4 Seth, *Wimbledon Green* (Montreal: D&Q, 2005), 16.

FIG. 6.5 Seth, *The Great Northern Brotherhood of Canadian Cartoonists* (Montreal: D&Q, 2009), 46.

These embellishments have an involuntary, almost compulsive quality, as of a child doodling idly in the margins, extending existing planes, filling in spaces. (This improvised play with conventions occurs at the level of narrative as well—anecdotes give way to apocrypha, adventures, quasi-academic analyses, and other additions.) It is appropriate that this type of play within the margins first appears in *Wimbledon Green*, which itself occupies a somewhat marginal position with respect to Seth's more polished works. For much of his career, Seth has been publishing sketchbook material along with his other work, not only narratives like *Wimbledon Green* and *The Great Northern Brotherhood* but also nonnarrative illustrations and sketches as well. The collection *Vernacular Drawings* contains over two hundred pages of work drawn from "Sketchbooks 1 to 6," and one of *Palookaville* 20's three sections consists of "Selections from Sketchbooks Seven & Eight." This material decenters that work that is more conventionally "finished" and tends to erode the boundary between public and private work. "Working in a sketchbook is always freeing," Seth explains, "because you never *have* to publish anything. It could take any form it likes. . . . You're aware that you *might* publish it. But if it works out, you'll figure out how to make it work in another form" (see page 205, emphases in original). The result of this process can be observed in the fully developed technical experimentation of a refined work like *George Sprott*.

In its scope, its conspicuous materiality, its capacious structure, its occasional ornate flourishes, and its profusion of available perspectives, *George Sprott* can comfortably be characterized as baroque. The term is used here without any pejorative connotations, to spotlight the work's formal and narrative plasticity: "baroque" provides another way of thinking about how Seth manages to convey "the capacity for endless interpolations" in the finite space of a book. This understanding of the protractible space of *George Sprott* draws on Gilles Deleuze's notion that "the Baroque invents the infinite work or process" (39). This is from *The Fold*, Deleuze's book on Leibniz and the baroque, in which he similarly states that "the Baroque fold unfurls all the way to infinity" (3). Deleuze also identifies the *unfold*, which he describes as "the continuation or extension of [the fold's] act, the condition of its manifestation" (40).

In certain contexts, these statements might seem abstract or opaque, but in the case of *George Sprott*, the reader must literally unfold large leaves in order to read them—a deliberate and somewhat delicate act that is haptically and narratively distinct from the conventional turning of pages. Here the *unfold* becomes a physical action performed by the reader, which does in fact extend the folded page and permit the manifestation of otherwise concealed panels. Unfolded, the foldout pages are in excess of themselves, extrusions from the familiar space of the book, which materialize the break from narrative linearity that their evocative sequences carry out. In these ways, the foldout section gestures toward the unbounded, irrepressible aspects of memory. The tactile experience of unfolding also fulfills the suggestion of tangibility made throughout *George Sprott* by drawn photographs, which sometimes overlap or appear with corners folded in a trompe l'oeil effect, as on the page titled "A Fresh Start" (trompe l'oeil is a hallmark of baroque art and architecture) (fig. 3.7).

It may be fruitful to pursue the potential affinity between the baroque and the "mannered quality" of Seth's work examined in previous chapters. Seth's baroque flourishes, of which the foldout section is the most overt, might be thought of as mannered qualities taken to a particular extreme. However, it is not just the excess of the physical page that suggests the infinite but also the profusion of unusually open-ended, evocative sequences. The reader is presented with six pages of drawn photographs, stream-of-conscious panels, and text plates that contain very distinctive, clipped language. Of particular note is Seth's use of the word "that," which repeatedly appears as a demonstrative pronoun—as in "that ball" or "that toy" or, more pointedly, "that child." As in other sequences where text plates form a dominant presence, the heavy black boxes establish a sort of cadence, and here their baroque deployment coincides with a hypnotic, mannered language. If "baroque" seems like too loaded a term, perhaps it would be better simply to say that the foldout section of *George Sprott* is especially dense and porous—indeed, it might be said to typify the book's particular brand of paratactic density and porosity.

Originally serialized in the weekly *New York Times Magazine*, *George Sprott* was published in 2009 as a large-format book containing many additional pages: illustrated intervals; two-page arctic spreads of icebergs and snowy landscapes; full-page photos (actual photos, not drawn photos) of cardboard models of some of Dominion's buildings; and sepia-toned sequences from George's life. These biographical interludes are less schematic than the bulk of the book, in which George's life seems one step removed, narrated by the unreliable narrator or through the anecdotes of secondary characters. The original pages drawn for the magazine are somewhat cramped, but the additional material is airy and open, and contributes significantly to the book's capacious feeling.

Arguably, *George Sprott* represents a development of the narrative approach that Seth improvised in his sketchbook with *Wimbledon Green*. Both books seem to take the very surface of the comics page—fragmented and almost infinitely flexible—as a model for narrative structure. The seamless inclusion of new material in *George Sprott* suggests an ideal literary space that might be expanded indefinitely—and it is ultimately the participation of the reader that makes such a space possible. The reader's capacity to bridge gaps and to incorporate (not to mention take pleasure in) unfamiliar or unexpected narrative fragments is one of the defining features of literature. In comics, this process is most in evidence on a smaller scale, from panel to panel: "For the comics reader," Thierry Groensteen states, "the fact of presupposing that there is a meaning necessarily leads him to search for the way that the panel he 'reads' is linked to the others" (*System of Comics* 113).

Readers find meaning not only between panels and between sequences, however, but even in the isolated image of a single-panel gag (discussed below), where the presupposition of meaning presents itself in terms of a presupposition of humor. To get the joke is to fulfill the role of the model reader that the cartoon has set out and to enter into the full world suggested by a diegetic fragment. The narrative density and porosity offered by even a single cartoon image make comics uniquely suited to the kind of flexibility that Seth so often displays in his storytelling.

The Single-Panel Gag

The single-panel gag cartoon, self-contained though it may be, rarely if ever appears in isolation. In magazines and newspapers, single-panel cartoons have always shared space with columns of text, advertisements, and other comics of various formats. In *It's a Good Life*, Seth reproduces the *mise-en-page* of magazines like the *Saturday Evening Post* and the *New Yorker*, into which he seamlessly incorporates Kalo's cartoons. In this way, Seth not only makes the gags that much more convincing as artifacts, he also acknowledges that the American single-panel cartoon is a specific form that does not exist in an ahistorical vacuum. The relation between the single-panel gag and its historical context is reciprocal: as suggested in chapter 1, the *New Yorker* owes much of its style to its cartoons, and vice versa. By inserting the works of his invented cartoonist into historical documents, Seth revises the reader's perception of history, and only when the reader has read the cartoons is the interpolation into the past complete. Part of what makes this anachronistic maneuver so potent is that it mirrors the semiotic operation of comics, and uses the reader's hermeneutic impulse to cement the bond (and blur the boundary) between public record and Seth's private, fabricated history.

The narrativity of the single-panel cartoon always seems to overflow its single panel, suggesting not only the space and time beyond the frame but also the overall context in which the frame exists. The same might be said of the photograph, but unlike the photograph the single-panel gag inclines toward

FIG. 6.6 Seth, *It's a Good Life, If You Don't Weaken* (Montreal: D&Q, 1996), 171.

narrative transparency rather than opacity. It may be the reader's projection of the narrative that realizes the gag, but all the necessary elements are already present in a latent form within the frame. Barbara Postema observes that "the single, static image contains intrinsic narrativity in a number of ways" (500). This is true of almost any sequential panel plucked out of its narrative context, but it is also true of a single-panel cartoon, the narrativity of which is not buttressed by sequential images.

The narrative context for a particular panel in a sequence is provided by ever-expanding orbits of potentially relevant information (e.g., other related works by the author, other unrelated works by the author, other works in a similar genre, canonical literary works, general literary conventions, historical events, etc.), but the most immediate context comes from adjacent panels. In the case of the single-panel cartoon, unconnected to other panels, the most immediate narrative context comes from the reader's experience of *other* single-panel cartoons. Familiarity with the conventions of the form—its economy, its typical topics and settings, its default point of view—is an important part of the reader's comprehension.

What may be the wittiest of the "Kalo" gags relies to a large extent on the reader's ability to make contextual leaps, both conventionally and culturally. The panel shows a familiar domestic scene: as a cross woman cleans up a broken lamp, she addresses a young boy who is standing in the corner of the room, facing the wall (fig. 6.6). (Of course, familiarity is a relative quality. Readers are expected to instantly recognize the furniture, wallpaper, decorations, etc., of the depicted room as well as the attire and, significantly, postures of the characters.) In a fraction of a second, the reader will infer a mother and son relationship between the two characters; although not explicitly stated, this relationship seems so strongly implied by all available information as to be effectively obvious. The caption—"I am *not* drunk with power!"—confirms and plays on the mother-son dynamic. Appreciation of this dynamic entails another inference, strongly implied by the structure of the caption and the emphasis on the word "not," that the mother is responding to a particular phrase used by the child. The single-panel gag cartoon, in its compactness, its verbal-visual density, and its combination of various cultural registers, exemplifies the way in which "different modes in multimodal media work together to provide the reader with clues to fill gaps and formulate hypotheses" (Kukkonen 40).

In this particular instance, the substance of the joke is absent from the panel. In diegetic time, it has occurred just prior to the scene that is made available to the reader. The child's precocious, hyperbolic accusation—which perfectly articulates a conventional reaction to parental authority—is the substance of the joke, and yet *not the joke itself*. If the same panel depicted the child saying "you are drunk with power," the effect would be much diminished. So what is the joke itself? It might be said that the joke is the relation between the mother and child, which exists in its full complexity only in the mind of the reader: not only the child's implied remark but the relation between the remark and the mother's childish retort, situated in a middle-class context. The gag draws its power from suggestion and works precisely because the reader must construct the full story. An understanding of narrative "as a cognitive construct" (Kukkonen 40) helps to account for the difficulty of locating the joke within the panel.

Construct, infer, formulate—such terms may be altogether too intentional, since the reading operation occurs so quickly and so instinctively. The texture of the single-panel gag makes a sudden transition from blurry to clear, hovering in a suspended state of obscurity before snapping into focus. The reader experiences the gag not as a hard-won insight but as an epiphanic burst of understanding. At issue is an aspect of the gag cartoon that is rarely remarked upon, likely because of its obviousness: the reader wants to get the joke. Some of the most successful gags enlist the reader's desire to make sense of the available information. Others, equally successful but in a different way, seem to lack any substantial punch line and depend mostly on the reader's expectation of humor. In another of Seth's Kalo cartoons, set on a windy urban sidewalk, a nonplussed police officer confronts a carefree man dressed only in undergarments, who says, "It's actually quite an amusing story, first my hat blew off ..." (*IAGL* 174). The joke here is not so much the man's circumstance as his lack of concern about it, and his blithe disregard for police authority. This is an example of the single-panel gag as dreamlike theater of absurd possibility, characterized by a sense of excess being contained or channeled into a single moment, a finite set of coordinates. A certain amount of Peter Arno–flavored class friction undergirds this gossamer gag, which Seth has aptly inserted into an issue of the *New Yorker*. In many ways it is a sight gag, well designed and illustrated with a light touch, with all the lines drawing attention to the speaker's oblivious face; the caption is almost superfluous. The contrasts are telling: the hunched, middle-class policeman grips a baton at his side; the relaxed, upper-class gentleman rests a closed umbrella on his shoulder (indeed, it is his lack of concern that most strongly implies his class position). Many gag cartoons rely on attitude and tone, particularly Arno's disengaged intimacy, and some seem to flatter the reader with their dryness—to appreciate a *New Yorker* cartoon is to fortify in a small but significant way one's status as a reader.

An Art of Suggestion

It bears repeating that there are many kinds of gaps in comics, more than in literature that does not incorporate drawing. In *Alternative Comics*, Charles Hatfield identifies fragmentation and instability as native strengths of the medium, arguing that "comic art is composed of several kinds of *tension*, in which various ways of reading—various interpretive options and potentialities—must be played against each other" (36). Like most media, comics are multimodal—and possibly more multimodal than most. For every mode of communication featured in a comics sequence, there is a corresponding gap; these various modes and their gaps, in tension and concert with each other, produce the singularly dense and porous texture of the medium. Of course, the most medium-specific gap on the comics page remains the gap between panels.

What is it that occurs between panels? For a detailed description, the most thorough source is still Groensteen's *System of Comics*. Groensteen explains that the gutter "marks the semantic solidarity of contiguous panels above all, both working through the codes of narrative and sequential drawings. Between the polysemic images, the polysyntactic gutter is the site of a reciprocal determination, and it is in this dialectic interaction that meaning is constructed, not without the active participation of the reader" (115). This description is dense with technical language, but not needlessly so, considering that Groensteen is attempting to dissect an invisible and almost instantaneous process. The "reciprocal determination" that takes place between images, the construction of meaning, does not actually require a visible gutter. Mario Saraceni observes that, occasionally, panels "are not separated by a gutter but only by the borders of the panels. However, in these cases the division between panels retains its importance, since it does not depend on the actual amount of physical space but on the narrative hiatus between the panels" (175n). As has been stated previously in other terms, the panels and the hiatuses between them are interdependent.

Sometimes Seth incorporates gaps into his sequences in a way that exceeds the expected spaces between panels: in certain instances, panels themselves serve as gaps, solid black voids. Such gaps do not behave in the same way as the negative spaces of the gutter, which tend to lead the reader's eye to the next image, operating as a steady force for forward momentum. Rather, these solid black panels tend to suspend narrative movement, operating as pauses. The reader may not be inclined to linger over these pauses, as they are sometimes positioned in the corners of pages, which can make them easier to overlook or regard as mere space fillers. In this sense, these voids become one of Seth's most understated textural techniques, affecting the "feel" of the page at an almost subconscious level. Nevertheless, when they appear amid Lily Matchcard's cluttered items, they stand out as noticeable blank spots.

Far more common than these solid black panels are Seth's distinctive text plates, black panels with white block text, which appear with increasing regularity over the course of his career. In *Wimbledon Green*, they often serve as transitional panels; in *George Sprott*, they usually contain dates, sound effects,

FIG. 6.7 Seth, *Palookaville* 20 (Montreal: D&Q, 2010), 1.

and fragments of speech or thought. In part 4 of *Clyde Fans*, these panels are used extensively and, it seems, exclusively to depict thoughts. The opening sequence establishes a technique of interspersing terse text plates with more conventional panels depicting illustrated action (fig. 6.7). The illustrated panels show disjointed images from a first-person perspective, so the black text plates produce a strong blinking effect, which structures the sequence and determines its sporadic rhythm. With regard to tempo, the text plates offer something of a counterpoint to the standard panels. Although both kinds of panels provide fragmented narratives, the illustrated part of the narrative moves at a hurried pace, even depicting the narrator's feet as he races from one location to another. By contrast, the choppy text covers little ground: "I remember the sound of my feet on the pavement as I ran, and turning the corner, blood rushing in my ears, like wind through a canyon. And I remember he wasn't there" (*PV* 20, 1). These two short sentences are spread out over an entire page in fragments, mingled with fragmentary images that also contain various kinds of text. These multiple layers of text interact with each other in a way that is ultimately at the discretion of the reader, although the foremost layers are the text plates and the onomatopoeia of the illustrated panels. Reduced to a linear sequence, the words appear thusly:

> I remember/the sound of my feet on the pavement/KLOP//KLOP/as I ran,/KLOP/ and turning the corner//KLOP/KLOP/blood rushing in my ears,/KLOP//like wind through a canyon./KLOP/And I remember//he wasn't there.

Although this purely textual notation gives some sense of rhythm, what it cannot capture is the way that words behave in the context of a comics page, the internal and external soundscapes that they can suggest, especially in tandem with cartoon images.

This sequence provides an exemplary instance of textural density/porosity: the standard panels and the text plates are interwoven for four pages, and rather than encumber each other they coexist without any confusion or sense of interruption. It is only at the end of the sequence that the two parallel modes appear to dovetail: the final panel features a cartoon tear against a solid black panel (*PV* 20, 4). Instead of appearing cluttered or overburdened with too much disparate visual information, the pages in fact seem quite spacious and cleanly laid out. In part, this is due to the high contrast between the two kinds of panels—the black blocks open up the page by providing explicit gaps between images (which supplement and complement the implicit gaps of the gutter). If the inner monologue were to appear in captions—within the panels instead of between them—the narrative would be entirely different,

FIG. 6.8 Seth, *George Sprott: 1894–1975* (Montreal: D&Q, 2009), n.p.

and the pages would likely seem cramped, less visually appealing. In some ways, Seth takes Will Eisner's dictum that "text reads as an image" (Eisner 2) to an extreme by isolating text fragments in their own highly legible units. Through this unique stratification of comics elements, Seth emphasizes the fragmented appearance of the page, but in doing so he reveals the ease with which the reader can put the pieces together. In this sense, parataxis is more than just discontinuity and fragmentation: it is a particular type of heightened juxtaposition that creates a field for readerly interpolation.

As Groensteen notes, each panel at once advances and suspends narrative movement. "The frame," he states, "is the agent of this double maneuver of progression/retention" (*System of Comics* 45). In this way, the frame is a kind of fulcrum between the diegesis of the panel and the intericonic void represented by the gap between panels. The surface of the comics page (what Groensteen more precisely labels the spatio-topia) coheres around various framing functions, which are typically carried out by literal frames that border images and make plain the gaps between them. An examination of the atypical instance—the frameless panel—may help to show the extent to which the coherence of the page depends on *implicit* framing.

One of the unnarrated sepia sequences in *George Sprott* features a number of frameless panels, in which a young George appears in isolation, almost as though he has stepped out of the diegesis and into the void of the gutter (fig. 6.8). A suggestive ground shadow gives these panels a hint of dimension, but George's environment—the richly rendered world of the narrative that persists in nearly all of the sequence's panels—has vanished along with the frame that normally contains it. These intermittent gaps in George's backdrop do not, however, disrupt the reading experience to any significant degree. Rather, they punctuate the sequence, lending emphasis and perhaps even a certain sense of timelessness to particular moments. Even though these panels are frameless (and in this sense constitute a structural/narrative interruption), they are nevertheless surrounded by the frames of other panels and by the physical boundary of the page's edge; their status as panels and their position in the sequence is never really at risk because it is expected that the reader will automatically make sense of the empty spots. In theory, all of the panels in a sequence could be frameless, which would slightly increase the interpretive burden placed on the reader but would likely not impede understanding of the narrative.

A somewhat obvious observation that may border on tautology: panels that have their own frames are also framed by the frames of adjacent panels. Indeed, it is this proliferation of frames that gives rise to the conventional gutter. "Bound to the contents that it encloses, the frame is no less attached to the frames that surround it" (Groensteen, *System of Comics* 43). Framing not only encloses a fragment of diegesis, ensuring the integrity of the panel (Groensteen, *System of Comics* 25), it also structures the relations among panels. In this sense, "framing" refers not only to particular functions of visible borders but also to the context that the juxtaposition of images provides. Groensteen identifies six distinct functions of the frame, but these functions interact and overlap to such an extent that their detailed elaboration does not contribute much to this chapter.[3] Still, in his discussion of what he calls "the expressive function" of the frame, Groensteen astutely observes that "the frame of the comics panel can connote or index the image that it encloses" (49). In this way, framing can provide information about how to read and interpret a panel. The soft, cloud-like borders of the dream sequence panels in *It's a Good Life* offer a somewhat superficial example, although far more subtle and inventive techniques are available to the comics author (for instance, Seth's use of drawn photographs and his method of fragmenting a single, continuous image into contiguous panels). One of the most understated and effective examples of expressive framing appears at the end of *Palookaville* 19, in the bedroom of Lily Matchcard.

"The frame," Groensteen asserts, "is always an invitation to stop and to scrutinize" (*System of Comics* 54). In the final pages of *Palookaville* 19, Seth offers the reader scores of uniform frames, laid out in regular rows with text captions, which invite a very deliberate, attentive reading. The reader may choose not to accept this invitation but will nevertheless be compelled to respond to it in some fashion—perhaps by skimming the pages casually and concentrating only on the most striking panels; perhaps by examining the images but generally ignoring the accompanying text; perhaps even by skipping the sequence entirely, flipping through to the very last page of *Palookaville* 19, where Seth opens up the page with a series of larger panels. Such atypical readings seem fairly unlikely, however, particularly for the reader who has arrived at this point in the *Clyde Fans* saga and is already accustomed to the measured pace of the ongoing story. In any case, the layout of the sequence and the events that precede it do not predispose the reader to inspect the illustrations while disregarding the text; likewise, it would be effectively impossible for the reader to pore over the captions without immediately, almost involuntarily absorbing the images that they describe.

It seems probable that Seth intends this sequence to induce what he has referred to in interviews as "sublime boredom" (see page 195), a borderline phenomenon that is always at risk of slipping into outright tedium. Sublime boredom is a feeling that will be familiar to admirers of Andrei Tarkovsky's long, unbroken shots, or the experimental films of Michael Snow, or even the exhaustive scene-setting descriptive passages found in certain kinds of genre fiction. Seth suggests that sublime boredom, as he conceives it, is by no means a negligible feeling, although it does occupy a marginal field of experience, "a thin line between things that are interesting and dull" (quoted in Dunley). Of course, apparently self-evident descriptors like "interesting" or "dull" encompass many conventions, assumptions, and subjective attitudes. Susan Sontag strongly asserts that "the charge of boredom is really hypocritical" and suggests that it masks another reaction:

> There is, in a sense, no such thing as boredom. Boredom is only another name for a certain species of frustration. And the new languages which the interesting art of our time speaks are frustrating. . . . [O]ur sensibilities may take time to catch up with the forms of pleasure that art in a given time may offer. (*Against Interpretation* 303)

For readers receptive to the pleasures of an intentionally slower pace, lingering gives way to luxuriating, and time seems to slow to an agreeably soporific crawl.

For a film to achieve this effect, it must usually approximate a more static medium by significantly reducing camera movement and extending the length of time between cuts. Comics, in their fundamental immobility, are in some ways much better suited to cultivating stillness in storytelling. Even in the most quickly paced comic, the reader always has the option to linger on a particular panel or narrative moment. It is, in fact, more than just an option available to the reader—it is an imperative of the medium, a constant invitation to appreciate both the movement and stillness of the sequence of panels, and the tension between the two. (This is the double maneuver of progression/retention to which Groensteen refers.) In comics, the species of frustration that Sontag describes can be understood as a result of friction between two contrasting storytelling modes or sensibilities: the more familiar one based on forward narrative movement, the other an extension of the potential for stillness.

Stories and sequences in which "nothing happens" tend to emphasize setting and tone over action and progression. Such works can achieve a meditative quality that derives precisely from their ambivalence toward the advancement of the plot, which significantly affects the sense of narrative texture. This approach courts the reader's indifference and seeks to cultivate the liminal state of mind that best accommodates reflection, reverie, and reminiscence. Still, much depends upon the individual reader's response, which remains basically unpredictable despite the author's attempts to guide it. Some will be attuned to Simon Matchcard's rhythms—indeed, some readers might find the annotated bedroom collection inventive and deeply satisfying—but it is not difficult to imagine those who will find his farewell to his mother dreary and overlong. In some ways, this sequence constitutes a significant authorial gamble on Seth's part, particularly since various lurid associations still cling to the medium of comics. By frustrating any expectation of hectic storytelling, Seth takes a marked turn away from the stereotype of disposable comics and toward something decidedly more contemplative. His work often requires close attention and is written to be read more than once. It meets that basic Wildean criterion voiced by Cyril in *The Decay of Lying*: "This is perhaps the best rough test of what is literature and what is not. If one cannot enjoy reading a book over and over again, there is no use reading it at all" (Wilde 784).

Here, again, the individual reader's capacity for enjoyment is paramount, and to imply that Seth's work places unusual demands on the "typical" reader of comic books is to make broad and unproductive assumptions. Is there such a thing as a typical reader, of comics, of poetry, of mass-market fiction? What evidence is there that any particular reader will be more inclined than another to appreciate action-oriented comics? It is possible that some readers will put aside *Palookaville* 19 out of boredom (or frustration) while others will return to it with consistent enthusiasm, but what is more likely is that each reader will experience a range of reactions, not only over the course of multiple rereadings but also within a single reading. Umberto Eco's *The Role of the Reader* helps to frame this discussion in terms of the interdependent relations between reader and text:

> To organize a text, its author has to rely upon a series of codes that assign given contents to the expressions he uses. To make his text communicative, the author has to assume that the ensemble of codes he relies upon is the same as that shared by his possible reader. The author has thus to foresee a model of the possible reader (hereafter Model Reader) supposedly able to deal interpretatively with the expressions in the same way as the author deals generatively with them. (Eco 7)

By this account, each text produces its own reader; indeed, "the text is nothing else but the semantic-pragmatic production of its own Model Reader" (Eco 10). This notion corresponds to the earlier suggestion (in chapter 1's discussion of authenticity) that Seth's books teach the reader how to read them.

In this respect, the work with the highest learning curve—in other words, the work that makes the most demands on the reader—continues to be *Clyde Fans*, especially in its latter sections. Where part 3, as discussed above, puts particular pressure on the reader's attention span, part 4 tends to increase the "hermeneutic burden" with sequences that require a significant amount of deduction and supposition based on context and background information. The reader who picks up *Palookaville* 20 without reading the previous ten installments is likely to be baffled by the opening sequence, which begins with a desperate dash around a city and ends in tears, all presented from the fragmented, first-person perspective of an unseen, unnamed narrator (fig. 6.7). Has someone died? Who is crying, and why? Even the devotee of *Clyde Fans* will experience some uncertainty—but this is one of the pleasures of the work, and of Seth's work in general, which is punctuated by moments of carefully orchestrated disorientation. In such instances, when the interaction between cartoonist and reader is at its most suspended (and, arguably, most literary), the reader becomes aware of actively filling narrative gaps. This is somewhat out of the ordinary because, widely acknowledged as it is that "the role of the reader becomes of most importance in between panels"

(Round, "Visual Perspective" 317), very often this action does not require a great deal of conscious effort. The increase in narrative gaps draws attention to the dense/porous texture of comics, and makes readerly interpolation into a more deliberate act.

Gaps automatically spring into existence as soon as multiple signs are placed in proximity; it might be said that juxtaposition is the fundamental (perhaps even inevitable) relation among proximate units in this system. Groensteen argues as much when he suggests that "the central element of comics, the first criteria in the foundational order, is *iconic solidarity*" (*System of Comics* 18). The simultaneous fragmentation and coherence of images on the comics page—which lends itself to parataxis—is a product of sequential juxtaposition. Postema goes so far as to suggest that the "construction based on juxtaposition makes the sequential form of the comic into the narrative form of images *par excellence*" (495). If this is so, then it is the visible narrative hiatuses generated by the juxtaposition of images that give comics their preeminent narrative potential (and contribute most palpably to the distinctive "texture" that this chapter attempts to describe).

However, this distinguishing feature—the visible gutter—can overshadow the other, less concrete gaps that also structure comics, for instance the various kinds of distance that exist between word and image. Groensteen quotes Jan Baetens and Pascal Lefèvre on the "temporal gap between the perception of the image, which is almost global and quasi-simultaneous, and the course of verbal signs, which is slower and in all cases more gradual" (quoted in *System of Comics* 132). (Seth deploys this tension to particular effect in *Clyde Fans*.)

The gaps that comics most share with traditional literature are those "spots of indeterminacy"—gaps in the represented world—that Roman Ingarden identifies as a crucial aspect of the ontology of the literary work of art, and which contribute significantly to what readers experience as the reality of the work. In comics, spots of indeterminacy and concrete gaps between images are by no means the same, but to some extent they may be considered functions of each other, and they often seem to overlap. Not every literary spot of indeterminacy in a comics narrative can be located in the gutter—but it is the rare gutter that does not constitute a spot of indeterminacy. To take a simple example from Seth's work: *Wimbledon Green* never offers the reader an image of the title character's mother, but this does not necessarily lead the reader to imagine her in the spaces between panels. Her physical appearance is indeterminate, but not in the same way that, for instance, Wimbledon Green's movement from one illustrated location in a panel to another in an adjacent panel is indeterminate.

Panels and gutters aside, spots of indeterminacy are also present in the very fabric of the cartoon medium. The most obvious point of contrast is the photographic medium, which offers images of an entirely different texture and type. "Reading comics," Stephan Packard suggests, "is among other things about mending the indexical lack of graphic signs" (115). This is one of the ways in which the reader is expected to "go beyond" the image in a panel, even before contending with the lack between panels. Seth does not shy away from the cartoon extremes of comics, using action lines, simplified facial expressions, and other such techniques with great dexterity and even subtlety. In Seth's work, cartoonish modes of expression combine with rich, delicate ink illustrations to produce a very potent visual tension that underscores the emotional range of the narratives. Lefèvre notes that "for the French comics scholar Pierre Fresnault-Deruelle, the comics medium is an art of suggestion, not of mimesis" (29). In his evocative approach to narrative, especially with respect to the conventions of the medium, Seth frequently exemplifies the art of suggestion.

An art of suggestion demands an appropriately suggestive mode of analysis; this chapter has endeavored to accommodate theoretical browsing and observations that are more heuristic than conclusive. Still, it is possible to draw together some suggestions about the formal capacities of comics and Seth's skillful manipulation of these capacities. Just as the reader of a single-panel gag wants to get the joke, the reader of a multipanel narrative is predisposed to ongoing interpolation, making of the juxtaposed fragments a coherent and meaningful sequence. This process is guided by explicit and implicit framing, which both suspends and progresses narrative movement. Seth's frequent distension of familiar framing functions and methods of juxtaposition amplifies narrative gaps and emphasizes the reader's role in filling them. However, Seth's inventive storytelling techniques do not simply make the reader "work harder" to construct a sequence of narrative events; they often call for a different reading practice entirely, one that is not exclusively geared toward plot progression. Browsing a full-page panorama that has been broken into contiguous panels, or accompanying a protagonist through a long, perambulatory sequence, the comics reader encounters new forms of medium-related pleasure and consequently becomes more aware of the medium-related conventions into which these pleasures insinuate themselves.

This investigation's continued attempt to repurpose terms like "mannered" and "baroque" is part of an effort to highlight the various ways in which Seth pushes his work to certain narrative limits. The structural potentialities of comics allow him to devise sequences that are uniquely dense and porous, qualities that often appear as two sides of the same coin. This dense/porous dynamic in Seth's work permits a reconsideration of the interdependence of fragmentation and coherence in comics, a new way of understanding the distinctive texture of the medium. Hatfield's contention that comics comprise various kinds of tension, which entail "various interpretive options and potentialities," can be understood as a description of how a uniquely dense/porous text engages the reader. (And vice versa: density and porosity can be understood as characteristic potentialities of the comics medium.)

At its most dense and/or porous, Seth's work engenders a heightened awareness of the gaps inherent in the medium of comics and encourages an unusually self-conscious form of readerly interpolation. Parataxis, "wherein discrete particulars are placed side by side" (Jennison 3), goes beyond mere narrative fragmentation; in this chapter, it refers to an amplification of the existing juxtaposition that structures comics. In effect, parataxis makes space for more unpredictable interpolation, priming the reader to construe fresh "correspondences, connections, asymmetries" (Jennison 3) between juxtaposed parts. By gently disorienting the reader, Seth draws attention to the reorientation of perspective that constantly takes place when assembling a coherent narrative. With each panel, each new fragment, the reader's sense of the text evolves slightly, and the spaces in between are an indispensable part of this process. Seth's work points to itself by emphasizing these gaps and reminds the reader that it is only through fragments that a coherent literary world can be suggested.

7

Forging Histories: Ghost Worlds and Invented Communities

In *It's a Good Life, If You Don't Weaken*, Seth evocatively describes the way that "bits and pieces" of the past seem to linger on in the present "like remnants of some ghost world—a vanished world" (43). This is from part 2 of the book, which was originally published as issue 5 of *Palookaville* in 1994. At this time, Daniel Clowes was already publishing parts of what would become his best-known work, *Ghost World*. For Seth, the notion of the ghost world is perhaps most productive as an analogy for history; for Clowes, the ghost world comes to serve as a thematic through line that underscores his characters' sense of loss and alienation. *Ghost World* seems to play on the expression "ghost town," commonly used to describe an abandoned place, cut off from other towns and also perhaps frozen in time—a circumscribed zone isolated both spatially and temporally. In this sense, the ghost *world* would be a boundless place, an alienated totality that is, paradoxically, both omnipresent and remote.

In another sense, it is quite useful to think of the fictional realities of literature as ghost worlds, which are enlivened by the reader. This not only helps to conceptualize the various strata of Seth's sometimes dense metafictional excursions, it also permits a fuller examination of the interdependent relationship between the historical and regional/national dimensions of his work. Seth is engaged in "historiographic metafiction," a term coined by Linda Hutcheon, which she defines as "fiction that is intensely, self-reflexively art, but is also grounded in historical, social, and political realities" (*Canadian Postmodern* 13). In works like *Wimbledon Green* and *The Great Northern Brotherhood of Canadian Cartoonists*, the fictional and historical ghost worlds are constituted primarily by invented communities, which Seth conjures by means of suggestive details that prompt the reader to imagine the whole.

Stuart Hall's contention that identities comprise different positions relative to narratives of the past is echoed by one of Eric Hobsbawm's remarks on community: "To be a member of any human community is to situate oneself with regard to one's (its) past, if only by rejecting it" (*On History* 10). Seth does not reject the past, but neither does he fully embrace it. Rather, he ambivalently situates himself in relation to the past by remaking it in fictional form—and in the process encourages the reader to take up a similarly ambivalent position. Hutcheon explains that historiographic metafiction "questions the nature and validity of the entire human process of writing—of both history and fiction. Its aim in so doing is to study how we know the past, how we *make* sense of it" (*Canadian Postmodern* 22). Her emphasis on the making of the past resonates strongly with the practices of both Seth and his characters.

Narrative Heterocosms

A more technical term for "ghost world" might be "heterocosm," a separate or alternative world. Hutcheon uses the word to denote the world of a fictional narrative (as in "the fictive heterocosm"), which she insists is "not a way of viewing reality, but a reality in its own right" (*Narcissistic Narrative* 90). Much the same reality claim could be made about the heterocosm found in nonfictional, historical accounts. In fact, it seems likely that many readers would sooner accept the historical heterocosm (in other words, "the past") as a reality in its own right. Although the past may be quite distinct from the present reality of the reader, it is nevertheless understood to be somehow continuous with that present reality—separate, but not alternative.

As discussed in previous chapters, Seth takes advantage of the credibility often attributed to historicizing discourses, using them to fortify his invented realities. This technique is extremely effective because fictive and historical accounts constitute highly compatible narrative heterocosms.[1] No doubt other types of heterocosms exist, each with varying degrees of narrativity. A discussion of a video game, for instance, could plausibly refer to the "ludic heterocosm" with which the player interacts, and such a heterocosm could have a strong narrative element. Conversely, an orchestral composition might be said to offer the listener access to an abstract sonic heterocosm that is essentially nonnarrative. For the purposes of this investigation, however, the term "heterocosm" refers to a *narrative* reality, a ghost world tied to a story.

In Seth's work, fictive and historical heterocosms often intersect and in some cases even become seemingly indistinguishable from each other. The credulous reader has little reason to doubt the veracity of the collection of cartoons, the "Famous Eleven," that appears at the end of *It's a Good Life*. Not only does Seth convincingly insert the gags into pages from period publications, he also provides a photograph of their author, Kalo, as well as a glossary that contains historical information on other cartoonists. More than this, he presents the entire Kalo fabrication within the broader context of a believable autobiographical narrative.

One of the distinguishing features of *It's a Good Life* is the protagonist's self-reflective commentary, a vein of autobiography that all but disappears from Seth's work in subsequent stories. However, even the most personal of these reflections is not conventionally autobiographical due to the fabricated nature of the story. "In the field of contemporary comic book production," Bart Beaty notes, "autobiography holds a promise to elevate the legitimacy of both the medium and the artist" (144). In *It's a Good Life*, Seth interrogates this notion of legitimacy by offering an apparently autobiographical story that centers on fictional events. Notably, *Palookaville* 20 closes with fourteen pages from Seth's sketchbook journal, a record of a trip to Calgary (discussed in chapter 4), the first unmistakably autobiographical material of significant length to appear in *Palookaville* since its earliest issues. (Seth goes on to include autobiographical sections in *Palookaville* 21 and 22 as well.)

What emerges most palpably in these journal entries is Seth's sense of loneliness and estrangement from the people he encounters in Calgary, a far cry from the camaraderie he feels with fellow cartoonist Chester Brown in *It's a Good Life*. Brown likewise depicts his relationships with Seth and Joe Matt in his autobiographical book *Paying for It*, and Matt provides a group portrait of the three in *Spent*. In these instances, autobiography seems less a route to artistic legitimacy than to artistic *community*. Seth even dedicates the nonautobiographical books *George Sprott* and *The Great Northern Brotherhood* to Brown and Matt, respectively—in the latter case, bestowing on Matt the title of "honourary Canadian." For the reader, the three authors form a community of cartoonists.

Even the reader who understands that John Kalloway is not an actual historical figure—and in turn wonders about the fictive dimensions of the rest of the plot of *It's a Good Life*—is still likely to accept as authentic Seth's investment in the cartoon medium, his preoccupation with the past, and his friendship with Brown. In these ways, the fictive heterocosm of *It's a Good Life* is emotionally grounded in the extraliterary reality of the author, which presumably overlaps with the world of the reader. To a certain extent, it is this presumption of continuity between realities that grants Seth's historical inventions/interventions their plausibility. Tied together are the ostensibly objective ghost world of the past, the present everyday reality shared by the author and the reader, and the more subjective ghost world of the autobiographical narrative. Seth's technique in *It's a Good Life* is to pretend that the fictive heterocosm is not separate or alternative at all, but is in fact consistent with the historical past and, by extension, the present.

This is not to say that Seth necessarily intends to deceive the reader. Particularly in subsequent books (which do not feature Seth as a protagonist and so are not explicitly bound to any autobiographical reality), it becomes clear that Seth is forging not just parallel histories but wholly alternative ones, each with "its own rules which govern the logic or motivation of its parts" (Hutcheon, *Narcissistic Narrative* 90). The appeal of *Wimbledon Green* derives in some ways from its self-containment. The reader has access to a thoroughly imagined world with a consistent internal logic (the obsession and compulsion of collecting and bibliomania), which extends from its single-minded characters to its accumulative story structure. The same could be said of the autonomous worlds of *George Sprott* and *The Great Northern Brotherhood*.

Other narratives feature self-containment of a different variety. One of the most arresting ghost worlds in Seth's work is also one of the most private and obscure: Simon Matchcard's dream world. A heterocosm within a heterocosm (a "metaheterocosm," although that term may be too clunky to be useful), this dream world is comparable to the metafictional comics that appear throughout Seth's work. It has even more in common, however, with the "frozen place" of Simon's novelty postcards, which appeals to him because it is removed from "mundane reality" (*PV* 18, 57). Although these dream worlds are intangible, they bleed over into Simon's waking reality in the form of fantasies and reveries. Seth's drawing style remains consistent, so Simon's private reality looks the same as the broader fictive heterocosm within which it appears. Nevertheless, it is rarely unclear to the reader which reality a particular sequence depicts, especially since the distinctive imagery of Simon's dreams becomes so familiar. In most cases, Seth uses narration, empty panels, and other, more elaborate transitions to explicitly toggle between Simon's mundane existence and his dream life.

Sometimes, however, the distinction between worlds does seem to collapse, as when Simon's toys speak to him (which may or may not be a sign of mounting dementia inherited from Lily Matchcard). The most ambiguous encroachment of the unreal into the everyday world is the uncanny sequence in which Simon—gripped with sudden paranoia—recedes into a crack in the wall and then realizes, too late: "I had become separated from myself" (fig. 2.4). Is this simply a nightmare, like the recurring dream of drowning to which Simon compares it? While it certainly has dreamlike qualities, it seems entirely unlike Simon's other dreams in overall tone and structure. Is it a paranoid delusion, further evidence of dementia? Seth does not offer the reader any clear indication about which stratum of reality is being depicted in this anxious sequence. Simon recounts the incident rationally, acknowledging its strangeness with no small amount of confusion and alarm. "About a month ago," Simon says at the beginning of the sequence, "I was sitting downstairs in the office" (*PV* 17, 46). This in itself may be a hint: the sequence is an instance of analepsis, a past event reported by Simon from the diegetic present. Unlike the scenes in which Simon talks with his toys, this unsettling episode is not part of the immediate present of the narrative. The reader may interpret the incident in any number of ways, but the literal meaning seems sufficiently potent: in a moment of anxiety, Simon is absorbed into the protective walls of his home.

In certain respects, the Matchcard family home, which provides a clearly delimited setting for much of *Clyde Fans*, constitutes a heterocosm of its own, which to the reader may sometimes seem like a crypt or haunted house. Its inhabitants, however, do not think of it as a ghost world: both Simon and Abe consider their home an oasis of reality in an otherwise hollow and illusive world. For Abe, what lies *outside* the house is the true ghost world, an alienated totality made up of fleeting relationships and empty roles such as "salesman, wheeler-dealer, pillar of society" (*Clyde Fans* 51–52). For Simon, the house becomes a protective shell that shields him from the practical, day-to-day ephemera that Abe endures, the change and progress that seem so at odds with the Matchcard temperament.

Against the inexorable forward movement of time, Simon manages to achieve what he calls a "stalemate" within the walls of his home. Time, he suggests, "can be halted. It can be held in place for short periods" (*PV* 18, 55). Simon makes the cryptic claim that he does not attain this state through any deliberate exertion but rather by means of "an effort that was, somehow, the opposite of will power" (*PV* 18, 56). Deliberate or not, this temporal exercise is of a piece with one of Simon's major preoccupations: the improbable persistence of a self that seems reborn with every passing moment. By residing in the threshold spaces of his home, and to such a degree that he considers the building a physical extension of himself, Simon feels that he is able to suspend time—although not indefinitely. His mother's imminent departure from the house serves as irrefutable proof that not only has the flow of time resumed but, as Simon says, "everything is winding down" (*PV* 18, 63).

Part 3 of *Clyde Fans* is taken up almost entirely by Simon's occasionally ambiguous but nonetheless consistent ruminations on time, which appear in caption narration. These circuitous musings—which repeatedly return in one way or another to the simultaneous continuity and discontinuity between

154   Ghost Worlds and Invented Communities

FIG. 7.1 Seth, *Palooka-ville* 3 (Montreal: Drawn and Quarterly, 1993), 3.

the past and present—accompany panels that depict Simon moving from room to room around the Matchcard home, tending to his mother, working, sketching, sometimes just wandering, thinking. Literally hundreds of panels offer the reader variations on the image of Simon in doorways and corridors, moving in and out of long shadows as he puzzles over the mutability of time, memory, and identity. The Matchcard family home comes to resemble a workshop or laboratory where Simon carries out various thought-experiments that test the nature of time, the most successful or instructive of which are not necessarily intentional.

    The reader has already been introduced to the spaces of the house in part 1 of *Clyde Fans*, which in some ways resembles a one-act play designed to show off a complex, detailed set. Through the lens of Simon's fixations, however, the house comes into sharper focus, and the reader gains a more intimate, in some cases almost claustrophobic sense of how its walls, passages, and rooms fit together. Chapter 1 describes this sense of space, which gradually accrues with each panel read, as "synesthetic": through the visual composition of elements within the panel, the cartoonist produces a nearly palpable impression of spatial relations in the world of the narrative. What Seth refers to as "spatial understanding" (see page 215) is a significant aspect of a cartoonist's drawing style and contributes considerably to the distinctive reality of the fictive heterocosm in comics. The spatial understanding that Seth imparts to the reader changes slightly from story to story—or even, in the case of a long-running series like *Clyde Fans*, over the course of a single narrative—but certain hard-to-define qualities remain consistent.

Ghost Worlds and Invented Communities 155

FIG. 7.2 Seth, *Palookaville* 19 (Montreal: D&Q, 2008), 85.

It may be analytically superficial (and somewhat indecorous) to set one of Seth's earliest pages alongside something more recent, but such a comparison dramatically demonstrates the evolution of his drawing style (figs. 7.1, 7.2). There is a tendency toward depth and dimension, qualities that have always been present in Seth's work but that increasingly define his composition within the panel. This investigation has characterized Seth's space in terms of its "softness" and "solidity"; chapter 5 noted the nearly tangible quality of the items collected in Lily Matchcard's bedroom; attention has also been paid to the materiality of the books themselves, carefully conceived objects that make haptic appeals to the reader with raised cover illustrations and foldout pages. With all this in mind, it begins to seem almost inevitable that Seth would plunge fully into three-dimensional creation, as he does with his cardboard models of Dominion City.

The Chalk City

The cardboard buildings make their first appearance in print in *George Sprott*, which features five large, full-page photographs of individual models. Each model—photographed in isolation against an empty white backdrop—appears opposite a standard page of comics panels that tell a story related to the building, in many cases "a Brief History of" the place. Although the models appear meticulously crafted, with detailed trimmings and carefully painted surfaces, they are not to scale, and no attempt has been made to disguise the

FIG. 7.3 Seth, *George Sprott: 1894–1975* (Montreal: D&Q, 2009), n.p.

fact that they have been constructed out of cardboard. The buildings are by no means sloppy, but they are literally rough around the edges: the fluted core of the cardboard is particularly visible at the corners of the structures, where corrugated sheets meet, and around the borders of glued-on windows and embellishments (fig. 7.3). Unlike their two-dimensional counterparts, these cardboard buildings are not seamless.

They do, however, share the decidedly cartoonish quality of Seth's drawings, appearing as a material extension of the distinctive style he has spent so many years refining in his comics. In some cases, the brushwork on a model is even more detailed than it would be in a two-dimensional drawing of the same building. A wall composed of interlocking bricks, for instance, might be indicated in a drawing by a handful of suggestive hatches; on Seth's models each individual brick is visible, painted onto the cardboard walls with an almost obsessive precision that demonstrates fidelity to a rather peculiar notion of verisimilitude. It is clear that Seth is not aiming for "realism" as such, but his characteristic attention to detail still helps to substantiate the reality of the ghost worlds that he creates.

The buildings featured in *George Sprott* are only a representative sample of a much larger project undertaken by Seth, which comprises approximately fifty Dominion City models as well as a wealth of sketchbook work. A section of *Palookaville* 20 is devoted to this "basement sort-of project" (44), and, judging by the material presented, a complete account of Seth's process could easily fill an entire book. In one sense, it already has: there are numerous extracts from "Encyclopedia Dominion," Seth's ledger workbook, which along with sketches of buildings includes notes, lore, stories, and scenes related to life in Dominion. One two-page spread features "Reference Books of Dominion" (*PV* 20, 57), each with a short synopsis and publication information, a familiar instance of an invented collection of books. These arcane volumes, such as a mid-nineteenth-century "City Directory" and an architectural history titled *The Chalk City*, stand in for the storied past that the reader imagines contained in their pages. Another sketchbook spread shows a more conventional comics sequence, narrated by George Sprott, which offers a tour of Dominion's "night spots" like the Edgewater Club and the Swan Room at the Forest Inn, locations not featured in *George Sprott* (*PV* 20, 57).

In addition to these sketchbook reproductions, *Palookaville* 20 also contains more than a dozen photographs of many of the fifty cardboard models, either individually (as in *George Sprott*) or grouped together to form makeshift city blocks. With their satisfying physicality yet cartoonish demeanor, the models are like miniature monuments, closed and mute, but exuding the same restrained energy as Seth's most polished comics. The sketches and notes are more openly energetic—voluble, peopled, and loose, with an evocative narrative depth—but lack the concrete, finished quality of the buildings. Ultimately, the cardboard models and the sketchbook histories are interdependent parts of the extensively imagined heterocosm that is Dominion City. Taken together, these disparate modes of world building provide a substantial and organic sense of place.

As Seth explains in the personal essay that accompanies the Dominion City documentation in *Palookaville* 20, the genesis of the project can be traced to a long-since-abandoned concept for a suite of stories. "There were five of them—five characters, five short stories. Nothing really linked them together, though. The characters never met, nor did the stories comment on each other. I thought it might be a nice idea to set all five stories in the same location" (*PV* 20, 41). Seth claims to have settled on Dominion—"the same city in which Simon Matchcard had failed to close" (41)—on a whim. In fact, this instinct toward continuity from project to project persists throughout Seth's career.

The front inside cover of the second issue of *Palookaville* (published in 1991) is a photograph of a lighthouse; the image of a lighthouse later becomes a fixture of the *Clyde Fans* saga, recurring both in Simon's dreams and in his sketchbook. If this seems like an insignificant repetition, perhaps even a simple coincidence, the inside cover of *Palookaville* 3 offers even stronger evidence of continuity: a novelty postcard with a manipulated photograph featuring an oversized fish, exactly the sort that Simon discovers in Dominion and begins to collect. Seth's inclination toward continuity yields a body of work that is unexpectedly coherent for a career that shows such a steady incline in artistic maturity. From this point of view, his work is an ongoing series of overlapping and sometimes interlocking worlds that reaches a particular culmination in the elaborated manifestations of Dominion City.

In 2005, the cardboard buildings were installed together as a city block to form the centerpiece of Seth's solo show at the Art Gallery of Ontario in Toronto. This exhibition (which also included comics pages) was the first to bring the models into a public space, marking what Seth describes as the transition of Dominion from private hobby to work of art. Neither context, however, fully demonstrates the literary depth or inhabitability of the imagined city. Even in its earliest state, according to Seth, the place had already begun to make another kind of transition: "day by day Dominion City became less of an artistic project and more of an interior landscape. I found myself walking its streets each night as I lay down to go to sleep" (*PV* 20, 42).

Appearing together in such close succession, these two striking statements tend to crowd each other, but both warrant further attention. First, the notion of the "interior landscape": this term perfectly conveys the dimensions of the project and also helps to account for its flexibility. More than a hobby or an art installation, Dominion City is an interior landscape that can take any number of exterior forms depending on the context (sketchbook, studio, gallery, etc.). In 2008, Dominion became the exclusive focus of a subsequent exhibition mounted in Waterloo, Ontario—an immersive, homey installation adorned with "flags, filing cabinets, oak swivel chairs and a giant portrait of 'Our Founder'" (*PV* 20, 53). Along with these unforced curatorial flourishes, Seth also created new work to complement his sketches and models, suggesting an interior landscape the full potential of which remains unexhausted.

Second, Seth's description of a particular somnambulistic impulse: each night, in mentally rehearsing the type of urban perambulation that often appears in his comics, Seth recasts the interior landscape as a kind of dreamscape. This brings to mind the meandering dreams of Simon Matchcard, in which he often wanders through urban spaces that may or may not be Dominion, occasionally encountering his mother. The photographs in *Palookaville*

Ghost Worlds and Invented Communities 159

FIG. 7.4 Seth, *Palookaville* 20 (Montreal: D&Q, 2010), 47.

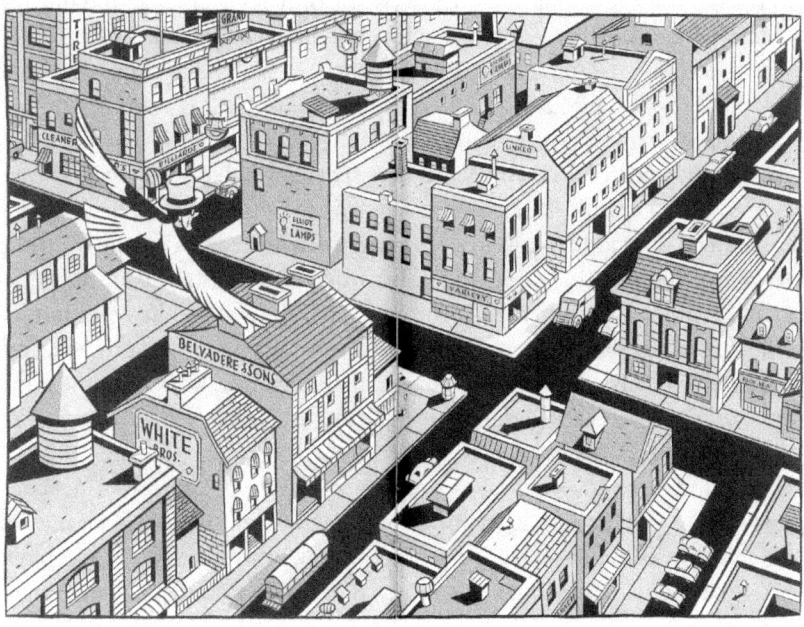

FIG. 7.5 Seth, *Palookaville* 18 (Montreal: D&Q, 2005), 68–69.

20 of the model city block strongly recall the aerial perspective of some of Simon's dreams (figs. 7.4, 7.5). It may also be worth noting that the practice of mentally navigating an interior space is one of the principal components of the method of loci—more colloquially known as a "memory palace"—the classical mnemonic device discovered by Simonides at the collapsing banquet hall. In the same way that an orator would use this art of memory by housing the parts of a speech in the various imagined locations of a memory palace, Seth houses the history of Dominion in the imagined city's buildings.

Some models embody a very specific period in the life of a building. The model of the Coronet Lecture Hall, for example, reproduces the building in its prime, sometime during the thirty-year period that George Sprott was giving his weekly talks (fig. 7.3). The facing page of comics panels offers "a Brief History of the Coronet Lecture Hall," depicting the precipitous decline of the site in the years following George's death. Ultimately, the building is torn down and replaced by a computer outlet. This compact chronicle of deterioration can be read as a highly specific example of "the special increase in density and concreteness of time markers," which Bakhtin argues is necessary for "the representability of events" (250). Within the larger context provided by the brief history of the building, the cardboard Coronet becomes a kind of time capsule, which contains a frozen segment of a much larger heterocosm.

Seth describes his model-building practice as "the kind of thing sad men cook up as they hit middle age. Like a train set . . . or putting ships in a bottle" (*PV* 20, 44). Behind the self-deprecation is a worthwhile comparison to other activities that entail the careful construction of alternative, separate (and usually miniature) worlds.[2] Such activities are very ordinary—familiar, domestic, amateur—but at the same time expressly intended as an escape from the everyday, a pastime that creates a ghost world which exists outside of everyday time. In this sense, there is a strong affinity between Seth's collection of cardboard models and Simon's collection of novelty postcards (and even, perhaps, Clyde Matchcard's collection of amateur taxidermy). Like Simon's postcards, Seth's models exceed mundane realism, and both collections eventually surpass their initial status as mere diversions.

Seth's model building serves as a useful case study for rather abstract concepts such as craft, scale, and manipulability. As three-dimensional anomalies in a chiefly two-dimensional artistic career, Seth's cardboard buildings often seem like modeled drawings, obviously handcrafted objects caught somewhere between model and cartoon. Whereas a drawn photograph by Seth is a cartoon approximation of a vestige of the real, his cardboard models might be regarded as real, three-dimensional representations of cartooning. Of course, it is difficult to say which version of a building is "real," particularly when the

FIG. 7.6 Seth, *The Great Northern Brotherhood of Canadian Cartoonists* (Montreal: D&Q, 2011), 6.

model and the drawing are side by side, as often happens in *George Sprott*. A page titled "5th Floor, End of the Hall" shows the reader George's suite of rooms on the top floor of the Radio Hotel; the cardboard model of the hotel, however, on the facing page, only appears to have a total of four stories. The model of the Radio Hotel is like a slightly distorted impression of the "actual" building (which perhaps only exists in the mind of the reader).

The sheer plasticity of these imagined buildings is even more apparent in the realization of the North Star Talking Picture House. Part of Seth's 2008 gallery show, the movie theater is "a human-sized cardboard version of one of the models—*not to actual scale*, but big enough that people could walk around inside" (*PV* 20, 53, emphasis added). Seth first constructed a cardboard model of the steepled building, of which the final, "life-size" construction is a more modest interpretation, suited to the confines of a gallery space. Nevertheless, the North Star cinema, complete with a working screen showing films selected by Seth, "turned out to be an ideal interior space (in both meanings of the phrase)" (*PV* 20, 54).

The Great Northern Brotherhood also features a variety of three-dimensional realizations and representations. In the opening pages, photographs show not only a cardboard model of the GNBCC clubhouse but also real-life objects like the club's well-worn presidential top hat and the Jasper award (fig. 7.6). These objects are not models or scale replicas; rather, they are materializations of invented items, "real" artifacts from the world of Seth's sketchbook. As such, they have more in common with the convincing counterfeit documents collected at the end of *It's a Good Life* than with the obviously handcrafted models of Dominion City buildings. Even though the models of Dominion are three dimensional, they are more like the sketched selections "from the library of Wimbledon Green" (fig. 5.1) than they are like these fully actualized GNBCC artifacts. In every instance—object, document, model, library selection—the thing forged serves as an evocative stand-in for something greater, a synecdoche of the complete collection or heterocosm that is too extensive to be perceived in its entirety.

Ambivalent Conceptions of Historiography

The most compelling community invented by Seth—livelier and more character driven than the interior cityscape of Dominion—may be the community of comic book collectors in *Wimbledon Green*. Here, the ostensibly stuffy world of auctions, price guides, and specialty bookshops is revealed to be the dynamic world of forgeries, lifelong searches, and unexpected reversals of fortune, all depicted in Seth's invitingly brisk sketchbook brushstrokes. And although these engaging aspects of the book certainly help to animate the characters, what really brings the community to life is Seth's portrayal of bibliophile politics. Whereas the history of Dominion resides in its distinctive but impartial buildings, it is the personal anecdotes told in *Wimbledon Green* that form a sort of talking history of the community, a history that is dominated by rivalry, rumor, and scandal.

The Coverloose Club provides a representative example: founded by "Cuts" Coupon as a sanctuary for comic book collectors, it deteriorated into little more than a clique when the other members vetoed Wimbledon Green's entry, to Coupon's dismay. Coupon attributes the club's behavior to "avarice, pettiness + jealously" (*WG* 107) but makes no reference to the persistent uncertainty surrounding Wimbledon Green. Amid accusations and conflicting information, there is much to suggest that Wimbledon Green is not quite who he claims to be. In part, it is this irresolvable ambiguity concerning the identity of the community's central figure, cast in sharp relief by occasional flashes of blunt condemnation, that gives *Wimbledon Green* its restless energy.

Ghost Worlds and Invented Communities 163

FIG. 7.7 Seth, *The Great Northern Brotherhood of Canadian Cartoonists* (Montreal: D&Q, 2011), 56.

The book also contains brief glimpses into the adjacent community of comic book artists, a particular segment of which becomes the focus of Seth's subsequent sketchbook story, *The Great Northern Brotherhood*. Seth's work has always been quietly Canadian, but in *The Great Northern Brotherhood* the national allegiances become explicit. Using a variation of the narrative technique developed in *It's a Good Life*, Seth reinforces his invented national history with references to actual Canadian cartoonists like Doug Wright and James Simpkins.

Along with extended assessments of metafictional comics and detailed descriptions of the brotherhood's sprawling clubhouse, Seth spends nine pages on Wright's popular strip *Nipper*, for which he clearly has genuine affection (fig. 7.7). The annual GNBCC award for best cartoonist, the Jasper (fig. 7.6), is a tribute to Simpkins's once nationally beloved, now nearly forgotten character Jasper the Bear. The reader who does not possess an encyclopedic knowledge of Canadian cartooning will probably not recognize names like Peter Whalley and George Feyer, and may assume that they too have been invented by Seth. Seth takes advantage of the relative obscurity of these real-life cartoonists, deftly incorporating them into a dense imbrication of historical fact and credible invention.

In this way, the central tension that emerges in reading *The Great Northern Brotherhood* is between the known and the unknown. This might fairly be described as epistemological ambivalence on the part of the reader, which is a product of the ontological ambiguity that is inherent in metafictional narratives. Seth accentuates the reader's ambivalence by appropriating historicizing discourses that typically connote epistemological certainty. In the opening pages of the book, Seth playfully anticipates (or perhaps even incites) the tension between known and unknown in his description of a bas-relief arch over the clubhouse entrance: "It's a Who's Who of Canadian cartoon characters. Some famous . . . some forgotten" (15). The reader with complete information (to borrow a fitting expression from game theory) knows that although some of the characters depicted in the arch may be relatively famous (Wright's Nipper) or forgotten (Simpkins's Chopper), many are actually Seth's inventions, which are strictly speaking neither famous nor forgotten.

Within the world of Canadian cartooning that Seth has invented, however, even his made-up cartoons exist in a hierarchy, some better known than others. By placing historical and fictive entities on the *same* spectrum between famous and forgotten, Seth once again yokes together fictive and historical heterocosms. About the bas-relief arch, Seth deadpans: "It's worth looking at carefully just to see who you can recognize" (16). The absurd implication is that failure of recognition signals not utter fabrication on Seth's part but simply the natural fading of certain artifacts from the collective pop cultural memory. This gambit has a sharp ironic edge because much of the real, *nonfabricated* history is so obscure. Throughout *The Great Northern Brotherhood*, even the most careful reader experiences occasional moments of literary-historical vertigo in which it is difficult to discern—or remember—which parts of Seth's history are invented. Seth gives new emphasis to the old motif of recognition/nonrecognition by making of it a game in which the reader is an active participant. The integration of real, esoteric Canadian history into an invented community is so seamless that for many readers—especially on the first reading—*The Great Northern Brotherhood* may have the effect of flattening all hierarchies, real or invented, into an ahistorical arcade. (In a final deadpan maneuver, the book closes with an alphabetical index, an entirely neutral list that does not distinguish between history and fabrication.)

Writing about Chris Ware's role in comics history, Jeet Heer reports that "Canadian cartoonist Seth, whose passion for old comics matches that of his friend Chris Ware, once noted that most cartoonists have to educate themselves in the history of comics" (4). In turn, they sometimes educate the reader. Heer positions Ware as a comics historian "engaged in an act of ancestor creation, of giving pedigree and lineage to his own work" (4). In many ways, Seth's literal invention of cartoonist predecessors is comparable to Ware's more conventional historical endeavor. In *It's a Good Life* and *The Great Northern Brotherhood*, Seth foregrounds his role as a comics history autodidact, but the knowledge he passes on to the reader blurs the boundary between fiction and nonfiction. These books constitute ironic versions of what Heer aptly calls "canon formation" in Ware's work (4). Both Ware and Seth are forging histories, but in different ways—Seth's work fully accommodates the double meaning of the word "forge" and in doing so points to the deliberate manipulation of material that even the most apparently neutral history entails. In *Metahistory*, Hayden White describes this process as the "selection and arrangement of data from the *unprocessed historical record* in the interest of rendering that record more comprehensible to an *audience* of a particular kind" (5, emphases in original).

It is the audience that finally realizes this arrangement of data as history. Seth's work frustrates this realization because the reader cannot participate in its history-making without simultaneously setting in motion other discursive modes—satire, metafiction—not traditionally associated with historical truth. White's very lucid remarks about "the conventional conceptions of historiography" help to account for this tension. "In the eighteenth century," he writes, "thinkers conventionally distinguished among three kinds of historiography: fabulous, true, and satirical" (*Metahistory* 49). These distinctions persist, indeed have become so entrenched that the twenty-first-century reader may regard the term "true history" as redundant and think of fabulous or satirical history simply as genres of fiction. Seth blends the three kinds of historiography together, which compels the reader to constantly take up new positions in relation to the text. In this way, Seth seems to cultivate something akin to what White calls a metahistorical consciousness, which "stands above, and adjudicates among, the claims which the three kinds of historiography (fabulous, satirical, and truthful) might make upon the reader" (*Metahistory* 51).

In Seth's work, this metahistorical consciousness usually has an ironic quality. As a result, satire—being a narrative manifestation of irony (*Metahistory* 8)—often seems to emerge as the foremost historiographical mode, even in those narratives that are not overtly satirical. For instance: the earnest, elegiac tone of *It's a Good Life* rarely takes on a satirical edge, but the mode of the work (i.e., fabulation presented as autobiographical truth) is highly ironic. *Wimbledon Green* on the other hand is outright satirical fabulation, an affectionate send-up of bibliomania, which employs historicizing discourses (chiefly anecdote) but which no one would mistake for a truthful history. Its companion volume, *The Great Northern Brotherhood*, is similarly fabulous but incorporates truth in a manner that destabilizes conventional historiographical distinctions; this very ambiguity, however, seems to invite a satirical resolution.

Each book offers a unique juxtaposition of the fabulous, truthful, and satirical, but Seth does not (cannot) actually impart either a metahistorical or ironic consciousness—readers will respond in different ways to the various claims made upon them by his work. In her rich, astute essay "Irony, Nostalgia, and the Postmodern," Linda Hutcheon describes such responses:

> Irony is not something *in* an object that you either "get" or fail to "get": irony "happens" for you (or, better, you *make* it "happen") when two meanings, one said and the other unsaid, come together, usually with a certain critical edge. Likewise, nostalgia is not something you "perceive" *in* an object; it is what you "feel" when two different temporal moments, past and present, come together for you. (emphases in original)

Hutcheon's straightforward, discerning account does much to refine and draw together certain strands of this investigation: first, it highlights the structural similarity between irony and nostalgia, both of which stem from ambivalence; second, it advances an appropriately process-oriented understanding of complex phenomena that resist rigid definition; third, in doing so, it helps to complicate the notion of "epistemological ambivalence" identified in the above discussion. It is not simply that the reader knows or does not know that, for instance, Kalo is a fictional character or that Doug Wright is an actual historical figure—it is that Seth's work engages readers in the process of *making* their own historical knowledge. Moreover, Seth's work prompts readers to make historical knowledge that is ironic, nostalgic, or otherwise ambivalent.

Nostalgia is itself a form of historical knowledge, not unlike memory. As Hutcheon suggests in her essay, it consists of "the past as imagined, as idealized through memory and desire." However, nostalgia is also a form of geographical knowledge: it operates both temporally *and* spatially, unable to separate geographical and historical origins. Originally a diagnosis of patriotic homesickness (Boym 3), nostalgia has always had geographical, which is to say national, stakes. Were Seth's more overtly Canadian stories not so saturated with irony and ambiguity, their geographically specific longing for the past might be in danger of becoming overdetermined as nationalist discourse.

Particularly in works like *George Sprott* and *The Great Northern Brotherhood*, nostalgia is often bound up with emblematic instances of Canadiana. The most obvious example is a literal emblem, the 1967 Canadian Centennial logo, which Seth uses as an insignia on the brass buttons of the GNBCC club jacket (*GNBCC* 97). Several pages later, there is a reference to the National Film Board of Canada, or NFB, an actual long-standing Canadian institution that Seth weaves into his invented history. Addressing the reader directly, the narrator insists: "You must remember, in grade school, watching those NFB cartoonist documentaries" (26). Here Seth invents a community of readers with a shared cultural memory—although, needless to say, the memory too has been invented by Seth.

In addition to these markers of official, institutional Canada, Seth's work also contains identifiably Canadian elements that are more atmospheric. In *Clyde Fans*, the collected items in Lily Matchcard's bedroom include several Inuit stone carvings (*PV* 19, 93), which encapsulate precisely the commodification and compartmentalization of aboriginal Canadian culture that becomes a sustained undercurrent of *George Sprott*. Another recurring feature of *George Sprott* is the arctic landscape, which appears not only in narrative episodes but also in the arresting two-page illustrations that punctuate the book. Northern geography appears in *The Great Northern Brotherhood* as well, but it is given a far less reverent treatment as the backdrop of the comically remote GNBCC Archive (in another flourish of hyperbolic Canadiana, the unlikely architecture of the Northern Archive is styled after igloos).

It is not surprising that a cartoonist would both utilize and satirize such potent imagery, bordering as it does on caricature, but this nevertheless suggests a series of questions: Is there some kernel of national identity that irony does not deflate? Aside from the sheer associative power that Inuit culture and arctic landscapes possess, what is it that makes them Canadian? From such historical and geographical specificities, is it possible to derive abstract elements of "Canadianness"? Grounded, as Hutcheon says, in "historical, social, and political realities" (*Canadian Postmodern* 13), Seth's historiographic metafictions readily assume a political tenor. Underlying the specific questions that particular works may prompt is a much broader question: Who claims the authority to conceive and designate national spaces and identities?

National Tendencies

In *The Canadian Identity*, originally published in 1961, historian W. L. Morton proposed that the "alternate penetration of the wilderness and return to civilization is the basic rhythm of Canadian life, and forms the basic elements of Canadian character" (5). Half a century later, this claim sounds more like mythmaking than measured historical analysis, but it nevertheless has a certain undeniable resonance. Like other cultural stereotypes, this notion of the basic "Canadian character" may dissolve on close examination but seems to cohere at a distance, powered by an irresistibly unambiguous essentialism. Morton imagines two archetypal geographies—wild and civilized—between which Canadians continually shuttle. This "basic rhythm" is reflected in "a country resting on paradoxes and anomalies" (51), for which the "evolution of the national identity" was "slow, obscure, and indefinite" (71). For Morton, Canadian identity is, essentially, a site of tensions and ambiguities.

In *Splitting Images: Contemporary Canadian Ironies* (1991), Hutcheon suggests that these ambiguities have done much to inform Canadian art and literature. "Obsessed, still, with articulating its identity," she writes, "Canada often speaks with a doubled voice, with the forked tongue of irony" (1). To some extent, Hutcheon is responding directly to Morton, whom she briefly cites, attempting to update and develop his claims. In the preface to *Splitting Images*, she offers Canadians an alternative to the endless search for a cohesive national identity: "What if we made a virtue out of our fence-sitting, bet-hedging sense of the difficult doubleness of being Canadian, yet North American, of being Canadian yet part of a multinational, global political economy? That virtue's name may well be irony" (vii). In many ways, Seth seems to embrace Hutcheon's proposal. The virtue of irony pervades his books, which do not strain toward national self-definition even when their stories have an explicitly Canadian dimension.

To return to the question posed at the end of the previous section, which speaks to the political implications of conceiving the nation: Seth's work serves as a counterpoint to apparently authoritative imaginings of national identity/geography (for instance, those asserted by historians like Morton). Seth's juxtaposition of differing conceptions of historiography also unsettles conventional notions of geography, providing an arena in which the reader is free to imagine not only unauthorized histories but also the unauthorized geographies in which they take place. His unassuming but hardly toothless approach is nowhere more on display than in his most ironically Canadian book, *The Great Northern Brotherhood of Canadian Cartoonists*.

The book opens with an epigraph attributed to the experimental cartoonist Henry Pefferlaw, one of Seth's most appealingly iconoclastic creations. According to Pefferlaw, "Canadians have a born advantage when it comes to cartooning because of their national tendency toward dullness" (*GNBCC* 1). Oddly, this sardonic statement strongly recalls Morton's entirely earnest claim that Canada is "governed only by compromise and kept strong only by moderation" (51). Here Morton seems comically temperate, a personification of the stereotypical Canadian dullness that Pefferlaw ironically invokes. Pefferlaw's droll aphorism is not just flatly ironic, however; it entails a range of ironies, the enumeration of which may help to demonstrate the rhetorical density of *The Great Northern Brotherhood*.

First and most obviously, the epigraph ironically praises Canadians for a rarely praised quality—dullness. Second, and less obviously, this irony is compounded by Pefferlaw's status as an experimental cartoonist (not revealed until much later in the book) whose nonnarrative comics could be described as willfully dull in their lack of conventional narrative action. With this in mind, the statement becomes doubly ironic: Pefferlaw's apparently sarcastic swipe may actually indicate esteem. Employing the self-conscious rhetoric of failure, his epigraph ironically inverts dull and interesting. As a writer, Pefferlaw has much in common with real-life artist Martin Vaughn-James, who only lived in Canada for a decade but produced a significant corpus of innovative short comics and book-length works during that period (Doug Wright Awards). Seth lists Vaughn-James's "darn near impenetrable" nonnarrative book *The Projector* as an item in his *Forty Cartoon Books of Interest* (44).³

Seth's own affinity for dullness in the form of "sublime boredom" adds a further dimension to the layered ironies of Pefferlaw's remark, which, despite its shifting significance, remains a statement about national identity. This convoluted, ambivalent brand of nationalism does seem characteristically Canadian, at least according to the terms set out by Morton and Hutcheon. Hutcheon is quick to note that irony is in no way uniquely Canadian, but she observes that there "seems little in Canada that is not (or has not been) inherently doubled and therefore at least structurally ripe for ironizing" (*Splitting Images* 15). Throughout *The Great Northern Brotherhood*, Seth demonstrates Canada's susceptibility to irony and satire, often with pointed (though not ungenerous) historical inventions.

One of the most indelible of Seth's invented comic book characters in *The Great Northern Brotherhood* is "Kao-Kuk of the Royal Canadian Astro-Men"—an Inuit astronaut. This marriage of occupation and cultural background has a cartoon logic that is strangely compelling: "The Eskimo, with his unique understanding of isolation ... and his experience with vast emptiness made him the perfect choice for space exploration" (*GNBCC* 46). Like Morton's conception of the basic Canadian disposition, this simplified understanding of "Eskimo" identity holds an essentialist fascination. Drawn into the momentum of the peculiar premise, the reader is suddenly complicit, fulfilling the caricature with personal assumptions and associations.

Even the character's name functions in this associative manner. Creator Bartley Munn (also, of course, invented by Seth) admits that Kao-Kuk is not authentically Inuit but rather a linguistic forgery that he felt "sounded Eskimo"

FIG. 7.8 Seth, *The Great Northern Brotherhood of Canadian Cartoonists* (Montreal: D&Q, 2011), 97.

(*GNBCC* 46). This telling detail further complicates *The Great Northern Brotherhood*'s ambivalent longing for a "Golden Age" of cartooning, evoking with subtle precision an era in which such culturally insensitive fabrication would go largely unnoticed. It also deftly conveys that particular strain of racism that lacks malice but is all the more insidious as a result. A white author sends an Inuit character into outer space: this scenario is a hyperbolic exemplification of the displacement and appropriation that characterizes pop culture's reimagining of communities that have become marginal. (Seth explores this white-Inuit dynamic in *George Sprott* as well, although not through the ironic lens of metafiction.)

In a complementary instance of metafictional hyperbole, Seth inverts Canada's putatively dominant culture with one of *The Great Northern Brotherhood*'s most outlandish characters, Canada Jack, who is loosely styled after nationalist heroes like Johnny Canuck.[4] Seth reports that Canada Jack was created in the 1960s by a mysterious cartoonist named Sol Gertzman. Some highlights include: a short-lived flying robot horse, a guest appearance by a poorly drawn Snoopy, an entire issue devoted to highway construction, and a caveman valet. As Seth says of his invented series: "They are certainly the oddest comic books ever made in Canada—a kind of folk art, almost" (*GNBCC* 95). Indeed, it is the sheer eccentricity of the stories that marks them as particularly Canadian (fig. 7.8). With his utterly unpredictable expressions of civic enthusiasm, Seth's Canada Jack is what Hutcheon might refer to as an "ex-centric," who is at once inside and outside the dominant culture (*Canadian Postmodern* 4). In this sense, Canada Jack is a nationalist hero—but it is a knowing, Pefferlavian nationalism that delights in ambivalent impulses. As Seth says elsewhere, in a description of one of the brotherhood's social clubs, it is "both grand *and* self-mocking" (*GNBCC* 70, emphasis in original).

A more delicate form of this ambivalent sentiment governs *George Sprott*, the fallible narrator of which personifies the doubt and disappointment behind George's "Gentleman Adventurer" facade. In its idiosyncratic, anti-epic narrative approach, *George Sprott* provides a noteworthy alternative to Chester Brown's much more straightforward Canadian comic-book biography, *Louis Riel* (2004), a carefully researched account of one of Canada's foremost revolutionary figures. Hutcheon names Riel as an "archetypal marginal ex-centric" (*Canadian Postmodern* 4). By contrast, George Sprott's particular brand of small-town marginality is based around a rather conservative archetype. Nevertheless, it is a conservative archetype that is enlivened by a spark of self-awareness. Pages such as the one titled "A Few Words from the Man Himself" (in which George addresses the reader directly with bons mots and aphorisms on a variety of topics) reveal a would-be iconoclast nagged by regret, aware of his limitations and of the ephemeral nature of his work. Seth imbues his small-town hero with the same clear-eyed intelligence discernible in his less successful characters.

With the "folk art" of Canada Jack, Seth tempers nationalism with camp; *George Sprott* exhibits nothing as strident as nationalism, so its exploration of the contradictions of the nation can afford to be implicit and nonverbal. Some

FIG. 7.9 Seth, *George Sprott: 1894–1975* (Montreal: D&Q, 2009), n.p.

of the most identifiably Canadian features of *George Sprott* are the two-page arctic landscape illustrations, which operate within the mode of undecidability even as they allude to the history of Canadian art. Seth's wintry tableaux owe a great deal to the later canvases of Lawren Harris, one of the foremost members of the Group of Seven, a pioneering collective of interwar Canadian landscape painters.

Morton makes specific reference to Harris's work in *The Canadian Identity* as an example of what he calls the "art of the hinterland" (109), a tradition that Seth clearly gestures toward in *George Sprott*. Harris's arctic paintings are often bright and translucent, distinguished by icy peaks and shafts of light that strongly suggest some form of spiritual ascension. Seth's allusive illustrations are more cryptic and opaque (fig. 7.9), moonlit panoramas that offer the reader a reprieve from the densely paneled, text-heavy pages that are typical of *George Sprott*. As an elaboration of his claims about the essential Canadian character, Morton points to "the existence in Canadian art and literature of distinctive qualities engendered by the experience of northern life" (109). In their resistance to sequential reading and interpretation, the large, mute, arctic hiatuses that Seth incorporates into *George Sprott* use the mystery of the image (in René Magritte's phrase) to evoke this northern experience. At the same time, these instances of undecidability are culturally anchored by their reference to Harris's depictions of the north.

Harris makes a more explicit appearance in *The Great Northern Brotherhood*. During the tour of the GNBCC archive, Seth discusses the Group of Seven's "connection to cartooning" (91). One of the archive's holdings is a "picture novel" by Harris, an artist's journal that documents a painting expedition (92). (The very believable title of this journal, *Pillar in the Sky*, may be lifted from *Snow Pillars in the Sky*, a 1915 landscape by Group of Seven member Tom Thomson.) The same page features a similar picture journal by Thoreau MacDonald, who, as Seth notes, was not actually a member of the Group of Seven but the son of founding member J. E. H. MacDonald. Through the manuscript attributed to Thoreau MacDonald, Seth once again reveals his affinity for the marginal or peripheral, the artist working largely in obscurity. He presents the "unpublished" (i.e., invented) work as "a simple record of his everyday life in Thornhill, Ontario. A quiet work—personal yet told with real restraint" (*GNBCC* 93). This is quite a fitting description of much of Seth's own work, from the specific Canadian setting to the sense of moderation.

Clyde Fans in particular is a model of regionalism and restraint, of quietly locating the universal in the specific and provincial. The province in this case is Ontario, and, as suggested in chapter 2, the Matchcard family saga can be regarded as "Southern Ontario Gothic"—a relatively recent development in the Gothic tradition. In *Eleven Canadian Novelists*, a 1973 collection of interviews by Graeme Gibson, noted Canadian author Timothy Findley remarks that Nathan Cohen (a Canadian theater critic) recognized the influence of southern Gothic literature in certain regional Canadian writing. Findley asserts: "Sure it's Southern Gothic: Southern *Ontario* Gothic" (Gibson 138, emphasis in original). The most internationally renowned writer of southern Ontario Gothic fiction is likely Alice Munro, another of the eleven Canadian novelists featured in the collection.

Gibson proposes that the region in which Munro's writing is rooted "might become a kind of mythical country, like the American South" (248). Munro concurs:

> Yes, I've thought of this, yes, probably because the writers who first excited me were the writers of the American South, because I felt there a country being depicted that was like my own.... [Southern Ontario] is rich in possibilities in this way. I mean the part of the country I come from is absolutely Gothic. (Gibson 248)

Perhaps it is no coincidence that Seth cites Munro as an example of a writer whose stories are at once deeply personal and restrained: "Her work has a great depth of understanding of human beings, but you don't get any sense of Alice herself. She's maintained a writerly distance somehow from it, but the work is very deep" (see page 214). Seth's comments suggest a correlation between reserved "writerly distance" and southern Ontario Gothic, which as a genre tends to hew quite closely to realism. This sense of unspoken emotional depth adds to the potency of the work's Gothic elements, which seem to represent a genuinely involuntary return of the repressed.

One of the most recognizably Gothic features of *Clyde Fans* is its portrayal of lineage, a fixation of the genre that almost inevitably takes a sinister form: "A cursed family inherits an unwelcome legacy" (Mighall 80). This is precisely the circumstance of the Matchcard family, each surviving member of which feels haunted by the legacy of Clyde. It is a powerful shared history, perhaps all the more so because it is left largely to the reader's imagination. Robert Mighall observes that "the idea of the Gothic carries a (pseudo-) historical inflection" (xv). This sense of pseudohistoricity is fundamental to Seth's overall aesthetic and to his method of unearthing invented pasts.

In his article on archives in contemporary comics, Jared Gardner makes reference to Daniel Clowes and Seth and offers careful readings of the similarly archaeological comics of Ben Katchor and Kim Deitch. However, he finds nothing Gothic in these diverse excavations of the past: "The phrase 'ghost world' is used by both Clowes and Seth," Gardner says, "and as we have seen it applies equally well to the work of Katchor and Deitch. But it is important to note that there is nothing gothic, nothing uncanny, in these scenes of haunting" (803). Needless to say, Gardner's claims are at odds with many of the observations of this investigation, which explicitly outline the Gothic and uncanny qualities of Seth's work. "Nothing is unsettled by the coexistence of past and present, text and image," Gardner insists. "Here the double-vision that allows present and past to coexist is not uncanny, but natural, inevitable, and responsible" (803). After persuasively arguing that "comics necessarily leave their binary tensions unresolved" (801), Gardner ultimately finds in the comics he examines not an irresolvable, generative tension between past and present but an everyday coexistence of the two. Although this coexistence can be quite ordinary, in Seth's work the familiar (and especially the domestic) often entails a Gothic-tinged return of the repressed.

In *Clyde Fans*, Gothic elements find their clearest personification in the fey and uncanny figure of Simon Matchcard, whose dreams, encounters, and behavior have already been discussed at some length, above and in previous chapters. Abe, the more grounded of the brothers, is more nostalgic than uncanny, but even his most practical concerns, often domestic or business related, take on a somewhat Gothic aspect. If, as Mighall suggests, the Gothic is an attitude to the past, then the same can be said of nostalgia and the uncanny. What nostalgia, the uncanny, and the Gothic have most in common is the past, to which they have variously ambivalent attitudes.

A Note on Modernism and Postmodernism

As a structural and aesthetic response to ambivalence, *Clyde Fans* seems to incline not only toward the Gothic but also significantly toward modernism. Often, Seth's approach to Simon and Abe's shared history brings to mind Virginia Woolf's striking image of the connected "caves" she digs out behind characters in *Mrs. Dalloway*, a quintessentially modernist novel (Woolf, *A Writer's Diary* 60). Chapter 2 attempts to highlight the interdependence of modernism and ambivalence. To some extent, ambivalence ("the great discovery of Freud") is understood as a characteristically modern phenomenon, and modernism is understood as the response to a swell of newly ambivalent impulses. Subsequently, ambivalence also figures prominently in postmodernism (as Hutcheon expertly observes).

Bart Beaty suggests that "comics are only now moving through a modernizing period but . . . they are doing so against a larger cultural backdrop of postmodernism" (11). Against assumptions that literary comics represent an inherently postmodern mingling of high and low culture—literature being high, comics being low—Beaty cogently remarks that "it is difficult to fully comprehend how comic books could move into postmodern culture without having paused first in modernism" (76). Much of Seth's work appears to share not only the concerns of modernism but a number of its techniques for addressing these concerns (for instance, the mode of undecidability), which are often related to ambivalence. In these respects, *George Sprott* may be Seth's most modern book, especially if read as a searching formal exercise in which fragmented storytelling creates an ambivalently elegiac mood.

By comparison, *The Great Northern Brotherhood* is quite gleefully postmodern, not only in its deployment of jostling metafictions but in the overall attitude to nationalism and national history that these fictions delineate. Seth's historiographic metafiction is invariably informed by irony and nostalgia; in "Irony, Nostalgia, and the Postmodern" Hutcheon brilliantly explores the manner in which the three phenomena relate to each other, observing that the postmodern "does indeed recall the past, but always with the kind of ironic double vision that acknowledges the final impossibility of indulging in nostalgia, even as it consciously evokes nostalgia's affective power." This ambivalent double vision is a hallmark of Seth's work, for instance in the quaint but unsettling racism of the Kao-Kuk premise. A less specific example of this double vision is provided by the overall narrative of *It's a Good Life*, the protagonist of which is ironically more sentimental about Kalo's work than Kalo himself. Hutcheon writes:

> In the postmodern, in other words, (and here is the source of the tension) nostalgia itself gets both called up, exploited, *and* ironized. This is a complicated (and postmodernly paradoxical) move that is both an ironizing of nostalgia itself, of the very urge to look backward for authenticity, and, at the same moment, a sometimes shameless invoking of the visceral power that attends the fulfillment of that urge. ("Irony, Nostalgia, and the Postmodern," emphasis in original)

Seth's search for Kalo points to a broader attempt to pin down an authentic past—a ghost world—that, ultimately, may not exist. Moreover, the figure of John Kalloway literally does not exist, except as a historiographical specter available through Seth's metafictional gag cartoons.

The complicated irony that Hutcheon describes is also a definitive element of *The Great Northern Brotherhood*, which offers the reader a moving target composed of constantly shuffling layers of truth and fabulation that never quite settle into an identifiable mode of historiography. In many ways, this disruption acts as rejoinder to familiar, institutional narratives of history, geography, and national identity by drawing attention to their construction. Metafiction is certainly the most identifiably postmodern technique in Seth's work, a fundamental narrative element as early as *It's a Good Life*, but postmodern playfulness alone does not account for the sheer charm of Seth's invented comics. Seth's metafictional comics are at their most lively when their blurring of familiar borders highlights the invented component of his communities.

Seth's incorporation of historicizing discourses (sometimes plain historical fact) into the portrayal of invented communities tends to collapse conventional historiographical hierarchies, leaving the reader in a kind of suspense—suspended, that is, between history and forgery. Often the forgeries offer fractional views that cumulatively suggest a comprehensive fictive heterocosm, much of which may remain unrepresented. Each cardboard model, for instance, manifests only a limited part of the history and geography that constitute the interior landscape of Dominion City. The notion of the interior landscape—*which is at once intangible and inhabitable*—engenders a richer understanding of the possibilities of the heterocosm, particularly in Seth's work.

If a meaningful distinction exists between the terms "heterocosm" and "ghost world" (used almost interchangeably in this chapter), it is that the latter has a less neutral connotation. Ghost worlds are haunted heterocosms, inflected with the return of the dead, the repressed, the past. In Seth's work, this haunting elicits an ambivalent longing, not only from his characters but from his readers. Just as irony is made by the reader when two meanings come together, nostalgia, Hutcheon says, "is what you 'feel' when two different temporal moments" come together. In this coming together, Hutcheon could just as easily be describing the "feeling" of history, of narrative progression, of the movement across a comics page. It is worth noting that the medium of comics fundamentally comprises the juxtaposition of meanings (as does irony) and the juxtaposition of temporal moments (as does nostalgia). Seth takes full advantage of these structural affinities, offering complex metahistories that amount to "a turning of the Ironic consciousness against Irony itself" (White, *Metahistory* xii). Without the complicity of the reader, however, this recursion is only a suggestion—it is ultimately the reader who must forge history.

Conclusion

Seth invites the reader to take a position between history and memory, to adopt an attitude toward the past that is characterized by ambivalence. In the preceding chapters, I identify a range of ambivalent impulses related to Seth's work, in particular an ambivalent longing for the past, which I occasionally refer to in a general way as nostalgia. This longing in fact takes many forms and has many sources, most of which on closer examination reveal an oppositional structure that arises from boundaries or gaps. The master-opposition between inside and outside exemplifies this structure at the broadest, most abstract level; more specific and concrete is the fundamental semiotic interdependence of panels and gutters on the comics page. Seth's work consistently engages with the crossing of boundaries and filling of gaps, and compels the reader to do likewise to make sense of his narrative modes of address (and sometimes even to make sense of narrative content). Seth's work resides somewhere between history and memory, and this ambivalence permeates every aspect of the narrative, from drawing style to story structure—each element solicits an act of interpolation, a contribution from the reader.

I have argued that the medium of comics induces a specific form of interpolation because it is essentially "founded on reticence" (Groensteen) and "composed of several kinds of tension" (Hatfield). Perhaps the most significant tension is the kind that arises between the panel and the gutter, which is often plainly visible on the page. Even in those instances where the gutter is only implied, and images abut without visible spaces to separate them, the comics page still generally presents itself as a vacillating arrangement of boundaries and borders that the reader must traverse. Linda Hutcheon's account of ambivalence remains unparalleled in its simplicity and broad applicability: "the desire to be on both sides of any border, deriving energy from the continual crossing" (*Canadian Postmodern* 162). Successful realization of the comics narrative depends on the reader's ability to construct a sequence out of adjacent images, in effect reading multiple moments at once. This entails a constant reinterpretation of previous panels in light of the panel currently being read, a constant reinterpolation into what has been.

This investigation tends to accept the Freudian premise that literature is a field of repressed impulses, the imaginary site of a return of the repressed. I borrow the phrase "ambivalent impulses" from Freud to designate a whole range of tendencies and behaviors borne out of repression (which are often related to return, repetition, and the passage of time). These ambivalent impulses saturate Seth's work, manifesting themselves in nostalgic perspectives and uncanny moments, in formal experiments that stretch the narrative capacity of comics, and even in Seth's distinctive, highly refined drawing style. Although ambivalence is not synonymous with ambiguity—which is the capacity for multiple interpretations of a literary detail—the two are closely related to each other. This book suggests a causal relationship, in which perceived ambiguity engenders a generative ambivalence in the reader. In this way, ambiguity produces an opening that the reader is prompted to fill by means of interpretation and interpolation. Seth's comics contain many overlapping ambiguities, simultaneously verbal and visual, structural and discursive, literary and historiographic. Charles Hatfield succinctly describes this multilayered complex of diverse elements as "the co-presence and interaction of various codes" (*Alternative Comics* 36). These codes each involve specific kinds of ambiguity, which demand a range of reading strategies in response to their "various interpretive options and potentialities" (36).

It is ultimately the reader who, in filling the gaps, serves as a site of articulation—a joint or junction—between the fragmentation and coherence of the comics narrative. Often the reader fulfills this role almost unconsciously, especially the reader who is already quite accustomed to the kind of narrative interpolation required by comics. Instances of particularly heightened parataxis elegantly disorient the reader and elicit a more deliberate and unpredictable mode of interpolation. The fragmentary foldout section of *George Sprott* comes closest to what Walter Benjamin famously calls "the chaos of memories" (*Illuminations* 60); a mixture of text plates, panels, and drawn photos, it becomes coherent only through the persistence of the reader. At its most dense and porous, Seth's work demonstrates a willingness to abandon traditional storytelling, trusting that the reader will make sense of indeterminate, sometimes cryptic sequences.

Despite Seth's formal inventiveness and sustained exploration of the capacities of comics as a medium, this investigation nevertheless aligns his work with the Chekhovian tradition of literary fiction, a tradition described in terms of "inbetweenness" and irony, particularly the irony of unfulfillment.

Conclusion 181

Through the irony of unfulfillment, the past and the passage of time come into increasingly sharp focus. Seth's characters often set themselves against the unremitting advance of time in their attempts to establish stable identities—which, as Stuart Hall suggests, are positions relative to the narratives of the past. In many instances, the process of collection allows characters to more effectively arbitrate between the past and present, and secure their identities by giving a fixed form to the chaos of memory. Following W. J. T. Mitchell, this book has often referred to memory/recollection as a medium, which is to say "a mechanism, a material and semiotic process subject to artifice and alteration" (192). It is likewise appropriate to speak of *collection* as a medium, and one that has much in common with the medium of memory. In Seth's work, it is the medium of comics that illuminates this commonality, a task to which it is uniquely suited because it shares significant structural similarities with both collection and memory.

As exercises in historiographic refraction, Seth's narratives of the past call for an alert response from the reader, who then gets caught up in the characters' repeated attempts to forestall loss by means of collection and recollection. The containment and compartmentalization at the heart of collection can be understood as expressions of the master-opposition between inside and outside, which manifests itself in terms of the selections and exclusions of the collector. As an intervention into the past, into memory and history, collection provides a model of meaning making that extends not only to Seth's method of collecting fragments into larger narratives but also to the acts of readerly interpolation that these narratives require.

Seth's strategy of prompting the reader to arbitrate between history and memory is most concretely demonstrated by his drawn photographs, which recast the historical objectivity typically ascribed to photography in the more subjective form of cartoon images. These dense meta-images combine the referential reticence of cartoons and photography, offering the reader representations that act as indices of an invented reality. This complex operation mirrors the larger thrust of Seth's work: he indexes a past that perhaps never existed but is nonetheless made real through the cooperation of the reader. As Karin Kukkonen suggests, the reality of the narrative is a cognitive construct of the reader.

Hutcheon uses the term "heterocosm" to designate such a reality, a separate or alternative world. For the reader, Seth's literary realities are "ghost worlds," fictive heterocosms that are haunted by the past. For Seth's characters, however, the term "ghost world" could just as easily refer to the past itself, the historical heterocosm from which the dead and the repressed return. Of course, this distinction between fictive and historical becomes quite murky in Seth's work, which provides many instructive instances of what Hutcheon calls "historiographic metafiction." This particularly ambiguous mode of literature works to uncover the various mechanisms (fictive, historical, etc.) that commonly construct the past. Seth often does this by setting different types of historiography against each other. Hayden White distinguishes between three kinds—fabulous, true, satirical—out of which Seth crafts subtle historiographic imbrications that provoke the reader toward a "metahistorical consciousness," an attitude to history that is governed by irony and ambivalence.

This strategy is not limited to the historiographic status of the plot. In Seth's work, even style becomes a metadiscourse, a set of attributes that often operates as a sort of running commentary on itself. In much the same way that an art historian might use the concept of style to create a generic chronology, Seth likewise uses style as a historicizing discourse, deploying a range of historically inflected points of reference to form a version of the past. In some cases, these are plainly visual references assimilated from the history of comics (for instance, a drawing style that bears the influence of particular cartoonists). However, Seth's style tends to crystallize around less specific elements—a certain handmade quality or autobiographical narrative register—which evoke a sense of authenticity that seems rooted in the past. If the appearance of authenticity in Seth's books occasionally takes an uncanny turn, it reflects a fundamental ambivalence toward this constructed past. His work is ambivalently nostalgic, straining toward an authentic past even as it recognizes the artifice necessary to conjure this past.

Of all the pasts that Seth conjures, the densest may be the one glimpsed in *Clyde Fans*, his most subtle and sustained meditation on memory and loss. *George Sprott* bristles with technical mastery and *Wimbledon Green* is a paragon of sketchbook vitality, but, arguably, *Clyde Fans* remains Seth's most profound work to date, in no small part because of the character of Simon Matchcard and the kind of comics storytelling he makes possible. This includes not only the striking dream sequences and ambiguous descents into dementia but also the remarkably understated section in which Simon describes the objects collected his mother's bedroom. Seth has expressed a particular affinity for this sequence and suggested that it may be an indication of work to come, even speculating on the possibility of a book composed entirely of descriptive storytelling (see page 195).

This growing ambivalence toward plot is one of the threads that runs through my interview with Seth, which includes many other musings about his creative process, his development as an artist, and his feelings about his own work and readers' reactions to it. Seth is a very generous interviewee, reflective and articulate, and I have incorporated many of his comments into the foregoing chapters—but some of his most telling and surprising reflections are tangential to the concerns of this investigation. The interview serves as a parallel inquiry, one that is looser and more accommodating, with some quite detailed remarks about page composition and methods of cartooning, and even specific materials—concrete observations that shed particular light on how Seth's comics actually get made.

Seth does not go so far as to *un*make the past in his work, but he does often leave it half-made, its narrative scaffolding exposed, inducing the reader to imagine the whole. In this way, Seth puts the reader in the position of the historian, who attempts to construct a coherent story out of various assorted fragments of the past. The particularly zealous reader of Seth's work may actually feel compelled to seek objective corroboration outside the text in an effort to discern truth from fabulation from satire. Even the more casual reader, however, will go beyond the text, filling spots of indeterminacy. Seth highlights the seams and borders of his stories, and openly examines the processes by which narratives of the past come to seem seamless.

Perhaps less explicit, but equally in evidence, is Seth's engagement with the concept of marginality itself and the spaces in which remembrance often takes place. Boundaries, borders, gutters, and gaps take on a marked significance, and the continual crossing of these boundaries gives rise to much of the uncertainty in Seth's work. Chief among ambivalent impulses is a complicated nostalgia, well aware of its own reactionary, restorative, and nationalistic inclinations and able to channel them toward productive ends. Seth ultimately turns the medium of memory on itself, using it as an instrument to examine longing, loss, and the processes of remembrance and making history.

Appendix: Interview with Seth

FIG. A.1 Ink stamp on an envelope sent by Seth to the author.

Sitting in the living room of Inkwell's End—Seth's home in Guelph, Ontario—I catch sight of a familiar object that immediately transports me into the world of *Clyde Fans*: a cheap ukulele, like the one that hangs in Lily Matchcard's bedroom, which I have only ever seen in cartoon form (fig 5.3). Here, on Seth's wall, in all its kitschy reality, hangs the actual item—and I cannot deny the little thrill of recognition, the promise of continuity between real and imagined lives, even if I must also admit that the object holds meaning for me precisely because of its fictional dimension.

This interview serves a number of purposes: to offset the density of theoretical analysis, to gesture toward those things beyond the scope of the preceding chapters, to include the kind of granular detail that a digressive conversation can accommodate, to give Seth the last word. But also, perhaps, to offer a glimpse of continuity between life and art, however imaginary it may be.

DANIEL MARRONE: When did you arrive in Toronto?

SETH: I got there about 1980, I think. And left around 1999 or 2000, something along those lines. Yeah, so it was a long stretch but I certainly fell in love with the city in the first ten years. There was nowhere I would have been happier. The next ten years not so much. It declined.

DM: What happened?

SETH: Well, it was a combination of two things. One is that I got into a bad relationship that lasted for nine years—now that's a long stretch. And . . . she didn't like Toronto and—well, it's a complicated story but basically she convinced me to leave Toronto and so we moved here to Guelph. And, uh, then we broke up. And so I just stayed here, and now I'm very comfortable here. But I probably would never have left if she hadn't pushed me to. But the truth is I was using the city a lot less in that ten years, besides the bad situation. I was staying in—like I was always in the house anyway. My real years of going out and exploring the city and doing things were the first ten.

DM: Yeah, you seem quite comfortably ensconced.

SETH: Oh yeah. I'll die here for sure. There's no chance I'll ever move again. It's like, I'm not—I hate moving, for one thing, so I—now that we've actually bought a house, I know I will never—even if I got like, you know, five million dollars, all I would do is maybe buy the other houses around here and knock them down.

DM: [laughs]

SETH: I wouldn't move, not a chance.

DM: . . . alright, let me see if I can segue smoothly into any of my questions here . . .

SETH: Sure.

DM: How much commercial illustration are you doing lately?

SETH: Not that much, really, anymore. The truth is that market is dead. It's funny, when I entered illustration in the eighties it was a very lucrative field. There were a lot of people doing it and I can remember how busy I was even within a year of starting out in illustration. But now, you know, ever since, well, since the Internet, basically. Magazines are all dying, and even the ones that are surviving don't have the ad revenue to pay for illustration half the time. I'm just grateful I'm not like a full-time illustrator. I know lots of people like that, and you can see them scrambling. Now, I mean, I have a regular gig I do every month for a magazine—I actually had two that I did every month, but I actually just quit one of them because I have other stuff I've got to get done and I can't do it all. I find that I do more book design now than I do illustration, which I like better but is a lot more work, is the problem. You know, it's more fun to design a book even if you're not interested in the book. It's really no fun to illustrate boring articles. That's just dull. So I only do a little bit, but I still do a fair amount of commercial work. I mean, I just took on a book design and illustration project that will last for like four books over four years, and that's going to be a lot of work and it's a project that will be interesting, but it's not something that I would have picked if they weren't going to pay me well. So, that's the kind of thing where I'd rather just work on my own work than do all these other things. But you gotta make a living.

DM: Do you feel the need to read the book front to back before starting the design?

SETH: It depends. These ones, definitely. Yeah, these are books that I will have to illustrate, and I'll have to do a good job on them, too. And I'm also going to be doing another book that's like a prose book that I'll be illustrating, and that one I definitely will read front to back as well. There are other things you can kind of fake through. It depends. But generally if you want to do a good job you have be familiar with the material. Even the boring illustration articles, you have to read them.

DM: So, do you mind if I ask what you're working on right now, in terms of your own personal work?

SETH: Well, right now, finishing *Clyde Fans*.

DM: Oh, great!

SETH: That's what I'm working on right now. So that's the project for the rest of this year and then, hopefully, it's onto a new book next year. So . . . that's a big project for me.

DM: Yeah . . . you seem to be putting out actually a lot of books recently.

SETH: It's funny, things just accumulate, sort of. I think if you just work on things every day, at some point they just come together. So it looks like a lot of stuff is coming together or coming out at the same time, but it's years of accumulation, really. I think that's always the way it is. People think, "Oh, you must be working so hard all the time," but if you put out a sketchbook, that's like six or seven years' work coming out. But I try to always keep busy is the truth.

DM: What's your daily schedule like?

SETH: Well, I get up around eight, I guess, and go down to the studio . . . if I'm smart and don't go to the computer first, I go right down to the studio and get to work. If I go to the computer, I probably don't get to work till about ten. Basically I just work until my wife comes home around dinnertime and then I go back to work after dinner till about eleven, and then we spend time together after that. So I work, I'd say, every day all day and all evening except on the weekends when I'll take a day or two off, usually. But it's the kind of thing—it's like, I want to be in the studio anyway, so I never feel like a pressure that I *need* to be there. I can't really think of anything I'd rather do than just sit in the studio anyway. It's funny, you don't plan your life in a way, but sometimes things—you realize when you get older, maybe subconsciously you did steer things in a direction, and you didn't realize it. When I was twenty years old, I wouldn't have realized that I was kind of re-creating my teenage life, for the rest of my life. Staying at home, sitting, listening to the radio or television or whatever and drawing all day: that's like what I did all through my teen years. And that was not really by choice, I was kind of an isolated teen. But then you realize that's what you're familiar with, and somehow you've re-created that life and that's what I do every day. It's the same life.

DM: Can you recall a time when you weren't drawing?

SETH: Yeah, for sure. There was a short period in the eighties. I went to art school in the early eighties and that's where I first—I wanted to be a cartoonist as a teenager, I knew that, but when I went to art school, that was probably when my life most changed . . . discovering new things, being a new person. I came to Toronto as a small-town boy, I met a lot of peers who were a lot more sophisticated and I got involved with the punk rock scene and suddenly I was going out to clubs. I started to have an outside life more than the drawing, and I can remember my interest in cartooning really was declining. The problem, too, was I just wasn't interested in the comics anymore, either. That was around the time that I—there's sort of a brief period between reading mainstream comic books in my late teens and then discovering people like the Hernandez brothers and Robert Crumb, and in that in-between window, when I was going to art school, I wasn't reading comics, I just wasn't interested in them anymore. But I still thought I wanted to be a cartoonist, although to be perfectly honest I didn't know what I was going to do anymore because I didn't want to go draw Spider-Man. But I didn't really—if I'd been left to my own devices, I'm not sure I ever would have figured it out. I needed those people to point the way. I needed to see the Hernandez brothers and say, "*Oh, I see what you could do.*" And so in those years I got way more interested, for a couple of years, in just going out and taking drugs and things like that. And, at that point, I can remember there was a day where I hadn't—I don't think I'd drawn in about a year. I dropped out of art school, and I remember every once and while I would go and sit at the drawing table and try and draw something, but I just wasn't interested. And I remember one day I just said to myself, "Well, I guess I'm not going to be a cartoonist. It was a pipe dream." And that was kind of shocking to me because I didn't have any backup plans. There was nothing else I'd planned to do in life. But the funny part of that is that very quickly after that it turned around. Within a couple of months of that I decided I had to straighten my life out, and so I decided to go back to art school, and that meant I had to get a portfolio together, and so I started sitting down and doing a portfolio. And right at that point, when I was drawing the comics in my portfolio, that's when I met up with the publisher of Vortex Comics, and that's when I started working on the *Mister X* comic. And after that it just sort of rolled on normally. There was a period there where it really didn't look like I was going to draw for a living. So you never know what's going to happen.

DM: When you first kind of got back into it, were there any cartoonists in particular that you were deliberately emulating?

SETH: Yeah, at that point, since I was really like—I hate to say the word, but I was a punk at the time—Jaime Hernandez was the person I was most interested in. It's funny, at the same time I was reading Gilbert [Hernandez]'s work, of course, and I was reading Crumb then, too, discovering all his work, and actually Edward Gorey was big at the time, too, for some reason. And I can remember trying a little bit to draw in some other styles. I didn't have a style of my own yet, but I can remember trying to draw a bit like Gorey and trying to draw a bit like Jaime and Crumb, you know, not really being able to pull it off. But Jaime was the one I was gravitating toward, and I think it was because his work was closest to what my own life was like at that point. And I think that naturally I was a sort of clean line sort of artist, and so he appealed to me instantly. And that kind of opened up a world—actually, getting involved with *Mister X* sort of opened up another world of discovering a lot of European cartoonists. And then going back and discovering the older artists—that was a period where I really started to look into cartooning and looking beyond the stuff I just knew as a teenager. But Jaime was *big* influence on me. Very . . . liberating, to see what he was doing. It was fun, and it was serious but it wasn't pretentious in any way. And that was really inspiring, for sure.

DM: Around what time did you kind of settle into what people might recognize as your distinctive style?

SETH: You mean like my drawing style?

DM: Yeah.

SETH: I guess it starts to come together—truthfully, I think it probably starts to come together right after I left *Mister X*, I suppose. Near the end of those comics, I was starting to understand what I was *trying* to do. It was a good apprenticeship period, because, I mean, I can't stand to look at any of that stuff but at least I wasn't writing it. So it's not painful—I'm divorced from the content—that element of the comics doesn't bother me, I didn't write them. I can't take any blame. That's fine. Even then, near the end of working on *Mister X*, I knew that wasn't the kind of comics I wanted to do. But I think during that period I was really trying to figure out . . . how to compose the pages was the big problem, and how to simplify the artwork to make it work.

It was a real shocker to me when I had the first issue of *Mister X* published, because that's when you really see your work for the first time. And I saw how many extraneous lines there were in every drawing and it was kind of a shock. There were little dots and fragments everywhere, I was just filling in space. If I drew a guy's head, for some reason I feel like I had to put a couple of little lines over here or there. That was a good lesson for me to cut back—only the absolutely necessary lines. But during that process I discovered Hergé's work, too—that and then, later, Peter Arno were the two big influences after Jaime, that taught me about the simplification of artwork. And that happened over a span of about five years, I guess. So by the time I quit *Mister X* and started to do illustration work, I was starting to approach the work differently. I was freed up from a certain kind of comic book realism—which even Jaime is somewhat connected to—into a freer world of sort of cartoon stylizations that appealed to me more and I think are more natural for me. Once I got away from any attempts at true realism—realism, for comics, there's not really much in the way of realism—that opened the door for me to really come to understand what I was doing and to free me to actually start thinking about drawing, cartooning as symbols and shapes, and not trying to create drawings of the real world. And that took about a five- to six- or seven-year period. And that took a lot of understanding of older cartoonists, and I think that's why I started to look back more and more at older stuff. And that's when my whole life, I think, started to turn toward looking backward.

DM: Was this around the same time that you were becoming proficient with a brush?

SETH: Yeah, pretty much. During that *Mister X* period I was trying to learn to use the brush, and that sort of came together by the end of that. Especially working in illustration, it's funny—thank god I recognized at that time the importance of having to learn it, because it's a real task. I'm not sure young cartoonists right now would feel they *have* to learn it . . . The computer offers such easy options to escape trying to figure out how to get that slick finish. I can remember looking at people like Hergé or Yves Chaland's work and trying to figure out how they could possibly get those brush lines that are straight lines—how do you get a straight line with a brush? Having to figure it out, having to come up with a method, that you could use a ruler and brush and actually get enough control to be able to do it—these were all skills that took years to acquire, really, but thank god that I was forced to do it, because it's not a pleasure to learn any craft. And I do worry that young cartoonists are probably not learning things as easily, just because they don't need to. They've got other options. And maybe it doesn't matter. Maybe some guy who was a

woodcutter would say it's a shame the next generation doesn't know how to make woodblocks. But maybe it doesn't matter.
DM: ... I have to think it matters, though.
SETH: It does matter to me. I must admit, I'm a bit of a devil's advocate of my own position because I have such a—my opinion of the world is all basically a knee-jerk reaction, that I don't like much that's new. And so I always have to think that my opinion is probably the least trustworthy of anyone's. I mean, I don't like the idea of replicating a brush on the computer, like a program that could just give you the brush lines rather than doing it yourself. There seems something about that that's morally wrong. Like, you've got to put the time in and *learn* to use those tools. But then, I'm sure that in a generation people just won't think that way.
DM: I suppose that's probably true. I just like to think that I'd be able to tell the difference.
SETH: Yeah.
DM: Maybe not in a single line, but looking at an entire work, somehow I'd know what was going on.
SETH: I feel that, but you know everything gets so sophisticated—you know someone will develop the program that allows it to be spontaneous enough that you can't figure out it's not real. It's funny ... there is a significant difference but it's hard to argue whether these things are better. That's the problem. I was watching an old movie from the seventies, the old Superman movie, not long ago, and I was looking at the special effects and thinking what a great deal of effort went in to making this glowing sun or whatever, whatever effects they had, and I thought just the sheer effort involved in it impresses me more than the computer effects of today. I'm not impressed by the computer effects, even though I recognize a huge amount of effort and skill and knowledge went into figuring this stuff out. But there's something unimpressive about it. The fact that some guy had to go get a can of gasoline and light something on fire and film it and then put it through an optical printer, blah blah blah ... that seems to me like a Herculean attempt that makes me more impressed with it than the gloss of the computer. And I feel that that's my main problem with almost all of the digital revolution, is I'm just not impressed with it. But I should be impressed. But somehow it leaves me cold.
DM: I think there's something about clunkiness, in material, and even sometimes in storytelling, in old movies. There's a certain clunkiness in tension with what's trying to be put across that gives something its substance.
SETH: Yeah, I think you're right. When things develop a formula that's rigid enough that it becomes boring, it is the elements of eccentricity that creep

into things or an inexactitude or humanness . . . when I was watching that Superman movie, I was thinking, "This movie is really corny," and there are some real bits in it that are just outright odd choices. I can't imagine—there's this scene where Superman is flying with Lois Lane and she's like reciting a poem in her head? And I was thinking, "Boy, this is corny." But I was also thinking, "I can't imagine this in a contemporary action film."
DM: It wouldn't even make it into the script.
SETH: Yeah, it was such a strange choice I thought, "That's kind of interesting."
DM: [shuffling papers] Have you come across much criticism of your work?
SETH: Well, I try to *not* read as much of it as I can, but of course you do come across it. The Internet—that's another thing about the Internet, it's opened a door to eavesdropping, basically, on people's thoughts, that you didn't have access to before. And, yeah, certainly I have seen a lot more criticism of my work because of the Internet than I did before. In a way, it's . . . well, it *is* a bad thing. It's simple: you don't want those opinions because they're not well-reasoned criticisms that are being aimed at you. But they sting, and they're often accurate. But they're said with the kind of meanness that you would say talking behind someone's back. I mean, I have those kinds of criticisms of other artists, too—I'll just dismiss people as boring or superficial or whatever, but I wouldn't write it down. If I was going to write a criticism, I would want it to be a bit more substantial. I will read some criticism that people have put online that *is* substantial, and I appreciate that even if it's negative. But the off-hand comments are the ones that hurt, actually. But I think the thing that most irritates me, as I've mentioned to you in emails, is the way that my work has just been boiled down to nostalgia. I mean, I understand why it is. And it's also because people aren't required to give as much thought to the work as I am. They see me, and they see that I'm living a kind of nostalgist's lifestyle, and so the work must be about the idea that things were better in the past. But I like to think it's never that simple. Even when I talk about the past in interviews, I try to make it a point never to say things were just better in the past. It's a very complicated issue. You can't say that things were better in 1935 than they are now; that's just a stupid position. You can argue about the relative merits of different aspects of culture. Certainly I wouldn't have been happy living as a cartoonist in 1930. It's a much better time to be a cartoonist right now. In fact, for most of the arts, this is the time that—we're born in this time, this is the time we belong to. But people think that because the work is about looking back that it's about dreaming about a golden era. And I've always tried, even in my earliest work, to make it clear that characters' thoughts—like even when it's me, that my own opinions are suspect. Even in something as old as *It's a Good Life*, I wanted to make it clear that even though I'm pining for the past,

that my own opinions are definitely undercut by what's going on in the story. But people generally just see it as a simple thing of Seth and his nostalgia. And that bothers me because it does really imply that I just think everything is better in the past and I'm longing for the past and my characters are longing for the past, and that's not true. But I am *interested* in the past and I am a person who's always thinking about their past, and my characters are like that, too. So that mix-up is irritating to me. I rarely see anything about me where the first line of the review doesn't have the word "nostalgia" in it in a way I don't like.

DM: [laughs] Yeah, admittedly, that *was* the starting point for my research back in my MA when I was looking at Daniel Clowes, and I was looking at what I was calling nostalgia in his work. And I've sort of backed off from the N word, but that was kind of the way in. You quickly discover that, as you say, it's much more than just pining.

SETH: Yeah, well Dan's an interesting case because, like many of the cartoonists I know, they are very much involved in the past—but I think Dan's avoided the whole negative stereotype of nostalgia that hounds a few cartoonists because his work has a built-in edge of cynicism that makes it very clear that even if his characters *are* pining for the past, that we don't sympathize with them truly. That "1966" ["MCMLXVI"] story—which I think is a great piece—we don't sympathize with the guy who's talking about how great 1966 is. Dan's been smart in separating himself from the characters in a really clear way. Even from the beginning, he's never earnestly applied himself to like "This is me," which I think is smart. I can't do that. I'm always very identified—the characters are me, my sympathies lie with them. To some degree. Usually I have some moral ambiguities toward them—but that's a smart move. Even somebody like Chris Ware hasn't succeeded really in separating himself from the characters. He gets labeled a nostalgist. Even someone like Ben Katchor gets labeled a nostalgist, and I think that—Ben's work is about a *sort* of a past, but it's really . . . it's hard to explain what Ben's work is about, but certainly not about a longing for the past.

DM: It's sort of like the New York I imagined in my childhood.

SETH: Mm-hmm, yeah, it's an alternate reality of some sort. It's so absurdist that it's hard to imagine that nostalgia's connected to it, but I think we've reached a point in the culture where an interest in past is seen as nostalgia. Nostalgia's a commodity now, it's like something easily sold and labeled. I'm not sure that was so true if you went back to say the 1970s. There certainly was a big nostalgia movement going on in the seventies, but I think it was recognized that people who did period pieces weren't necessarily nostalgists. I mean, nobody would have called *The Godfather* a "nostalgia" film, even though it was set in the past. Now, if you were to do like a gangster film set in the forties, there would be some sort of veneer of retro-nostalgia to it, which is unpleasant.

DM: Can you think of any influences of yours that might surprise readers?

SETH: It's hard to say. When *you* like something, you think it's natural, but I know that a lot of my own interests are not—if you knew me, you'd see that I have really wide tastes. I'm sure my readers would be surprised how much I like old B movies, for example. It doesn't really fit into the "1930s guy" image I've got. But I wouldn't really say any of that stuff is an influence. Those are just things I'm interested in. Jack Kirby certainly remains someone I have a deep interest in—it's hard to say whether he's an influence at this point. I never sit down and try and draw like Jack Kirby. I still study his work, though. I look at how he composed panels, and that's still interesting, but I can't say that a lot of that is really applicable to what I do any longer.

DM: What is the enduring appeal there?

SETH: Well, beyond *actual* nostalgia—and that's a case where I *would* have real nostalgia for Kirby's work because I loved it so much as a child—it's just that he was such a great visual cartoonist. There's some potency in the work that's different to me than when I look at other cartoonists I love, too. Like I love, say, Harold Gray or Chester Gould, but they don't have that same personal connection for me as Kirby does, even though I would like their work better if had to sit down and read it. There's something in Kirby's work that—I guess it's like we all have certain foods we like to eat, there's a flavor. And Kirby has a certain flavor that really appeals to me. It's funny how you can like a lot of art, but there are certain people that just immediately rise to the surface and you put them in a special pantheon. I have a sort of pantheon of artists that I like more than other artists, and not all of them necessarily—there's only a few cartoonists in that group. For some reason, these people click with you in some way. Glenn Gould would be on that list. But it's not because I'm a great lover of piano music, it's just something about Gould clicked with me. Henry Darger is someone who's one of my favorite artists, yet I think most people would not see any Henry Darger in my work. I think sometimes it's a combination of the life story and the artist and the art. Stanley Spencer is a British artist I have a deep affinity toward. And also another British artist named L. S. Lowry. These are guys who are big in my list of favorites, but most cartoonists—I have my people who influenced me and I love, but they don't all necessarily make it into this top list of artists that mean the most to me. Crumb does. Crumb rises above almost any cartoonist I'm interested in. Crumb and [Charles] Schulz. They sit together at different ends of a spectrum. It's funny, though: I really don't think people would see much Crumb in my work. There's none of that freedom. None of that kind of..."let it all hang out" earnestness. I'm just too uptight for that... kind of revealing qualities. I think that that's really valuable, and I think when was younger I was thinking I was working toward that, but I never was. That was just an illusion. Schulz I think people might see more of in my work. The simplicity of it, the clear line approach. Even sometimes the way he paces things, I think, has somehow got into how I move the characters...

DM: Yeah, I wanted to ask you about pacing, because it seems so important to your work in ways that maybe is less apparent in other work. I mean, how would you kind of define "pacing," with respect to comics?

SETH: Well, for me, the storytelling *is* the comic. When people talk about what particular qualities do comics have that other media don't, the main thing is the way you can control the flow of time. The compression or decompression of time. And that's all in the pacing. And I think, ideally, I would like to slow the pacing down as slow as humanly possible. The problem, of course, is that you're limited by your ability to draw it. Every time I do a page where a character walks from one room to another, I always think, "Maybe it should've been *two* pages." But the truth is, it's a thin line between—I think of a thing I call "sublime boredom," which is a boredom that is a good thing. And then if you go a little too far you pass into actual boredom. And it's tricky to know where that thin line is.

DM: It's a fine balance. I mean, it's probably different for different readers, too.

SETH: Exactly. I was reading—somebody was saying somewhere once—in one of the chapters of *Clyde Fans*, recently, I had like a six-page sequence at the end where the character goes through the items in the mother's bedroom. Somebody made a comment, something like, "This could have been like three pages shorter." And when I was working on it I was thinking it should have been twenty pages longer. I love that sort of thing. More and more, as I'm moving on, I find I'm more interested in the description than I am in the plot. And I'm realizing I think that's where my work is going, ultimately, into description... rather than characters. I like describing things. I think the next book is going to be just almost all description. And that means—you realize it's all about slowing down. I like slowed-down storytelling, but it's tricky on how you handle it. The George Sprott book didn't have that much sloweddown storytelling, even though each segment is kind of like, nothing happens. It's like, you had to get a lot of nothing into one page. So if I were to do that as a comic, if I just had freedom of space like *Clyde Fans*, each of those one pages would've probably been about thirty pages long. I would've really added in a lot more of what I call the storytelling. You want that feeling—there's a kind of a magic feeling in comics, the way your eye moves across the page that allows you to invest meaning into images. So if on those George Sprott pages

I've got George in one panel walking through the snow, in the next panel he's back in the television studio. You didn't have much space to do things there. I would have liked to have put like three pages in there, really slow that down. Show the sequence of walking through the snow, have the narration go along with it, have some silent panels in there . . . you get a feeling to reading them. I think after a while every cartoonist just has a rhythm they're familiar with. There is kind of an unspoken staccato that goes along with how a page reads, and you can kind of break that in certain ways, stretch out a long note here. If you have like four little panels and then a long one, it changes the kind of rhythm of reading, the feeling of it. And that's, to me, the real magic of comics. There's lots of other elements, of course, on how they work, but that's the main thing that interests me about them. I'm not interested in drawing in a real sense. Every once and a while I realize I better put something in here that looks like "real drawing" in it. But, ultimately, the kind of bravad—bravura? bravado? what's the word I'm looking for?

DM: I think both work.

SETH: That kind of really impressive drawing that comic fans like—I like to look at it, too, but I don't really think of that as important in any way in comic storytelling. When I look at an old, say, Jack Davis comic or something, any of those classic comic illustrators, I can be impressed. Like, "Wow, look at this big vista they drew" or all these characters or whatever, that's impressive. But truthfully, I think comics are most effective when they aren't just about telling the story, and that means every once and a while you might want to pull out a two-page spread to show the city or to show a room crammed full of people. But most of the time it's the simplicity of how the things move from panel to panel that's of interest. You get caught up in the drawing, that's where you get lost. I think a lot of young cartoonists, they actually have to learn that. I did, too. It's like you're afraid people will think you *can't* draw. There's so much emphasis put on being a "good artist" that you kind of have to pull it back and realize it's not about showing people you can draw. You can do that on the cover. It's about telling the story in an effective manner. And for me that means telling it quietly.

DM: You've got those—in *George Sprott*—those kind of arctic spreads. Could you talk a little bit about that?

SETH: Well that was pretty much exactly what I was talking about earlier—I had been forced to design each of those pages as very crammed. And even those, the actual editing of them, when I sat down and wrote them, and then broke them down, each of those pages I tried to just work out as panels and then see how many panels it would be, and it was always—I think I could do about a maximum of thirty panels on a page.

DM: Which is a lot.

SETH: It's a lot, yeah. Squeezed in small. [telephone rings] Oh, just a sec. Actually, I'll let the machine get that.

DM: Are you sure?

SETH: Yeah, because I know—it's either phone sales or my agent going to want to have a conversation, so I'll call him later. At about thirty panels, so that was maximum. Small panels. But each time after I wrote it was about ninety panels. So it would be like a massive amount of editing, and even there you try and fight to get in like one silent panel there somewhere. But the thing is, since I knew that was so dense, each of those pages, I felt like I had to have some way to open the book up. So that's primarily why I have those big double-page spreads. I want people to be able to read that, and then you turn the page and you get like a big long pause.

DM: It's like a palate cleanser, almost.

SETH: Yeah, exactly. And that's also why I added in the shorter strips, where they're not so dense. Because I wanted to break away into some actual— what I call naturalistic storytelling, where the characters, you follow them around. I mean, I think that's what initially interested me in cartooning, was natural storytelling, where you follow someone walking around and you see it as if you're a ghost walking with them. I always thought that that was the strength of comic storytelling, that kind of progression, and that's why old comics like *Superman* were not good comics, because they didn't really follow the characters much. They jump from one big scene to another. Superman's in his apartment, and then in the next panel he's on the moon. Because they just describe it, they say, "He flew out the window and went to the moon." So you think, "That's bad cartooning." But now I'm not so sure about that anymore. Now I feel like you can do both. As I say, as I'm getting more into description I'm realizing that—for a while, I just thought narration was bad, you shouldn't use narration unless it's interior dialogue. Now I'm thinking, it's okay to describe things. You just gotta be careful that when you're doing it the storytelling underneath the descriptions is somehow interesting on its own. As I'm thinking more and more about how I just want to write about places, or describe things, rather than show them, I'm realizing that you can do both. You can find a way to keep the storytelling lively. Like what I did in *Wimbledon Green*, where you have a variety of approaches. You can have people talking directly to the camera, you can have naturalistic storytelling, and you can have straight description. And they can kind of work together. I think when I was younger I thought, "It has to be that naturalistic storytelling."

DM: It's funny that you say "camera." Is that kind of how you think of it?

SETH: I don't, but it's the way that we've learned to see it. You talk about comics, you always end up using film terms. You say a medium shot or a long shot. There's really no other terms for them.

DM: I mean, to me it almost seems more natural than speaking to a camera. There's no technology that the character's addressing, it's just right straight to the reader. It seems almost native to the medium somehow.

SETH: It's funny, I agree. You know, when *Wimbledon Green* came out, a few people said it was done like a documentary. And I hadn't thought of it in those terms, because I just thought the characters were talking to the reader. But people do see it as talking to the camera. And, as you saw, I use the term myself because—I think we're so used to watching film and television that we tend to think in those terms. But in comics I think it's a natural thing to have the characters talk directly to the reader. God knows when they started that, but I imagine that even back in the twenties there must have been a bit of that. But now it seems like after the underground, after people like Harvey Pekar, et cetera, that seems like a completely normal—even newspaper strips, I'm sure there are characters that speak directly to the audience. Yet somehow I think people see that as a filmic technique, breaking the fourth wall kind of thing.

DM: *Are* there any filmic techniques that kind of crept in or just that you sort of absorbed without realizing it?

SETH: I think a lot of my cartooning in the beginning was very much based on film technique. Mostly, though, that's because I grew up studying mainstream cartoonists. And so if you're drawing comics as a teenager and you're looking at Marvel comics, a lot of that stuff, how they actually tell the story, is based on film. A lot of those cartoonists deliberately tried to incorporate the same techniques. You see it, even a guy like Kirby, clearly he watched a lot of movies. I don't think I really thought about it for a while. Those early *Mister X*s are just completely—that type of teenage storytelling is surfacing in that work. It wasn't till later, when I started to step back and think of the medium itself and realize there's no reason why you need to have an establishing shot like in a film before you start. And that you need to keep the scene interesting by moving the camera around. That's something that really got into my brain early—if a guy's sitting in a chair, you should be going around the chair while they're talking, it's boring just to have the same shot over and over again. But I think most cartoonists eventually come to realize that there's nothing wrong with using rigid grids or repetition. That stuff all works fine. I think there's been a bit of a knee-jerk reaction *against* filmic approaches. I think that maybe in the last fifteen years cartoonists have sort of felt like maybe it was a betrayal of comics to tell it in a . . . what's the word I was going to use? I guess, filmic is the word for . . .

DM: ... sort of, cinematic ...
SETH: ... yeah, cinematic. But I think it can't be avoided on a certain level. I think what I was calling naturalistic storytelling—it makes perfect sense that you should follow a character in some sense. It's not necessarily an emulation of a camera to follow someone walking through, to cut to different shots. This is an editing process we've gotten used to, and I think that we see the world in that manner to some degree and so you have to use it sometimes. You *could* do everything like *Blondie*—you know, it's all proscenium arch and you're constantly following full-figured characters from a side view—and that would probably be very true to cartooning. But it is limiting and it does cut back ... sometimes I think you want to pull in to a closer shot on a face because that has some sort of iconic power to it, that you're not going to get by always having them the same size. I know Chris Ware talked a lot about that. And he still talks a lot about using the comics medium in its purest form, but if you really look at Chris's work, it's full of close-ups and all that sort of stuff, too. You can't avoid it. I think that that has great power. To be inside a character's head, to see that head blown up large, it implies that you're—how do I put this?—you get that sort of sensory experience of *being* the character's head. And that is something that can only be done by presenting a large, iconic image on the page. You can't do it by having it constantly within that proscenium arch.
DM: How long have you known Chris Ware?
SETH: I guess since sometime in the late nineties, I suppose. Yeah, we met when I went through on a book tour down there, and just became friends. Very influential person. But no one would be surprised by that. Chris had a big influence on me.
DM: Like personally on your work.
SETH: Oh yeah, totally. When I met Chris in like the late nineties, it was a wake-up call, really. I went to his house, and I'd read his first couple of issues and I was impressed with them. But somewhere in my mind I thought he was just doing a lot of that work with computers. All this type—when I actually saw the level of craft in what he was doing, it really made me sit up and say, "I've got to work harder." I think he had an effect like that on a *lot* of cartoonists, where they said, "Boy ..."
DM: Really kind of galvanized ...
SETH: Oh absolutely. Chris is the figure that will be remembered from this period, there's no doubt about it. I think initially everyone was taken aback by Chris's ability. And his intelligence. And I think in time each of the cartoonists—we've all had to deal with Chris's work, we've had to realize we'll never beat him at his own game. And so you just have to do your own work and forget about Chris Ware. But I think he was a very galvanizing person—he was

kind of like Crumb in that sense. I think Crumb changed the whole underground medium just by being Crumb in the center of it. And I think Chris had that effect, too. The funny thing is, he affected the older cartoonists, and I think Crumb did that in a way, too. I think people like [Harvey] Kurtzman—I think they recognized instantly that here was someone of great transformative power in the medium. I can tell, artists like [Art] Spiegelman, they've been affected by Chris as much as his own contemporaries. He's just a big figure. And fortunately he's a very humble person—that's not something that I think is a concern of his. Because he could be very smug.

DM: Yeah, he certainly doesn't come across as smug.

SETH: No, not in the least. It's his saving grace. But certainly Chris—it wasn't just his skill, it was also his depth of understanding of the comics medium, that made me think deeper, too. It really did make me think about why I was approaching certain kinds of storytelling. I have an affinity for slowing it down and keeping it quiet, and I was interested in that almost from the beginning, but I'm not sure I'd given it as much thought as I could have. Chris was good in that sense that he really made everybody sit and think about what they were doing, and why they were doing it.

DM: I wonder if you could talk more about that tension between storytelling and describing.

SETH: Okay, well, basically I think, as I was saying, when I started out I felt that the strength in cartooning was in showing and not telling. And even while I, for example, loved Lynda Barry—she was like a favorite cartoonist of mine—I always felt like Lynda was relying too much on narration for me to really emulate that approach. And as I was saying, with those old comics, where they would *tell* you things rather than show you, I thought the secret in real, good cartooning—why cartooning is good—is if you actually just show things happening. And that meant I really tried to have as few transitions as possible. So, a character gets up in the morning, they get out of bed, they walk to the bathroom, they walk downstairs—and you follow them, and you don't try to just jump between scenes. And that's a kind of storytelling that I think is very effective at creating—not a believable world, but immersing you into the world of the character. It takes you in, in a way. Whereas the other kinds of storytelling actually *are* more distant. But the thing is, that is a very specific approach, and it is actually pretty tedious to draw. I mean, you *want* to jump between scenes. And I think around the time when I did *Wimbledon Green*, it showed me that there was actually a great power in doing short sequences that you just sort of set together, and let them create their own dynamic by being together. But as for the tension between that and the descriptive form, it took me a while but eventually I came to realize that narration has a power to it. There was lots of cartooning I was reading that was heavily narrated and I didn't have a prejudice against it. Like Dan's work is remarkably full of narration, every panel usually—he does a lot more narration than he does naturalistic storytelling. Well, maybe not so much anymore. Something like *Mister Wonderful* has got a lot of naturalism in it, a lot of characters walking around and talking, rather than just narration. And Ben Katchor is full of narrative. And I love both those cartoonists. But I think I had a real prejudice against doing it myself. Only when I started to use it more did I realize that in a way it's my natural voice. I'm not a quiet person, I'm actually a very talkative person and I have a desire to describe things and talk about them. And I felt that was an element of my personality that was frustrated in trying to do the work, because I wanted to write and talk about things. That sequence I described—describing the mother's room—there's a power to description, by bringing it to the surface, that's different from just allowing the pictures to tell the story. Yes, you can draw the room, and show the accumulated detail, which I was doing as well, and allow the reader to make assumptions based on that. That's one of the powers of cartooning—someone is wearing a hat, you don't have to describe the hat, they just have a hat on, and so the reader knows they have a hat. But you might want to bring the hat forward and say what's interesting about this hat. And that's where a lot of my interest actually lies. The city I've been making up for years—the city of Dominion—that's all just about description. When I write in my notebooks about it, I'm writing down facts, and visual descriptions of things. I'm talking about how elements fit together and realizing that's where my work is going. Going about, describing places and events and circumstances, more than showing them. And the trick is to find a balance between the two. Because you can't have just—there's nothing more boring than saying "the So-and-So Building" and drawing a picture of that building, "It's on Smith Street" and then drawing a sign that says "Smith Street." Sometimes you have to do that, but too much of that is really dull, and then you start to say, "Why even draw it at all?" So what you need to do is find that happy tension between the two. What's interesting is that when you're drawing description-based work, that's when the strip comes alive in ways you didn't plan. For example, I just got a magazine in [Seth gets up] that I did a six-page story for. It came today, actually. [returns with issue no. 82 of *Canadian Notes and Queries*] This strip I did here on—*Jocko*, it's called. It's a strip I just did about these little gumball machine things. And this is this little character that appears in these little books that are in these gumball things, and his name is Jocko and he's a little Scotsman. So when I was drawing it, I wrote out the dialogue first . . . it's all description, basically, talking about who owned the company and how he came up with the idea for these little books. When I was drawing it out—it mentions, why did he pick a little Scotsman character? And so as I was drawing it, this little tramp appeared in the drawings, asking for spare change, which becomes like a funny point of him seeing this Scottish tramp and he's getting the idea for the character. Now that wasn't in my mind at all when I was writing it, that only comes together as you're drawing it. Description sort of takes on a separate life of its own when you're actually drawing it out, when you're breaking it down. There's a different part of the brain involved somehow in drawing and writing. So a lot of times I will sit down and type out a script of dialogue between characters. Like the sequence I'm working on right now, there's a long conversation between the two brothers in *Clyde Fans*, and that's all just typed out. But when you actually sit down and start drawing it, breaking it down in comics, that's when somehow a new alchemy gets involved that it takes on a different life—that is why you're not writing a novel. Stuff happens in the pictures that make it interesting. Most of the stuff I write down here, it's not interesting—it wouldn't be interesting as a short story. Like I say, there's a certain kind of alchemy that occurs when you draw pictures, different things happen by making sequences form.

DM: It's not simply illustrated prose.

SETH: Yeah. Like somehow with talking about the gumball machine, having the kid go and get the gumball and having it come out and seeing it open and seeing the little booklet—there's something in the actual movement of a sequence that brings things to life. They create a parallel kind of storytelling that goes with the narration, and that to me is really interesting at the moment. Maybe more so than the naturalistic storytelling I'd been doing previously.

DM: When you lay out the panels of a scene, are you working quite intentionally, or more instinctively . . . ?

SETH: Kind of instinctively. I mean, initially, *always* instinctively. Then I might decide to work harder and take that same sequence—when you break down, you do thumbnail pages, a quick thumbnail. You might say, "That looks pretty good" or you might say, "Let's do that again" and work it through. Sometimes you realize the central panel—say you've got a nine-panel grid, and the middle panel would be panel five. But you might find that panel six, where you drew something, that really should be the center of the page. You'll find a way to shift your storytelling, cut something out, or expand something else. Sometimes pages, there's an architecture to them that develops and you'll see that it needs to be a certain way, or you'll realize, "There's a nice repetition going on here, I should break this into two pages instead of one." It all kind of happens as you're doing it. And it always just starts with pure instinct, moving the story along, and then you realize that there's a design element that has to be taken into account. I think comics are often compared to film or literature or a combination of the two, but I really think they're closer to poetry and graphic design. And I think it's because they are really about compression and about moving things around, like the way that you do when you design things. Moving images around, moving shapes around. So that compression of time and that moving of the shapes is why you make pages look the way they do. In something like this, these are pretty straightforward—obviously I put a big picture in there because I thought that would be nice graphically. But sometimes—here's a good example: while you're drawing it you'll realize that the flame of the sign will tie in well with him lighting the match here. Or you'll realize that you can align the three figures here simply. Or over on this page here, you'll realize this is the perfect spot to open the page up, having a silent panel there frees it up, and the same thing over here, where suddenly you can take all the density of all the architecture that's around the single figure there in the center and that will kind of bring it to life. But you don't know that when you start designing the page, it just sort of happens as you're doodling it out.

DM: The silent panel seems like a kind of favorite of yours, a sort of treat to include for yourself.

SETH: It is, yeah. Because I think cartooning has always been about brevity of space, you don't have a lot of space. Most cartoonists had to work in short spaces, so they weren't often given that luxury. It's actually a great luxury to have silent sequences, too, where you can—the *Clyde Fans* part I'm working on right now has several pages of characters walking down stairs, things like that. That's like a luxury cartoonists in the past did not have. If you had six pages, you could not devote even a panel to a silent moment. And I think because of that, I've always had a fascination for the power that a single image has when surrounded by a lot of text. Suddenly that one panel just pops. It adds a moment of profundity to almost any sequence. It's funny that way. But I have a real fondness for it. And it's funny how a single drawing is not a silent panel. Like if you see an illustration, it's not silent. But in the middle of a comic strip, something without any dialogue in it is silent somehow.

DM: What would you say about like a silent, single-panel gag strip? I mean, it wouldn't be a strip . . .

SETH: Yeah, that's funny. It wouldn't really seem silent in that way to me. I mean, all cartooning in a strange way isn't fully quiet. It takes a real effort to create actual silence in a comic strip because there's always some implied sense of motion and noise in a drawing. And certainly in a gag cartoon, even if there's no dialogue, it feels noisy to me, I guess because it's humorous. It's always a humorous situation. Maybe if it was the right kind of drawing. Maybe if it was a character sitting in a chair in a darkened room, it might feel silent, even if it was funny. But usually they feel—I think it's because they're kind of broad . . .

DM: . . . you can almost hear the punch of the . . .

SETH: Yeah, exactly. Whereas—I think a lot of it has to do with sequence. Something about sequence where you . . . Hmm, it's funny. It's sequence, but it's not just that. I can imagine in some of Doug Wright's strips, for example, which are all entirely without words, they're all pantomime, not all of it feels silent. Only once in a while is there a panel that implies quiet.

DM: Hmm. And how does he achieve that?

SETH: Usually I think it's circumstantial. Like a shot of the father peering into the darkened room with the children sleeping, or maybe the kids looking out the window as snow is coming down. It has to be something that the actual content implies silence as well. A shot of the kids running through the house, that's very noisy. A lot of it has to do with rhythm, I suppose. There's always an implied rhythm and so it's hard to actually create real silence because that rhythm's still moving you through the strip always.

DM: How does serial publication affect structure and rhythm when you're putting these things together?

SETH: It does. And I think I'm only just starting to get away from that now. Even with the first hardcover of *Palookaville*, that *Clyde Fans* sequence in there is like pretty much what I would have done in a regular comic. Because the length of those comics did affect how I thought of each segment in terms of how it's going to fit together. I know when I first started *Palookaville*, I felt like having a whole issue to tell a story with was a lot of space. And then in the next issue or two I did a couple that were a two-part story. And then I did like a six-part or something. In each of those, each issue became a chapter, because that space determined what a chapter would be. When I moved on to *Clyde Fans*, I realized I needed more space, so they would be *part* of a chapter. But the thing about that was you're even then structuring them to have some kind of a moment at the end. And so that affects it, too. Now, working on this piece that I'm working on right now, I finally feel a little freed up, that this will just be the end of that other chapter. So it will be as long as it is, it doesn't really matter. I think the books that follow, I will be a little more freed from that as well. They will take just the space they require. But I think that space limitations have always affected the way people think about what they're working on, and certainly affected me. That twenty-four-page sequence of a comic book was pretty much what I thought of as a chunk you work in.

DM: How would you compare it to a sketchbook story like *Wimbledon Green*?

SETH: Well, actually, *Wimbledon Green*, now that you say it, that was releasing me from that, now that I think about it. Because I wasn't concerned about that at all. If it was a one-pager, it was fine, if it was five-pager, it was fine. I think that kind of storytelling actually frees you from that to some degree. Working in a sketchbook is always freeing because you never *have* to publish anything. It could take any form it likes. If it works out—I mean, you're aware that you *might* publish it. But if it works out, you'll figure out how to make it work in another form. And I suppose even *George Sprott* to some degree, although that was really determined by the form of the magazine. But then compiling it later was kind of freeing, to figure out some other way to use the space. But they are physical objects, these books, and that does have an effect on your thinking, for sure.

DM: At what point did you decide that you wanted your books to be real objects?

SETH: Probably not immediately. But certainly by the time I was working on *It's a Good Life*, I was becoming more interested in the design of things. Even then it was still formative, I was really learning at that point. And when I look at my first collection, my first book collection, I didn't know what I was doing and there's all kinds of obvious errors. But I can see I was making some attempts to do certain things. I was starting to understand that the actual design elements in the book that go around the story are important to setting the tone of the story. There's a bit of that in *Good Life*. And I think that's something that's been increasingly more interesting to me as time goes on. I think because the cartoonists of my generation came out of that world of newsprint comic strips or comic books, it took us a while to understand that design was important. I can remember Chester Brown and I, when we would talk about comics back in the eighties, we never talked about design. It was always just about storytelling. The only design that you really gave much thought to was that it would have a cover. And the choices made in picking a cover were part of a process of getting away from the idea of a comic book cover. To make things inherently *not* an exciting image. So much of what a comic book cover was about was picking some potent moment from the story, and I think Chester and I were both trying to avoid that. And you look at Crumb's work and you see he's one of the first guys who started to do that—pick something that was not a moment per se. If you look at some of those *Mr. Natural* comics or something, Mr. Natural might just be on the cover with leaves falling or something. That in a way was like a big shift for the comic book. That was certainly inspirational to me, when Crumb would take an atypical moment. And Crumb was interested in design. But I don't think I recognized that when I was young, I just saw that he was doing interesting things with how he was putting his comic books together. It was later I realized that Crumb might have been one of the first comic book artists to really be interested in design in a way that applies to the modern aesthetic. But ... what was I talking about? Where did this start from?

DM: ... now I don't even recall ... we were talking about your books as objects.

SETH: Oh, yeah, that's right. That really comes later. Now I'm very concerned with that, which is also worrying because the book seems to be in a state of decline right now. It's worth wondering what's going to happen. I mean, I'm pretty sure I can continue to make books until I die, but whether they will be the primary way your work is released ... that's worrisome.

DM: It is worrisome. I can barely stand to read comics on a screen.

SETH: Yeah, it's not an experience I like.

DM: People keep talking about how much they love their Kindles or whatever ...

SETH: Yeah, I'm clearly not the audience for that stuff. And it's like I'm actively hostile to it, too. So I can't imagine I'll *have* a Kindle, unless it's the only way to read certain people's work and it may be. But the funny thing is, I'm really just not interested in doing my own work for that, but I'm worried that that's what it's going to be in ten years—it's gonna be like that's the only way that people will read your work. And at that point what I'll be trying to do is continue to have a book published of it, but I'll be aware that that's like a vanity project, just to go in the closet.

DM: Oh, that's depressing.

SETH: Or to sell to other collectors who are still concerned about books. It seems strange to me that the book could have *possibly* passed so quickly into something that isn't vital in the culture anymore. After a thousand years. It's surprising. It just seems a mistake. It's funny, the book is just a perfect delivery system. It's just not the same for me, to look at something electronically.

DM: Until I can eat on top of a Kindle ...

SETH: Yeah, exactly. They're an integral part of everyday life.

DM: What are you reading right now?

SETH: Well, let's see, what *am* I reading right now? I just finished a book called—what's it called?—*The Country of the Pointed Firs* [by Sarah Orne Jewett]. Which is a book from around the turn of the last century, I guess. A sort bucolic set of interconnected stories. A bit kind of *Winesburg, Ohio*-ish. But a lot gentler. And I also just finished reading—what was it?—*The Bridge of San Del Rey*, something like that [actually, *San Luis Rey*], a Thornton Wilder book. Yeah, I just picked it up at Goodwill, it was like a hundred and fifty pages, so it was a quick read. It was actually pretty good. Somewhere in my mind I'd always got that book mixed up with *The Bridge over the River Kwai* so I thought, I'm not interested in that sort of military story, but it wasn't. Comic-wise, though, I'm reading whatever graphic novels have just come out. Dan's *Mister Wonderful*; I just finished Lynda Barry's two collections.

DM: So you try to keep very up-to-date?

SETH: Yeah, I'm probably more up-to-date than people might think. I follow all the young cartoonists that are interesting—I have a huge stack of graphic novels that are always the new stuff to wade through. I'm paying attention to any young cartoonist who's interesting.

DM: Any bright lights on the horizon?

SETH: Yeah, there's a couple of really great guys. There's a guy from Britain right now I'm crazy about named Jon McNaught, who has a book—actually, he has two books out. One's called *Birchfield Close* and the other's called *Pebble Island*. And he's quite young, I think he's only like twenty-three or something. And he's using a really beautiful slowed-down storytelling. Very much to my taste. Let's see, who else am I interested in right now? Well, there's a handful of guys who you probably wouldn't even count as the younger guys anymore. People like—I think Kevin Huizenga is brilliant. Sammy Harkham's super interesting, his last comic *Crickets* was really good. The funny thing about that last comic, *Crickets*—if this was like 1989, there would be so much discussion of it. But there's so much stuff coming out now that people are spoiled.

DM: Yeah, it's hard to keep track of everything.

SETH: Yeah, for sure.

DM: Which of your works would you recommend someone starting with, if they were just coming to your work?

SETH: Well, for me, I like—*George Sprott* is the work I would give to someone. But you know I really don't get the impression that that's the work of mine that people like the best, at all.

DM: Really?

SETH: Yeah, I find that, generally, the two things I notice is—people like *It's a Good Life, If You Don't Weaken*, which is a book I can't even look at anymore. It's a very young book.

DM: I suppose the storytelling's very accessible.

SETH: Yeah, it is.

DM: It's not broken up . . .

SETH: Yeah. And every time I look at it I find—well, for me, it's too young. I can see the young person I was when I wrote it.

DM: And you don't care for what you see?

SETH: No, it's like—certainly things I can see I'm trying too hard, and the drawing looks awful to me, and there's all kinds of moments that bother me. It's earnest in the wrong ways and not honest enough in other ways. It's fine for what it is, but it's a not a book for me. Which is the funny thing about writing books, is that you write them because they're the books you want to read, and then they're books you will never enjoy under any circumstances.

And the other one people seem to like is *Wimbledon Green*. A lot of people say that's their favorite book. I think because it's fun.

DM: Yeah, it has such an energy to it, I guess.

SETH: And in some ways, I like that, and in other ways, I'm like, "Well, that's kind of a refutation of what I actually want to do with my work." It's like what I *really* want to do is not work that people are interested in. But that's okay. *Clyde Fans*, in a way, is not a book I would recommend to start with because it's a big, disjointed work in a way. And when it's done, I think it will make sense as a single narrative. But in some ways, it's a big long book of me figuring out what I want to do. And I think the next book after that is the book probably that will be—well, of course it's the book I'm most interested in now, because it's the one I'm planning. But I also think that it might be the book that I've been building up to do. That I've had to figure out how to do my own work, and it's just starting to come to me now. Like working in this strip here—that's kind of where I'm headed, which is being able to jump from one piece of description to another and build like a complicated thread of places and ideas. And I think that that's going to be what my work has always been about, but I didn't know it. I was trying to get a plot into everything. Now I realize that my work isn't probably about having a plot.

DM: How many years have you been working on *Clyde Fans*?

SETH: Well, certainly over ten years. Maybe even coming up on fifteen, I'm not sure. I mean, I started thinking about those characters probably by about 1994 or something. Probably didn't start drawing them until the late nineties. The thing is, remarkably, the story has not changed that much from my initial plans. It's just become subtler in my mind as each year has gone on. So as I finally reach each point as I'm working on it, those *were* the points I was planning to get to, but they have changed somewhat in my thinking. And, in fact, it's funny that the last part, which was part 3, when I finally finished that I realized that it came out the way I was planning it but that's not what I want anymore. I've actually gone back, and reedited that and changed some of it. And now, okay, "that's closer to what it should be like." So when the collection finally comes out, it will be a little bit more cohesive. That section was a little bit gangly.

[recording pauses]

[recording resumes]

DM: I wanted to ask you about misanthropy and self-loathing and antisocial tendencies that seem to crop up in your work.

SETH: Sure. Yeah, it's funny... well, how would I put this? I think it's a typical trait among cartoonists that they had a kind of upbringing—well, where they ended up feeling kind of isolated or outcast or something. It's not surprising, it's the typical comic book kind of experience. And I think it leads to a certain type, that does end up working in this kind of cartooning. I guess basically my point is that the kind of cartoonists who do the kind of work that we do—in my peer group—seem to be of a type. And part of the type, I think, is that there's a complicated balance between a kind of self-loathing, mixed with a certain kind of narcissistic arrogance, too. It's not just self-loathing, because you can't produce art if you just don't like yourself. You have to have some sort of confidence that there's a reason you're putting the artwork out there, too. You see more extreme versions of it in some people than others. There are people like Al Columbia, who has some sort of severe problem about actually releasing the work. And I think that gets caught up in the kind of perfectionism that comes from self-loathing, too. But I actually think that it's an important balance to have, because it keeps you in check in a weird way. And I find that most of the cartoonists I talk to, even the ones that it's not that pronounced in—someone like Chester Brown doesn't have very much self-loathing at all. He's actually pretty confident in his own weird way.

DM: Yeah, I just read *Paying for It*.

SETH: [laughs] Oh, yeah. It's an interesting book.

DM: He's almost like ... compulsively articulate.

SETH: Yeah. Yeah, exactly. And he's almost, in a strange way, unwilling to go into certain emotional areas. It's like: it's not gonna happen. But even Chester has that strange thing that happens when you're working which is that you start to develop an idea that this is really good, what you're working on, that it's really great, that it's the best thing you've ever done ... and then you take the mood swing to where it's the worst. "It's terrible, how can I even release this?" And I think that kind of combination between the two is important, to keep the work in balance. Because if you think things are too good, that's a not a good way to learn about your own work. But the funny thing is, I find I joke about self-loathing, but it really comes in when it's connected to social interaction, I think. And I think that's why the types I'm talking about—partly why we're cartoonists is that you spend a lot of time alone. And I think that that time alone is actually—it's a complicated thing, because I would say that being by yourself is when you are most authentically yourself *but* it's also a comfortable situation where you're not *really* presented with the complications of being yourself. That comes into play when you deal with other people. You're always comfortable when you're with yourself, because you don't have the conflict that comes with dealing with others. Of course, the problem with dealing with others, I find, is that that creates a distraction from the core of who you are. There's something about experience experienced alone that is deeper than experience with other people, because you're distracted by your persona. The very nature of talking to other people is a distraction. And I find that, mostly, when self-loathing is most potent to me is when I've been out involved in social activities of any sort. I come back, and it's worse at some times than others, but you have a kind of inability to let go of the experience, to keep going over them, it's very unpleasant.

DM: I'm thinking now of that sketchbook anecdote that you included at the end of *Palookaville* 20, the Calgary authors' festival.

SETH: That's a classic example, yeah. And the truth is, that does happen to me, although there are times when you're happier and times when you're less happy. That was kind of a grim period for me, too. I wasn't very happy during that time.

DM: Although, it plays like high comedy, somehow . . .

SETH: [laughs] I know. Well, it's always over the top, in a weird way. That obsession with yourself is always a bit unpleasant, too. But the funny thing is that, for me, the thing I'm most interested in *is* myself. I mean, I'm sitting in a room all alone all the time, and picking over the details of my own existence, constantly. And that is the most interesting thing to me. Every once in a while you're reminded that there's people experiencing really complicated things out there in the world and that your little interior drama is probably not that important. But somehow that's the luxury of living in this culture, to be able to sit and worry about these minor little existential worries. But I do think that that's an almost unavoidable character type for the sort of person who's sort of overly involved with looking back all the time. I'm not sure why I'm so interested in looking back. It's not just to earlier time periods, it's looking back in my own life, mostly. But nothing is really as interesting to me as the past. The present is interesting to me because it's connected to the past. When I go out, if I'm walking down the street and it's a nice sunny day, I'm feeling the overlays of the other sunny days from the past that have remained in my memory that are potent. And it's that interconnection of one overlay over the other that makes that experience pleasurable to me. I don't really feel that everyone's like that. I think a lot of people do actually kind of enjoy living in the moment more. But to me the real pleasure comes from sending out these kind of psychic feelers that feel around for the past. I see an old house, I like to see the crumbling steps on it, somehow that feels good to me. To feel that iconic sense of the past is alive around you. I'm not sure why that is. It's a fetish, almost. It's a fetishistic interest in the Western past of a hundred and fifty years, for some reason. I'm not sure I could really rationalize it as having any great meaning, but certainly that informs every thought of my waking days, usually.

DM: I wanted to ask you, as well, about background characters and strangers. Because even in like *Palookaville* number 1, you've got scenes where you've got the strangers kind of crowding around the big event. And in *Good Life*, you've got the Seth character kind of looking at these strangers passing by and making little judgments and wondering, "What's their deal?"

SETH: It's funny, now that you say it, I probably haven't given as much thought to that over the years and I'm thinking maybe that had a lot more to do with me living in the city back then. Because I'm realizing I don't do much of that anymore with my work. In fact, I realize I draw an awful lot of empty scenes now. And it may have to do with the shift from moving from an urban environment to a more rural environment. Certainly, on the weekend, the thing I do most is drive out of town to the country. And I do know that— somewhere someone commented on something that was like the absence of people in these drawings, in city scenes, and it hadn't occurred to me that I didn't draw anybody in the street, because I hadn't been thinking of it. I was just thinking of streets themselves. I think it may have had a lot to do with the fact that when I was younger and living in the city I probably *was* more interested in people than I am now. Certainly when I moved to Toronto as a young person that was one of the great, life-changing experiences, was to be around so many people. And I was very naïve in those years, coming from a small town, so being in a big city like Toronto was like remarkably eye opening. I don't think I really do pay as much attention to people any longer, and do try to avoid them in general. I know when I go downtown here, I try to actually take routes where I won't see any people. I usually walk on the railroad tracks, which is very safe because no one's ever up there except maybe some hobos, and they're not looking to talk to you, so it's fine.

DM: [laughs] So, it's really contact you're hoping to avoid.

SETH: It is, yeah. It's funny, that's part of that—what we were talking about— that social anxiety. It's funny, I can *deal* with talking to anybody, it's not a problem. And I never really have any kind of awkward thing that's awful. Of course, you say things and later you think, "That was stupid," but everybody has that and it's not trauma. But the funny thing is, any kind of social contact—I do kind of dread it in a way. When I go downtown, I don't really *want* to talk to a teller at the bank. It's all a little . . . fraught with anxiety. Even though there's nothing to be anxious about, and it's all forgotten the second you leave. Phoning someone, anything like that, I don't like to do. I've gotten used to spending my time entirely by myself and that's really comfortable. It ties in again to what I was saying, this feeling that that's your authentic self. And that when you're talking to other people, there's some facade—I think,

actually, that's a lot of what my work—I kind of dream that the work will ultimately spell out who's under the facade. But it doesn't really seem to do it.
DM: No?
SETH: No, that doesn't really get at it. I did a documentary with the National Film Board over the last few years, and I'd hate for the director to hear this but it was not entirely a good experience for me.
DM: [laughs] Oh, really?
SETH: I mean, I think he knows that. He had a different approach than I would...
DM: Right.
SETH: I felt like what I wanted was that they would film me long enough that somehow...
DM: The real you would...
SETH: The real—yeah, and it never happened. In fact, I think it was less me than ever.
DM: Because you felt the need to perform...
SETH: Yeah, it puts you on the spot, makes you feel like a performer of some sort, and it really wasn't working for me. Yeah, so, we'll see. I hope to god he can pull it together, but I have my worries. Yeah, it felt pretty awkward, and when he would leave I would have a severe depression afterward for a week, because it was—talk about social anxiety, that really felt like, "Oh god, not only did that go badly...
DM and SETH: "It's all on film."
SETH: ...and they're going to edit that together somehow? I've told him, too, I will only watch it once. If I could say I wouldn't watch it at all, I would, but that's just too rude. For someone who put that much time into a film. But I think watching it once will traumatize me for life.
DM: Was he a great fan, or was he kind of commissioned by the board...?
SETH: No, he was a fan, and at first I thought it might just be a perfect thing. He's a really nice guy. I mean, I like him. But as time went on, I thought, "This is not what I would do." His way of handling it—it was more focused on style than I was comfortable with. That might sound odd from someone as art directed as myself—but I think I wanted something different. Like, just forget about the style. I don't care about the lighting, I don't need the whole thing to look like it's set in 1940. That's what I *don't* want. That's my worry. That I'll end up being simply Mr. Nostalgia—Mr. 1940s. We'll see. My only hope is that he's also—there's also going to be a series of animated sequences through it.
DM: Oh!
SETH: I'm hoping that might...that might pull it together, maybe. We'll see.
DM: Have you done animation in the past?

SETH: No. And in this sense I'm really not doing much, either. He's doing it all. But maybe that will pull the thing together. I'm hoping that will distract away from the other stuff.
DM: I'm trying to imagine your work in motion.
SETH: The little bits I've seen, he's done limited kind of stuff so far, and it seemed promising. But I'm not really interested in animation in the sense of seeing my own work animated. And I suspect if they actually have some sequences where they go into more full animation, I'm not going to like it. I can't see those characters walking, somehow.
DM: Is it that it seems somehow superfluous? Or just not right somehow.
SETH: I think if I was interested in animation, it wouldn't be to animate what I would draw. Somehow that seems boring to me. Like I certainly wouldn't do a cartoon with characters walking around. I can see maybe doing like—about place, I can see drawing buildings and moving around somewhere. Trying to set up some sense of being somewhere. But the idea of drawing a couple of my characters and having them walking along and talking and stuff, that just seems dull in a way and . . . kind of vulgar, sort of. I wouldn't like it, I don't think. I'm talking off the top of my head here. And I'm sure there will be stuff like that in the film. I don't actually know. But I'm letting it out of my hands, like "It's not my project. They can't blame *me* if it's a bad documentary." The worst they can say is that I'm a terrible subject. And so that's fine.
DM: [laughs] It seems somehow unlikely that they'll actually say that.
SETH: Well, they might. We'll see. The problem is, being the subject of a documentary, what you really worry about is that people will basically watch it and say you're an asshole.
DM: Right.
SETH: [laughing] And I think there's a possibility. I think this may be one of those things where you shake your head at the end and—I've seen a few documentaries where people just came off as unlikable. And not because they were real jerks—I've seen those, of course, where you're watching someone who's the head of a skinhead movement, of course they're a jerk—but I mean I saw a documentary about the cartoonist Bruce McCall. Guy who works for the *New Yorker*. And at the end of that, I just thought, "I don't like this guy." And I'm worried that's what this is going to be like.
DM: That's how you're going to come off.
SETH: I have a feeling. Or, the worst case scenario is you just come off stupid. You just look like—they put the wrong stuff together, stupid things came out of your mouth and at the end you just shudder.
DM: [laughs] Would that be like the harshest criticism you could think of? If someone said, "Oh, his work is just stupid."

SETH: Yeah. I think so, yeah. I think the thing that most worries me, if I really let myself worry about it, is that as time goes on the work will be seen as superficial. And I can't control that, is the funny thing. What you want the work to do, ideally, is to transmit some depth of experience, of what you felt while you were alive. But you're a part of the time you live in and you're a result of many influences—as time goes by, the work could become mannered and start to be unreadable to future audiences. And also seem precious or pretentious or empty or all kinds of things, and you can't see it in your own work. I'm already aware of certain elements in my own work that I can't control. It does have a mannered quality to it, and at its worst it becomes sort of fey in a way that I don't like. I'd like it to have a real kind of . . . I'd like it to have an honesty rather than an earnestness, and that's difficult to get into the work. I'm not an open person like somebody like Crumb. Crumb's laying it all on the line and that works somehow for him, and I feel that that will continue to transmit as time goes on. I'm not sure that the work I'm doing will have that quality. But you can only do the work you do. There's nothing you can do about it.

DM: Can you think of anyone you might hold up as a model of being honest but also sort of restrained?

SETH: Hmm . . .

DM: Not necessarily cartoonists, just any writer or . . .

SETH: Let me think about that for a moment. Well, Alice Munro would be a good example, because her work has a great depth of understanding of human beings, but you don't get any sense of Alice herself. She's maintained a writerly distance somehow from it, but the work is very deep. But I'd have to think about it to come up with the ideal answer to that question.

DM: Is that distance a quality you think would be useful for a writer-cartoonist, is that kind of necessary?

SETH: I don't know if it's necessary. You get different quality of work from it, though. Cartoonists, for some reason, tend to have a desire to I think infuse their own personality into the work, maybe more than writers do. Writers are a little more comfortable with that distance. It may have to do with the fact that you draw it, and that makes it somehow . . . it's more connected to you than a writing style. A drawing style is sort of a representation of—artists are touchy about their drawing style. I've actually found that other cartoonists want to pretend that they didn't come up with it, that it just sort of happened by accident. I think cartoonists sort of look at it like it's a fashion statement or something. Picking a drawing style, developing a drawing style is like wearing a fancy outfit, and they're a little ashamed that they've put that much effort into coming up with it. Most *guys* want to pretend that everything they've done is just, "Whatever . . ."

DM: Somehow organic, or inevitable ...
SETH: Exactly.
DM: Do you have a pretty good sense of the development of your own style?
SETH: Oh, yeah. Yeah, it was always very calculated. Every step of the way was a process of incorporating something you learned from some other artist or making some decision to simplify. In fact, I think most drawing style is based on *how* you choose to simplify. And the stylizations you *build* out of those simplifications. Every cartoonist starts picking a series of noses they draw, for example. And they stylize that and a system develops. And that simplification process is where your style comes from, the combination of a million of these little elements put through a kind of ... Systematic Stylization Machine, which makes it all of the same stamp. The parts all fit together.
DM: Can you think of an early plateau, when a lot of these things felt like they were really coming together for the first time for you?
SETH: Well, it really was like right around the end of *Mister X*, beginning of the illustration career. I think that's when I started to understand how I was simplifying and started to make a more conscious choice about how to make the elements work together. And then I think probably a few years later when I started to understand how to compose a panel better. And those things are really connected to each other. How you compose space within the panel is as big a part of your drawing style as what kind of faces you draw. I think if you really look at cartoonists you'll start to see that they have a kind of spatial understanding they work with, which is really different from artist to artist. Somebody like Chester—who often draws in a kind of deep space—the characters exist in a fully realized reality. You can *sense* the streets going back.
DM: Yeah, there's a real volume.
SETH: Yeah, exactly. Somebody like Dan—it's shallow, the characters are standing in like a picture box, almost. They're almost always on a flat surface. Somebody like Chris Ware—as much deep space as he can get into it, the drawing's too iconic to really feel like you're in the real world. He's moving around big blocks, sort of, and the characters are in among these things. This stuff is so integral to their *feeling*, their style. But generally when people think "style," they think like, "Well, they use cross-hatching" or "he's got a slick brush" or whatever. But I think that's the surface of the style. The real style is how you construct the actual panels, and how the space moves around.
DM: Whose panel composition do you really admire?
SETH: Well ... I'm actually pretty impressed with Ben Katchor's compositional skills. He has a real kind of spontaneous look to the work, but the panels are actually really smartly composed. And if you really study how he's doing things, he's leading your eye through those pages really cleverly

and he really—he has a blocky, kind of clunky understanding of how things sit together that I find very impressive. But when it really comes down to it, who I probably spent most of my life studying, it's probably someone like Hergé. Hergé is probably where I learned more about panel composition. And some of the guys who followed in his wake, like Yves Chaland, were pretty influential in those early years. And Peter Arno. Those guys, I mention them a lot because even though I don't look at them the way I used to, they were really formative. I can remember Arno being very influential for me for understanding how characters could be shapes, in a way. That sounds pretty straightforward but, actually, looking at something like Hergé, they're pretty illustrative, it's pretty obvious they're *drawings*, in a way. When I first looked at Arno's work, they were almost a bit two-dimensional. He used the washes to make things solid, but he's really carving those figures out with a brush, and that was very . . . that was something that really taught me how to approach drawing in a different way. Something I needed to learn at that point.

DM: A friend of mine wanted me to ask you a very specific material question.
SETH: Sure.
DM: I don't even know really what to ask—brushes, paper, tools . . .
SETH: Oh, it's very simple. Like old cartoonists, I work with the most primary of tools. I work with a #4 brush, and I work with India ink; I draw with HB pencils and nonreproduceable blue pencils; I work on a light table, which is a little different than most people. I'll work out the page as a thumbnail, I'll draw out the grid I'm going to use, and then I'll draw each panel individually—tracing over top of each other to get it just right—and then I'll tape it onto the page, and then I'll do the next panel, blah blah blah. And then I'll see, as they're going up, if they work. It's an easy method—you can just tear a panel off and say, "That character should be a little higher or a little lower." And that way, rather than drawing on the board—where you make a lot of mistakes and you have to erase and then you start to ruin the surface. So when that page is done, you just take that page and put it on the back of a good piece of paper, put that on the light table, and then I can ink without ever disturbing the surface of the paper. And I use Wite-Out. Lots of Wite-Out. There's lots of corrections made to everything. That's something I'm trying to get away from. And it's not because—when people see the amount of Wite-Out I use, they think I'm making a lot of mistakes. It's not actually any mistakes; what it is is perfectionism. A desire to control the art too much. And that's why something like *Wimbledon Green* or this other book that's coming out this year, this *GNB Double C* book—I'm able to do that without all the correcting, because I've already told myself right away that I'm not concerned with it being perfect. I'm trying to find some way to meet a happy medium between

the two. Because I don't enjoy the perfectionism. But it's hard when I do that finished comic page not to fix up *every little thing*, to fix every little hair you don't quite like, to thin out a line a little bit. And when you start working that way, that means that while you're inking, you're actually planning on fixing it, so you're not as concerned with making it a finished drawing to begin with. So, you do a line, you just *let* it go out the edge of the panel, because you're gonna fix it later, anyway. You're going to fix every line with a bit of Wite-Out. So I'm trying—I keep telling myself that the next work will be the one where I kind of let go of that, but we'll see. I'm definitely going to carry it through to the end of *Clyde Fans* and then I'm going to try and get rid of that.

DM: How big is everything before it's reduced?

SETH: Well, it used to be much bigger. I'd say when I started *Clyde Fans*, each of the pages was about *that* big [indicates dimensions with hands]. But now it's down to about that big [moves hands closer together]. So it's only about double or something. Yeah, I've been progressively working smaller and smaller as the years go by. I think it's because I've discovered that something like this [*Jocko* strip] is only about eleven by seventeen, the actual page, about that big. I've discovered that I like filling the space better when the spaces are smaller. It allows me to be a little more iconic. To do a drawing like this little empty room, there, if I was drawing the panel this big [moves hands to enlarged dimensions], I'd be tempted to put more stuff in it. And you don't need it. So the smaller you draw, the more it allows you to actually work with simpler shapes.

DM: And something sort of enormous like *George Sprott*—you get the sense, opening that, that it's almost actual size.

SETH: Some of it was actual size, for sure. Yeah, actually all of it was actual size except for the pages I did for the . . .

DM: For the magazine?

SETH: Yeah, those I did bigger because there were just too many panels per page. Everything else I did for it afterward—those sepia pages, the big drawings—those were done actual size. And generally I'm getting closer to working actual size. I like to work small, now. The sketchbook stuff is small, it's like a sketchbook *size*. So if you've got twenty panels in a sketchbook, that's pretty small. A character's head is that big [indicates with thumb and forefinger]. But that *is* freeing. A lot of working with a brush is working in big shapes, too. So working in little shapes is very simple.

DM: Does it annoy you at all when readers with a less trained eye tell you how much they like *Wimbledon Green*, and how loose it is and . . . ?

SETH: Yeah. It does bother you a bit because part of you thinks, "What's the point of doing the other work?"

DM: Right. "What am I putting all of this effort into it for?"

SETH: But the flip side of that is you always know you're only doing that for yourself anyway. There's some weird fetishistic quality to artwork anyway, it's like you're trying to create this perfect object for *yourself*. There's something in it—that's why you go back and fix a panel that's perfectly fine. Because you know it will bother you to see it later. No one else will ever notice it. In fact, if I was to say to almost anybody—like with one of those pages—"Pick your favorite drawing on that page," I would guarantee that they would almost always pick the drawing I like the least.

DM: [laughs] It's like a magic trick, like an awful...

SETH: [laughs] Exactly. So you can't really think about that too much. And truthfully I try not to think about what anyone—it's funny... what do I not like? I don't care if people don't like the work. It doesn't really bother me and I accept that, and I kind of take it for granted.

DM: Just because it's not for everyone?

SETH: Yeah. Yeah, and I know I'm not crafting the work in a way to make it what people would like. Even the work of people I *do* really like, I know why I like it and I know I'm not doing that. I look at somebody—like Dan's work—I know why I'm engaged with it, and I'm not putting that into my work.

DM: Right, you're not trying to engage someone in that specific way.

SETH: Yeah. I'm *going* for something that's kind of boring in a way. I like things that have—like I say, on the edge of boring. And I know that that's not going to engage most people, and I even know people who like the sort of thing I like might not care for it. But that's where it's going and it's—nothing I can do about it... beyond do work I'm not that interested in. You have to do what you want to do. In fact, I realize as time goes on I'm moving into a direction that *I'm* excited about, thinking, "Oh boy, I'm going to do a whole book that's just description." Every once and a while I think, "Maybe nobody wants to read that. Maybe that guy was right when he said three pages was enough of that stuff," and I want to do like three *hundred* pages of it now. But what are you gonna do? You—you bet on the fact that what you're interested in, someone else will be interested in. And you have to do it that way. And that's the only work that ultimately can matter. People often say—and I've had this experience—working with someone else will make the work more interesting sometimes, for other people. They'll make suggestions and you're like, "Oh, yeah, that does make it better." But I can't work that way. It's got to be—if it's going to be worse work, at least it's my work. Those are choices you have to make. I don't know what started me on this—I can't remember the question. Oh, I guess it was about readers and their opinions. It's like, you're happy that they like something, and you can see why and you feel good

about it—like when people like *Wimbledon Green*, I think that's nice. I mean, I enjoyed working on it and it was meant to be fun, and it's nice to know that some element of your sense of humor actually got out into your work in some way. But I guess I never did want it to be better than the other stuff I was trying *harder* on. But you end up learning from that anyway, and some of that ends up getting incorporated into the other work. And I like to think that what I learned doing *Wimbledon Green* will make this next book a book that they'll like more than, say, the other books, because maybe there's a bit more freedom in it than what I've been doing in *Clyde Fans*, for example. Each one is a bit of a process.
[end of interview]

Notes

Introduction

1. "Juxtaposed pictorial and other images in deliberate sequence, intended to convey information and/or produce an aesthetic response in the viewer" (McCloud 9).
2. Groensteen also uses the term "closure," but in a different way: for Groensteen, closure is a function of the panel's frame, which works "to close the panel" and "enclose a fragment of space-time belonging to the diegesis" (*System of Comics* 40).
3. At the beginning of the interview, Seth provides a fuller account of his time in Toronto and his reasons for leaving.
4. Vortex Comics is also known for publishing Chester Brown's innovative comic book *Yummy Fur*, before that series moved to Drawn and Quarterly.

Chapter 1

1. See Grennan for a reading of the tonal and temporal relation between Seth and Arno vis-à-vis *Clyde Fans*.
2. The coffee-table anthology, edited by Robert Mankoff, actually only contains 2,004 of the more than 68,000 cartoons included in the accompanying digital archive.
3. Seth's comment may call to mind the comics and concrete poetry of experimental Canadian poet bpNichol, but he is in fact referring to the familiar rhythms of comics as popular as *Peanuts* (see Marc Ngui's interview with Seth in *Carousel*).

Chapter 2

1. In *Ezra Pound and the Making of Modernism*, William Pratt goes so far as to suggest that "Imagism, the movement [Pound] launched in 1912, was the beginning of what came to be called Modernism" (5).
2. Fans of Seth will recognize the character as a homonymous double of Jimmy Frise, the creator of a highly regarded but largely forgotten strip, *Birdseye Center*. In the glossary

of *It's a Good Life*, Seth describes Frise as "undoubtedly the finest Canadian cartoonist of the past" (180).

Chapter 3

1. This correspondence can also be observed in other comics that deal explicitly with the past, for instance Alison Bechdel's memoir *Fun Home*, each chapter of which has a title page with a drawn photograph.
2. In the case of Simon's manipulated novelty postcards, they are decidedly kitsch.

Chapter 4

1. In "Rhetoric of the Image," his well-known reading of advertising images, Roland Barthes suggests that rhetoric appears as "the signifying aspect of ideology" (49).
2. With the exception of nonrepresentational experiments in cartooning, the majority of comics are still concerned with fairly traditional storytelling. "Abstract Comics," such as those collected by Andrei Molotiu in his 2009 anthology of the same name, tend to exploit the tension between the absence of story development and the conventionally narrative structure and sequence of the comics grid.
3. Notably, an abbreviated form of this irony animates Peter Arno's work, in which Iain Topliss finds a "comic world of disillusionment, failed purposes, and actuality's falling short of expectation" (24). See chapter 1.
4. Ball's use of the term "rhetoric" relies on "the distinction that is traditionally drawn between 'natural' and 'rhetorical' expression" (Richards 11).

Chapter 5

1. Despite the semantic overlap, "remembrance" did not emerge as a derivation of the verb "remember," as might be assumed.
2. In its renown and caliber, the Webb collection resembles the great library of Robert Hoe III, fifty years in the making, which was dissolved shortly after his death (Basbanes, *Gentle Madness* 173–74). One of this collection's most notable items was a vellum Gutenberg Bible, sold in 1911 for $50,000 to Henry E. Huntington, "a stately man with a bushy moustache" (181) and a likely physical template for Wimbledon Green.
3. Chester Brown has also explored his relationship with pornography collection in his memoir *The Playboy*, which is dedicated to Seth.
4. See Julia Round's *Gothic in Comics and Graphic Novels* for an insightful consideration of the gutter as a crypt-like space. Round conceives "the events of the gutter as more properly belonging to the Derridean crypt: a sealed space that is the 'interior' of each panel" (100); she reinforces this redefinition by using the term "gutter/crypt" (101).

Chapter 6

1. See chapter 2 for a parallel discussion of "the mode of undecidability" in modernist poetry and Seth's work.
2. In the first volume of his history of the comic strip, David Kunzle presents a late fifteenth-century northern Italian engraving—not divided into panels—that features multiple juxtaposed episodes from the martyrdom of an infant saint (*History of the Comic Strip*, vol. 1, 25).
3. Groensteen's six functions of the frame are: the function of closure; the separative function; the rhythmic function; the structuring function; the expressive function; and the readerly function (*System of Comics* 39–57). Groensteen himself notes: "The function of closure and the separative function are, in truth, nothing but the same function" (45).

Chapter 7

1. In the opening pages of *Metahistory*, Hayden White explicitly refers to "the fictive character of historical reconstructions" (1–2).
2. Seth's remark also contains a highly abbreviated set of assumptions about the roles that age and gender play in the pursuit of the hobbies to which he refers. Left unsaid is the corresponding class assumption: the man with the train set in his basement is not only middle aged but likely also middle class. The implications of the stereotypical profile of the hobbyist, however, lie outside the concerns of this chapter.
3. *The Projector* was first published in 1971 by Coach House Books, the Canadian avant-garde press that was also home to bpNichol. Coach House's reissue of Vaughn-James's 1975 book *The Cage* features an introduction by Seth.
4. Here, the boundary between historical truth and fabulation becomes exceedingly porous: in the mid-1940s, freelance artist George Menendez Rae created a very straitlaced, "realistic" Nazi-fighting hero named Canada Jack ("Guardians of the North").

Bibliography

Primary Texts

Seth. *Bannock, Beans, and Black Tea: Memories of a Prince Edward Island Childhood during the Depression*. Montreal: Drawn and Quarterly, 2004.
———. *Clyde Fans: Book 1*. Montreal: Drawn and Quarterly, 2004.
———. *Forty Cartoon Books of Interest*. Oakland: Buenaventura Press, 2006.
———. *George Sprott: 1894–1975*. Montreal: Drawn and Quarterly, 2009.
———. *The Great Northern Brotherhood of Canadian Cartoonists*. Montreal: Drawn and Quarterly, 2011.
———. Interview by Daniel Marrone, August 8, 2011.
———. *It's a Good Life, If You Don't Weaken*. Montreal: Drawn and Quarterly, 1996.
———. *Palookaville*. 22 vols. to date. Montreal: Drawn and Quarterly, 1991–.
———. *Vernacular Drawings*. Montreal: Drawn and Quarterly, 2002.
———. *Wimbledon Green: The Greatest Comic Book Collector in the World*. Montreal: Drawn and Quarterly, 2005.

Secondary Texts

Alpers, Svetlana. "Style Is What You Make It: The Visual Arts Once Again." In Lang, *The Concept of Style*, 137–62.
Baetens, Jan, ed. *The Graphic Novel*. Leuven: Leuven University Press, 2001.
Bakhtin, M. M. *The Dialogic Imagination: Four Essays by M. M. Bakhtin*. Edited by Michael Holquist. Translated by Caryl Emerson and Michael Holquist. Austin: University of Texas Press, 2004.
Ball, David M. "Chris Ware's Failures." In Ball and Kuhlman, *The Comics of Chris Ware*, 45–61.
Ball, David M., and Martha B. Kuhlman, eds. *The Comics of Chris Ware: Drawing Is a Way of Thinking*. Jackson: University Press of Mississippi, 2010.
Barthes, Roland. "Rhetoric of the Image." In *Image Music Text*. Translated by Stephen Heath. London: Fontana Press, 1987.

Basbanes, Nicholas A. *Among the Gently Mad: Strategies and Perspectives for the Book Hunter in the Twenty-First Century*. New York: Henry Holt, 2002.

———. *A Gentle Madness: Bibliophiles, Bibliomanes, and the Eternal Passion for Books*. New York: Henry Holt, 1995.

———. *Patience and Fortitude: A Roving Chronicle of Book People, Book Places, and Book Culture*. New York: HarperCollins, 2001.

Bauman, Zygmunt. *Modernity and Ambivalence*. Cambridge: Polity Press, 1993.

Beaty, Bart. *Unpopular Culture: Transforming the European Comic Book in the 1990s*. Toronto: University of Toronto Press, 2007.

Bechdel, Alison. *Fun Home: A Family Tragicomic*. London: Jonathan Cape, 2006.

Benjamin, Walter. *The Arcades Project*. Translated by Howard Eiland and Kevin McLaughlin. Cambridge, MA: Belknap Press of Harvard University Press, 2002.

———. *Illuminations*. Translated by Harry Zohn. New York: Schocken Books, 2007.

———. *Reflections: Essays, Aphorisms, Autobiographical Writings*. Translated by Edmund Jephcott. New York: Schocken Books, 2007.

Boym, Svetlana. *The Future of Nostalgia*. New York: Basic Books, 2001.

Brown, Chester. *Ed the Happy Clown: A Graphic Novel*. Montreal: Drawn and Quarterly, 2012.

———. *Louis Riel*. Montreal: Drawn and Quarterly, 2004.

———. *Paying for It: A Comic-Strip Memoir about Being a John*. Montreal: Drawn and Quarterly, 2011.

———. *The Playboy: A Comic Book*. Montreal: Drawn and Quarterly, 2002.

———. *Yummy Fur*. 24 vols. Toronto: Vortex Comics, 1986–1991.

———. *Yummy Fur*. 8 vols. Montreal: Drawn and Quarterly, 1991–1994.

Buhle, Paul. "History and Comics." *Reviews in American History* 35.2 (June 2007): 315–23.

Burgin, Victor. "Looking at Photographs." In Wells, *The Photography Reader*, 130–37.

Chaplin, Charlie, dir. *City Lights*. United Artists, 1931.

Cicero, Marcus Tullius. *De Oratore*. Translated by E. W. Sutton. Cambridge, MA: Harvard University Press, 1967.

Clowes, Daniel. *David Boring*. New York: Pantheon Books, 2000.

———. *Ghost World*. Seattle: Fantagraphics, 1997.

Crane, Stephen. *The Complete Poems of Stephen Crane*. Edited by Joseph Katz. Ithaca, NY: Cornell University Press, 1972.

Davies, Ruth. *The Great Books of Russia*. Norman: University of Oklahoma Press, 1968.

Deleuze, Gilles. *The Fold: Leibniz and the Baroque*. Translated by Tom Conley. London: Continuum, 2006.

Derrida, Jacques. Foreword to *The Wolf Man's Magic Word*, by Nicolas Abraham and Maria Torok, xi–xlviii. Minneapolis: University of Minnesota Press, 1986.

Doane, Janice, and Devon Hodges. *Nostalgia and Sexual Difference: The Resistance to Contemporary Feminism*. New York: Methuen, 1987.

Doug Wright Awards. "Martin Vaughn-James (1943–2009)." Doug Wright Awards, 2012. At http://www.wrightawards.ca/giants-of-the-north/previous-inductees/martin-vaughn-james.

Dunley, Kathleen. "Conversations with Seth, Attention Revisited." *Comics Grid*, May 5, 2011. At http://blog.comicsgrid.com/2011/05/conversations-with-seth-attention-revisited/.
Eco, Umberto. *The Role of the Reader: Explorations in the Semiotics of Texts*. London: Hutchinson, 1981.
Eisner, Will. *Comics and Sequential Art: Principles and Practices from the Legendary Cartoonist*. New York: W. W. Norton, 2008.
Empson, William. *Seven Types of Ambiguity*. London: Penguin, 1973.
Freud, Sigmund. "Mourning and Melancholia." In *The Standard Edition of the Complete Psychological Works of Sigmund Freud*, vol. 14, translated and edited James Strachey et al., 237–58. London: Hogarth Press, 1981.
———. *Totem and Taboo: Some Points of Agreement between the Mental Lives of Savages and Neurotics*. Translated by James Strachey. New York: W. W. Norton, 1950.
———. "The Uncanny." In *The Standard Edition of the Complete Psychological Works of Sigmund Freud*, vol. 17, translated and edited by James Strachey et al., 219–52. London: Hogarth Press, 1981.
Gardner, Jared. "Archives, Collectors, and the New Media Work of Comics." *Modern Fiction Studies* 51.4 (2006): 787–806.
Gibson, Graeme. *Eleven Canadian Novelists*. Toronto: House of Anansi Press, 1973.
Grennan, Simon. "Demonstrating *Discours*: Two Comic Strip Projects in Self-Constraint." *Studies in Comics* 2.2 (2012): 295–316.
Groensteen, Thierry. *The System of Comics*. Translated by Bart Beaty and Nick Nguyen. Jackson: University Press of Mississippi, 2007.
———. "Why Are Comics Still in Search of Cultural Legitimization?" In Heer and Worcester, *A Comics Studies Reader*, 3–11.
"Guardians of the North, Superhero Profiles: Canada Jack." Library and Archives Canada. At http://epe.lac-bac.gc.ca/100/200/301/lac-bac/guardians_north-ef/2009/www.collectionscanada.gc.ca/superheroes/t3-303-e.html.
Guibert, Emmanuel, Didier Lefèvre, and Frédéric Lemercier. *Le Photographe*. 3 vols. Marcinelle, Belgium: Aire Libre Dupuis, 2003–2006.
Hall, Stuart. "Cultural Identity and Diaspora." In *Identity: Community, Culture, Difference*, edited by Jonathan Rutherford, 223–37. London: Lawrence and Wishart, 1990.
Hatfield, Charles. *Alternative Comics: An Emerging Literature*. Jackson: University Press of Mississippi, 2005.
———. "'It's Not the House I Lived In': Seth's Comics and the Problem of Nostalgia." Popular Culture Association conference, Toronto, March 16, 2002.
———. "Same as It Never Was: Nostalgia in Contemporary Comics." Popular Culture Association conference, Philadelphia, April 14, 2001.
Heer, Jeet. "Inventing Cartoon Ancestors: Ware and the Comics Canon." In Ball and Kuhlman, *The Comics of Chris Ware*, 3–13.
Heer, Jeet, and Kent Worcester, eds. *Arguing Comics: Literary Masters on a Popular Medium*. Jackson: University Press of Mississippi, 2004.
———. *A Comics Studies Reader*. Jackson: University Press of Mississippi, 2009.
Hobsbawm, Eric J. *The Age of Empire: 1875–1914*. New York: Pantheon Books, 1987.

———. *On History*. London: Weidenfeld and Nicolson, 1997.
Hutcheon, Linda. *The Canadian Postmodern: A Study of Contemporary English-Canadian Fiction*. Toronto: Oxford University Press, 1988.
———. "Irony, Nostalgia, and the Postmodern." University of Toronto, January 19, 1998. At http://library.utoronto.ca/utel/criticism/hutchinp.html.
———. *Narcissistic Narrative: The Metafictional Paradox*. New York: Routledge, 1980.
———. *Splitting Images: Contemporary Canadian Ironies*. Toronto: Oxford University Press, 1991.
Ingarden, Roman. *The Literary Work of Art*. Translated by George G. Grabowicz. Evanston, IL: Northwestern University Press, 1973.
Jenkins, Keith. *Re-thinking History*. London: Routledge, 1991.
Jennison, Ruth. *The Zukofsky Era: Modernity, Margins, and the Avant-Garde*. Baltimore: Johns Hopkins University Press, 2012.
Juno, Andrea, ed. *Dangerous Drawings*. New York: Juno Books, 1997.
Kannenberg, Gene, Jr. "The Comics of Chris Ware: Text, Image, and Visual Narrative Strategies." In Varnum and Gibbons, *The Language of Comics*, 174–97.
Kracauer, Siegfried. *Theory of Film: The Redemption of Physical Reality*. London: Oxford University Press, 1976.
Krell, David Farrell. *Of Memory, Reminiscence, and Writing: On the Verge*. Bloomington: Indiana University Press, 1990.
Kukkonen, Karin. "Comics as a Test Case for Transmedial Narratology." *SubStance* 40.1 (2011): 34–52.
Kunzle, David. *History of the Comic Strip*. Vol. 1, *The Early Comic Strip: Narrative Strips and Picture Stories in the European Broadsheet from c. 1450 to 1825*. Berkeley: University of California Press, 1973.
———. *History of the Comic Strip*. Vol. 2, *The Nineteenth Century*. Berkeley: University of California Press, 1990.
Lang, Berel, ed. *The Concept of Style*. Ithaca, NY: Cornell University Press, 1987.
Lapushin, Radislav. *"Dew on the Grass": The Poetics of Inbetweenness in Chekhov*. New York: Peter Lang, 2010.
Lefèvre, Pascal. "Some Medium-Specific Qualities of Graphic Sequences." *SubStance* 40.1 (2011): 14–33.
Linville, Susan E. *History Films, Women, and Freud's Uncanny*. Austin: University of Texas Press, 2004.
Lodge, David. *After Bakhtin: Essays on Fiction and Criticism*. London: Routledge, 1990.
Mankoff, Robert, ed. *The Complete Cartoons of the New Yorker*. New York: Black Dog and Leventhal, 2006.
Matt, Joe. *Spent*. Montreal: Drawn and Quarterly, 2007.
McCloud, Scott. *Understanding Comics: The Invisible Art*. New York: HarperPerennial, 1993.
Metz, Christian. "Photography and Fetish." *October* 34 (Autumn 1985): 81–90.
Mighall, Robert. *A Geography of Victorian Graphic Fiction: Mapping History's Nightmares*. New York: Oxford University Press, 1999.
Miller, Ann. *Reading Bande Dessinée: Critical Approaches to French-Language Comic Strip*. Bristol, England: Intellect, 2007.

Mitchell, W. J. T. *Picture Theory: Essays on Verbal and Visual Representation.* Chicago: University of Chicago Press, 1994.

Mitscherling, Jeff. *Roman Ingarden's Ontology and Aesthetics.* Ottawa: University of Ottawa Press, 1997.

Molotiu, Andrei. *Abstract Comics: The Anthology.* Seattle: Fantagraphics, 2009.

Morton, W. L. *The Canadian Identity.* Toronto: University of Toronto Press, 1973.

Motter, Dean, Jaime Hernandez, et al. *Mister X.* Series 1, 14 vols. Toronto: Vortex Comics, 1984–1988.

Mullins, Katie. "Questioning Comics: Women and Autocritique in Seth's *It's a Good Life, If You Don't Weaken*." *Canadian Literature* 203 (Winter 2009): 11–27.

Munslow, Alun. *Narrative and History.* New York: Palgrave Macmillan, 2007.

Ngui, Marc. "Poetry, Design and Comics: An Interview with Seth." *Carousel* 19 (Spring–Summer 2006): 17–24.

O'Malley, Bryan Lee. *Scott Pilgrim.* 6 vols. Portland, OR: Oni Press, 2010.

Orlando, Francesco. *Obsolete Objects in the Literary Imagination: Ruins, Relics, Rarities, Rubbish, Uninhabited Places, and Hidden Treasures.* Translated by Gabriel Pihas et al. New Haven, CT: Yale University Press, 2006.

Packard, Stephan. "Reflections of the Cartoon." *International Journal of Comic Art* 8.2 (2006): 113–25.

Pearce, Susan M. *Collecting in Contemporary Practice.* London: Sage Publications, 1998.

Pedri, Nancy. "When Photographs Aren't Quite Enough: Reflections on Photography and Cartooning in *Le Photographe*." *ImageTexT: Interdisciplinary Comics Studies* 6.1 (2011): n.p. At http://www.english.ufl.edu/imagetext/archives/v6_1/pedri/.

Perloff, Marjorie. *The Poetics of Indeterminacy: Rimbaud to Cage.* Princeton, NJ: Princeton University Press, 1981.

Peters, John Durham. "The Gaps of Which Communication Is Made." *Critical Studies in Mass Communication* 11.2 (1994): 117–40.

Postema, Barbara. "Draw a Thousand Words: Signification and Narration in Comics Images." *International Journal of Comic Art* 9.1 (2007): 487–501.

Pratt, William. *Ezra Pound and the Making of Modernism.* Brooklyn: AMS Press, 2007.

Quartermain, Peter. "Parataxis in Basil Bunting and Louis Zukofsky." *Durham University Journal* (1995): 54–70.

Richards, Jennifer. *Rhetoric.* London: Routledge, 2008.

Rifkind, Candida. "Drawn from Memory: Comics Artists and Intergenerational Auto/biography." *Canadian Review of American Studies* 38.3 (2008): 399–427.

Round, Julia. *Gothic in Comics and Graphic Novels: A Critical Approach.* Jefferson, NC: McFarland, 2014.

———. "Visual Perspective and Narrative Voice in Comics: Redefining Literary Terminology." *International Journal of Comic Art* 9.2 (2007): 316–29.

Royle, Nicholas. *The Uncanny.* New York: Routledge, 2005.

Russo, Mary. "Female Grotesques: Carnival and Theory." In *Writing on the Body: Female Embodiment and Feminist Theory*, edited by Katie Conboy, Nadia Medina, and Sarah Stanbury, 318–36. New York: Columbia University Press, 1997.

Saraceni, Mario. "Relatedness: Aspects of Textual Connectivity in Comics." In Baetens, *The Graphic Novel*, 167–80.
Screech, Matthew. *Masters of the Ninth Art: Bandes Dessinées and Franco-Belgian Identity*. Liverpool: Liverpool University Press, 2005.
Shapton, Leanne. *Important Artifacts and Personal Property from the Collection of Lenore Doolan and Harold Morris, Including Books, Street Fashion, and Jewelry*. London: Bloomsbury, 2009.
Sontag, Susan. *Against Interpretation and Other Essays*. New York: Farrar, Straus & Giroux, 1986.
———. *On Photography*. London: Penguin, 2002.
Tagg, John. *The Burden of Representation: Essays on Photographies and Histories*. Minneapolis: University of Minnesota Press, 1993.
Taylor, Craig. "Modern Life Is Rubbish: Acclaimed Cartoonist Seth Turns Alienation into Art." *Quill and Quire* 70.5 (May 2004): 14–15.
Topliss, Iain. *The Comic Worlds of Peter Arno, William Steig, Charles Addams, and Saul Steinberg*. Baltimore: Johns Hopkins University Press, 2005.
Trilling, Lionel. *Sincerity and Authenticity*. London: Oxford Paperbacks, 1974.
Varnum, Robin, and Christina T. Gibbons, eds. *The Language of Comics: Word and Image*. Jackson: University Press of Mississippi, 2001.
Vaughn-James, Martin. *The Cage*. 1975. With an introduction by Seth. Toronto: Coach House Books, 2013.
———. *The Projector*. Toronto: Coach House Books, 1971.
Walton, Kendall L. "Style and the Products and Processes of Art." In Lang, *The Concept of Style*, 72–103.
Wells, Liz, ed. *The Photography Reader*. London: Routledge, 2003.
White, Hayden. "Masterclass Lecture." Birkbeck College, University of London, February 20, 2012.
———. *Metahistory: The Historical Imagination in the Nineteenth Century*. Baltimore: Johns Hopkins University Press, 1973.
Wilde, Oscar. *Collected Works of Oscar Wilde*. Ware, Hertfordshire, England: Wordsworth Editions, 1997.
Wilson, Janelle L. *Nostalgia: Sanctuary of Meaning*. Lewisburg, PA: Bucknell University Press, 2005.
Wollen, Peter. "Fire and Ice." In Wells, *The Photography Reader*, 76–81.
Woolf, Virginia. *Mrs. Dalloway*. London: Hogarth Press, 1925.
———. *A Writer's Diary: Being Extracts from the Diary of Virginia Woolf*. Edited by Leonard Woolf. London: Hogarth Press, 1969.
Wright, Edgar, dir. *Scott Pilgrim vs. the World*. Universal Pictures, 2010.

Index

Abraham, Nicolas, 117
Alpers, Svetlana, 20
ambiguity, 17, 44–47, 52, 56–57, 164, 166, 168, 180
ambivalence: and ambiguity, 17, 44–45; ambivalent impulses, 11, 16, 17, 41–42, 47, 52, 56–57, 175, 179, 180, 183; ambivalent longing, 4, 15, 77, 170, 177; ambivalent nostalgia, 5, 15, 16, 21, 39, 53, 95, 175, 179, 182; and appearance, 23, 39, 51; definitions of, 41–44, 179; generative capacity of, 5, 11, 43–44, 45, 56–57, 60, 78; and modernity, 42–43, 175; and value, 88, 96
anecdote, 17, 90, 91, 132, 133, 162, 165
Aristotle, 6, 97, 104
Arno, Peter, 16, 24–28, 29, 30, 38, 39, 137, 190, 216
artifice, 5, 22, 29, 39, 51, 100, 182
authenticity, 16, 20, 21–23, 26, 27, 28, 29, 39, 51, 53, 81, 145, 182
autobiography, 23, 151

Baetens, Jan, 146
Bakhtin, M. M., 160
baroque, 132–33, 147
Barry, Lynda, 200, 206
Basbanes, Nicholas A., 98–99, 102, 104, 106, 108, 113
Bauman, Zygmunt, 17, 42, 43, 44, 56, 98
Beaty, Bart, 23, 151, 175
Benjamin, Walter, 3, 16, 123, 180

Benveniste, Émile, 21
boredom, 122, 143, 145, 169, 195
Boym, Svetlana, 4–5, 21, 41, 52, 53, 56, 111, 166
Brown, Chester, 14, 26, 38, 68, 105, 106, 124, 151, 171, 205, 209, 215
browsing, 113, 123–24, 127, 147
Buhle, Paul, 15
Burgin, Victor, 71

cardboard models, 35, 133, 155, 156–58, 159, 160–62, 176
cartooning: as a form 3, 6, 7, 8, 9–10, 31, 39, 52, 60–61, 69, 73, 79–80, 123, 134, 147, 181; in practice, 6, 19, 22, 24–27, 29, 73, 100, 168
catalogs (invented), 100–103, 157
Chaland, Yves, 190, 216
Chekhov, Anton, 17, 80–81, 84, 95, 180
Cicero, 6, 98
clear line. See *ligne claire*
closure, 8, 9, 121
Clowes, Daniel, 14, 15, 31, 38, 39, 52, 89, 149, 174, 193, 201, 206, 215, 218
Clyde Fans, 13; and browsing, 124; and collection, 17, 98, 102, 108–10, 114–18, 167; and descriptive storytelling, 182, 195; and Dominion, 13, 49, 81–82; and drawn photographs, 63–64, 67–69, 71–72, 76; and failure, 89, 91, 92–94; Gothic tendencies of, 53, 54, 55, 173, 174; Grennan's use of, 15, 21; and the Matchcard home,

231

33, 41, 153, 154; and modernism, 175; and parataxis, 143, 145; Seth's work on, 187, 202, 203, 204, 208, 217, 219; and speech, 47; style of, 31–32, 34, 36; and texture, 140; and time, 153

coherence, 11, 17, 65, 107, 122, 125, 127, 128, 141–42, 146, 147–48, 180, 183

collection: bedroom of Lily Matchcard, 108, 109, 100, 111–12, 113–14, 116, 121, 143, 144, 155, 167, 182; in *Clyde Fans*, 98, 102, 107–19; and Derridean crypts, 11, 117–18; and editing, 105–6; and forgetting, 107–8; in *George Sprott*, 87, 106, 107, 110; in *Great Northern Brotherhood*, 87, 106; and identity, 99, 119, 181; in *It's a Good Life*, 25, 68, 87, 99–100, 106; and obsolete objects, 87, 114; of photographs, 71, 72; of Simon's postcards, 72, 114–15, 158, 160; of Simon's sketches, 49, 50, 115; structural affinity with comics, 15, 71, 98, 106, 119, 121, 181; in *Wimbledon Green*, 13, 87, 88, 98, 100–102, 104, 106, 107

composition. *See* page composition; panel composition

compulsion, 4, 49, 52, 85, 94–95, 98, 105, 114, 129, 132, 152. *See also* obsession

Crane, Stephen, 81–82

Crumb, Robert, 28, 188, 189, 194, 200, 205, 214

crypt, 5, 11, 117–18, 153

Daguerre, Louis, 59
Darger, Henry, 194
Davies, Ruth, 80, 84, 95
Deleuze, Gilles, 12, 132
Derrida, Jacques, 11, 117–18
descriptive storytelling, 108, 113–14, 182, 195, 197, 200–202, 208, 218
design: book design, 19, 32, 186–87; graphic design, 36, 44, 46, 202–3, 205; page design, 10, 19, 36, 38, 127
Doane, Janice, 22
Dominion City, 13, 35, 49, 81, 88, 93, 115, 133, 155, 156, 157, 158, 159, 160, 162, 176, 201

drawing style: and composition, 38; consistency of, 20, 152, 154; development of, 26–27, 29–30, 36, 38, 154–56, 189, 214–15; historicizing effect of, 21, 73, 179, 182; influence of Arno on, 26–27, 30; seamlessness of, 23, 29, 32, 39, 80, 156

Drawn and Quarterly, 12–13

drawn photographs, 17; in *Clyde Fans*, 63, 64, 65, 68–69, 71, 72; in *George Sprott*, 74, 75, 76, 85, 110, 133, 180; and interpolation, 69, 78; in *It's a Good Life*, 76; as meta-images, 61, 65, 73; in *Palookaville*, 70, 71; referential status of, 60–61, 71, 73, 77, 160, 181; in *Wimbledon Green*, 76; yearbook format, 70, 71

dream sequences, 31, 38, 44, 47, 48, 49, 126, 127, 142, 152, 158, 160, 182

duration, 17, 46–47, 57, 61–62, 63

Eco, Umberto, 16, 99, 104, 107, 108, 145
editing, 105–6
Eisner, Will, 9, 141

failure: corporeal failure, 87–88; financial failure, 88–89; narrative failure, 84–86; rhetoric of failure, 89–90, 95, 169; and Simon Matchcard, 81–82, 91, 93–94; and success, 17, 82, 88, 89, 95–96
film, 8, 36, 61–63, 124, 143, 144, 198, 202
Findley, Timothy, 173
flaneur, 123, 124–25
Forty Cartoon Books of Interest, 14, 169
frames, 9, 22, 59, 61, 62, 73, 98, 130, 134, 141–43
framing, 61, 62, 122, 124, 141–43, 147
Freud, Sigmund, 11, 17, 41, 43, 53, 55, 94, 117, 175
Frise, Jimmy, 105

gaps: between panels, 55–56, 69, 98, 113, 130, 138, 140, 141; in comics, 7, 9, 10, 16, 98, 106, 121, 124, 136, 137–38, 145–46, 148, 179, 180, 183; in communication,

7; in literature, 7; in narrative, 16, 124, 130, 145–46, 147. *See also* spots of indeterminacy
Gardner, Jared, 15, 98, 106, 174
George Sprott, 14; arctic tableaux, 34, 35, 133, 167, 172, 196; Canadian culture, 166–67, 171–72; CKCK, 76, 87, 89; foldout section, 17, 35, 52, 75, 110, 132–33, 155, 180; "A Fresh Start," 50, 74, 75, 85, 133; "George Is Born," 127, 128–29; narrator of, 14, 23, 34, 50, 51, 52, 75, 84–86, 127, 128, 133, 171; physical properties of, 34–35, 133, 155, 182; sepia sequences, 46, 133, 141, 142, 217; Seth's work on, 195–96, 205, 217. *See also* Sprott, George
Ghost World, 31, 52, 149
Gibbons, Christina, 8–9
Gorey, Edward, 30, 189
Gothic, 11, 53–55, 173–75
Gould, Glenn, 194
Great Northern Brotherhood of Canadian Cartoonists, The, 14; Canada Jack, 170, 171; and collection, 87, 106; Jasper award, 161, 162, 163; Kao-Kuk, 130, 131, 169, 176; metafictional aspects, 127, 149, 164–66, 175, 176; national dimensions, 4, 163–64, 166, 167, 168–71, 173; sketchbook composition, 29, 132
Green, Wimbledon, 14, 41, 76, 99, 100–104, 107, 130, 146, 162
Grennan, Simon, 15, 21
Groensteen, Thierry: arthrology, 9; comics as a system, 6–7, 9, 10, 77; framing, 142–43; iconic solidarity, 146; and McCloud, 9; medium-related pleasure, 20, 147; panels, 7, 9, 46–47, 62, 98, 134, 138, 141, 144; redundancy, 50; reticence, 77, 179; spatio-topical system, 9, 36, 47, 110, 141
Group of Seven, The, 172–73
gutter, 8, 9, 62, 69, 98, 113, 121, 129–30, 138, 140, 142, 146, 179, 183

Hall, Stuart, 99, 119, 150, 181
Harris, Lawren, 172–73

Hatfield, Charles, 4, 6, 7, 10, 14–15, 137, 148, 179, 180
Heer, Jeet, 7, 164–65
Hergé, 30, 38, 39, 80, 190, 216
Hernandez, Gilbert, 188, 189
Hernandez, Jaime, 188, 189
heterocosm, 17, 150, 151–52, 153, 154, 157, 160, 162, 164, 176–77, 181
historiographic metafiction, 3, 16, 17, 149–50, 167, 175, 182
historiography, conventional conceptions of, 165–66, 168, 176, 182
history: abbreviation of, 72, 77; and collection, 99; construction of, 5, 134, 150, 160, 162–65, 174, 177, 182, 183; and geography, 53, 176; and memory, 3, 5, 16, 60, 75, 78, 100, 179, 181
Hobsbawm, Eric, 3, 150
Hodges, Devon, 22
Hofer, Johannes, 4
home. *See* Matchcard family home
homecoming, 4, 41, 108, 116
homosociality, 106
Hutcheon, Linda: *Canadian Postmodern*, 3, 17, 43, 149, 150, 167, 171, 179; "Irony, Nostalgia, and the Postmodern," 45, 166, 175–76, 177; *Narcissistic Narrative*, 150, 152, 181–82; *Splitting Images*, 168–69

illustration, 9–10, 14, 19, 31, 167, 172, 186–87, 190, 215
imagetext, 6, 16, 98
immobility, 8, 63, 68, 107, 119, 144. *See also* stillness
inbetweenness, 80, 95, 180
Ingarden, Roman, 7, 146
inside-outside relations, 43, 49, 56, 77–78, 98, 99, 106, 117–18, 119, 171, 179, 181
interior landscape, 17, 158, 162, 176
interpolation, 15–16, 62, 69, 113, 123, 130, 134, 141, 146, 147, 148, 179–80, 181
irony: and ambivalence, 15, 45, 182; and Canada, 167, 168–69; "Irony, Nostalgia, and the Postmodern," 45, 166, 175–76,

177; irony of unfulfillment, 80–81, 95, 180–81; in metafiction, 164–66
It's a Good Life, If You Don't Weaken, 13, 46–47; and authenticity, 22, 29; autobiographical elements of, 13, 23, 151–52; as autocritique, 15; and collection, 99–100, 106; and drawn photographs, 68, 76; and failure, 82, 83; framing, 142; ghost worlds, 149; glossary of, 24, 151; Kalo cartoons, 24, 25, 26, 29, 134, 135, 151, 162, 176; Seth's work on, 192, 205, 207, 211; shading, 30–31; snapshot of Kalo, 61, 65; strangers, 122, 123, 124, 125

Jenkins, Keith, 5
Jennison, Ruth, 121, 148
Jonah, 22, 88
juxtaposition, 5, 8, 9, 121, 122, 127, 141, 142, 146, 147, 148, 166, 168, 177

Kalloway, John, 13, 76, 82, 100, 151, 176
Kalo, 13, 24–25, 26, 29, 61, 65–66, 76, 82, 89, 100, 134, 136, 137, 151, 166, 176
Kannenberg, Gene, Jr., 36
Katchor, Ben, 4, 38, 174, 193, 201, 215
Kirby, Jack, 38, 194, 198
Kracauer, Siegfried, 60, 77
Krell, David, 6
Kukkonen, Karin, 136–37, 181
Kurtzman, Harvey, 200

Lapushin, Radislav, 80
Lefèvre, Pascal, 146, 147
Lessing, Gotthold, 8
lexis, 61–62
ligne claire, 30, 32, 195
Linville, Susan, 53
Lodge, David, 42, 43–44
longing for the past, 3–5, 16, 21, 22, 77, 88, 166, 179, 193. *See also* nostalgia

Magritte, René, 44, 172
mannered quality, 29, 39, 51–52, 56, 133, 147, 214

margins, 121, 122, 124, 132, 143
Matchcard, Abraham, 13, 47, 63, 67, 72, 76, 86, 89, 91, 108, 114, 115, 116, 119, 124, 153, 174, 175
Matchcard, Clyde, 13, 68–69, 118–19, 160, 174
Matchcard, Lily: bedroom of, 102, 108, 109, 110, 111–12, 113–14, 116, 121, 138, 143, 144, 155, 167, 185; and Simon, 106, 119, 152, 153, 158
Matchcard, Simon: and Abraham Matchcard, 13, 86, 116, 175; collection of postcards, 72, 115, 152, 160; collection of toys, 47, 49, 116, 152; Dominion, 13, 49, 81–82, 92–94, 115, 158–60; inner life of, 47–49, 55, 127, 152, 158–60; and the Matchcard family home, 31, 54, 55, 115, 116, 117–18, 153–54, 155; mother's bedroom, 108, 109, 110, 111–12, 113–14, 182; sketching habit, 49, 94, 158; time, 107–8, 115, 153–54
Matchcard family home, 13, 31, 33, 41, 108, 115, 116, 117–18, 124, 153–54, 155
Matt, Joe, 14, 105, 106, 151
McCloud, Scott, 6, 8, 9, 45, 121, 123
Melville, Herman, 89
memory as a medium, 5–6, 16, 17, 60, 181, 183
memory palace. *See* method of loci
metafiction, 25, 77, 100, 127, 149, 150, 152, 163–64, 165, 167, 171, 175, 176, 182. *See also* historiographic metafiction
metahistorical consciousness, 17, 165–66, 182
method of loci, 6, 160
Metz, Christian, 61–63, 73, 75
Mighall, Robert, 53, 174–75
Miller, Ann, 30
Miller, Arthur, 82
Mister X, 12, 189–90, 198, 215
Mitchell, W. J. T., 5, 6, 10, 16, 59, 77, 97–98, 181
Mitscherling, Jeff, 7
models. *See* cardboard models
modernity, 5, 17, 27, 42, 43, 44, 46, 52, 56, 121, 175
Mouly, Françoise, 12

Morton, W. L., 167–68, 169, 172
Mullins, Katie, 15
Munro, Alice, 173, 214
Munslow, Alun, 5

narratology, 15, 21
National Film Board of Canada, 167, 212
national identity, 4, 5, 55, 82, 149, 163, 166–69, 171, 175, 176
New Yorker, 14, 24, 26, 28, 134, 137, 213
New York Times Magazine, 14, 35, 133
nostalgia, 4–5, 41, 179; approaches to studying, 11, 52; armchair nostalgia, 111; and authenticity, 21–22, 39; and comics, 3–4, 14–15; "Irony, Nostalgia, and the Postmodern," 45, 166, 175–76, 177; and photography, 60; reflective nostalgia, 5, 21; restorative nostalgia, 5; Seth's reaction to the label of, 192–94; and the uncanny, 53, 56, 174–75

obsession, 4, 41, 49, 52, 94, 95, 108, 114, 152, 156, 168. *See also* compulsion
Obsolete Objects in the Literary Imagination, 11, 42, 87–88
Orlando, Francesco, 11, 17, 42, 53, 56, 87–88, 96, 114

pace, 46, 124, 140, 143, 144
Packard, Stephan, 147
page: discontinuity of comics page, 10, 17, 61, 62–63, 65, 78, 115, 121, 125, 127, 141, 146; page composition, 36, 89; page layout, 10, 34, 36, 38, 129, 130, 143; potentialities of comics page, 10, 11, 36, 45, 68, 122, 123, 133, 140, 202–3; surface of, 10, 19, 22, 56, 78, 128–30, 133, 141–42, 177; structure of comics page, 6, 8, 9, 43, 56, 62–63, 71, 72, 98, 113, 121, 128–30, 138, 179
Palookaville, 12, 13, 29, 35–36, 204; issue 1, 90–91, 122, 211; issues 2–3, 154, 158; issues 4–9, 13, 149; issues 10–15, 13; issue 16, 49, 89–90, 107, 118; issue 17, 48, 49, 50, 54, 55; issue 18, 159; issue 19, 33, 34, 36, 109, 111, 112, 117, 126, 127, 143, 145, 155; issue 20, 61, 66, 67, 69, 70, 71, 90, 102, 103, 132, 139, 145, 151, 157, 158, 159, 160, 204, 210; issue 21, 151; issue 22, 151
panels, 9; duration, 62; frameless panels, 142; full-page panels, 66, 67–68; and gaps, 8, 9, 98, 121, 130, 138, 141, 146–47, 179; at once separate and linked, 8, 10, 65, 78, 125–27, 142, 180; panel composition, 38, 122, 123, 124, 154, 155, 194, 215–16; panel transitions, 9, 45–47, 56, 196; physical attributes, 72, 73, 75, 130; progression/retention, 47, 56, 107, 141, 144; as units in the system of comics, 7, 9, 10, 61, 62, 65, 98, 125–27, 134, 148. *See also* single-panel cartoon
Panter, Gary, 30
parataxis, 121, 122, 127, 133, 141, 146, 148, 180
Pearce, Susan, 99
Pedri, Nancy, 60, 65, 71
Pefferlaw, Henry, 168–69, 171
Peirce, C. S., 61
Perloff, Marjorie, 44
Peters, John Durham, 7
photography, 17, 59; group photos, 76, 77; photographic frame, 62, 71, 73; referential status of, 60, 61, 63, 65, 66, 68, 71, 77–78, 147, 181; and time, 60, 62, 63, 65, 73, 75, 77, 134
poetry, 36, 44, 46, 81, 121, 203
postcards, 72, 93, 110, 114–15, 152, 158, 160
Postema, Barbara, 135, 146
postmodernism, 43, 175–76. *See also* metafiction
Pound, Ezra, 44, 121
preservation, 104, 107, 114, 115, 119
Proust, Marcel, 60, 77

Quartermain, Peter, 127

Remi, George. *See* Hergé
repetition, 4, 49–50, 56, 95, 129, 153, 180, 198; of images, 25, 34, 38, 49, 52, 77, 94, 115, 127, 129

return of the repressed, 11, 43, 52, 53, 56, 87, 94, 96, 174, 177, 180, 181
rhythm, 10, 46–47, 52, 113, 140, 196, 204
Richards, Jennifer, 79
Rifkind, Candida, 15
Round, Julia, 145–46
Royal Ontario Museum, 99–100, 123
Royle, Nicholas, 53
Russo, Mary, 71

Saraceni, Mario, 138
satire, 22, 165–66, 167, 169, 182, 183
Schulz, Charles, 194–95
Screech, Matthew, 30, 32
shading, 19, 30–32, 123, 130
shadow, 31–32, 33, 142
Shapton, Leanne, 102
"silent" panels, 76, 79, 196, 197, 203–4
Simonides of Ceos, 5–6, 160
Simpkins, James, 163, 164
single-panel cartoon, 17, 25–26, 28, 62, 122, 134, 135–37, 147, 203
Sontag, Susan: *Against Interpretation*, 19, 20–21, 23, 38–39, 143, 144; *On Photography*, 60, 61, 62, 63, 66, 68, 72–73, 76, 77, 78
Southern Ontario Gothic, 53, 173–74
speech balloon, 10, 47, 124
Spiegelman, Art, 12, 15, 200
spots of indeterminacy, 7–8, 9, 45, 146–47, 183
Sprott, Daisy, 86, 88
Sprott, George: appearance in Seth's sketchbook, 157; career, 23, 49–51, 76–77, 88, 95, 160; death, 86, 160; "George Is Born," 127, 128–29; hotel suite, 16; Institute of Polar Studies, 35; memories, 75, 110; regrets, 84, 95, 171; unacknowledged daughter, 76, 88; young George, 46, 142. See also *George Sprott*
Stein, Gertrude, 44
Steinberg, Saul, 26

stillness, 63–65, 73, 78, 144
style: concept of, 19–22; structure of, 27, 38. See also drawing style

Tagg, John, 60
taxidermy, 118, 160
television, 50–51, 60, 76–77
tempo, 123–24, 125, 140
text plates, 46, 75, 116–17, 133, 138, 139–40, 180
Tomine, Adrian, 28, 52
Topliss, Iain, 24, 26, 27–28, 39
Torok, Maria, 117
Trilling, Lionel, 21

uncanny, 11, 17, 29, 49, 53, 56, 94, 116, 127, 152, 174–75, 180, 182
undecidability, 44, 49, 57, 172, 175
unheimlich, 53. See also uncanny

Varnum, Robin, 8–9
Vaughn-James, Martin, 169
Vernacular Drawings, 14, 29, 132

Walton, Kendall L., 20
Ware, Chris, 4, 14, 15, 28, 36, 38, 39, 89–90, 95, 164–65, 193, 199–200, 215
White, Hayden, 17, 41, 165, 182
Whitey, 93–94
Wilde, Oscar, 39, 144
Williams, William Carlos, 44, 121
Wilson, Janelle L., 11
Wimbledon Green, 13–14; and anecdote, 37, 38, 162, 198; cartoonists, 87, 89; and collection, 15, 17, 84, 98–99, 100, 101–4, 107, 110, 162, 165; Coverloose Club, 76, 162; Jonah, 22, 88; metafiction, 127, 149, 165; physical properties of, 32, 34, 35, 130–31, 132; "Rivals of Wimbledon Green," 130, 131; Seth's introduction to, 85, 89, 90, 98; as a sketchbook story, 29, 30, 34, 132, 133, 182, 204, 216, 217, 219; structure of, 34,

98, 102, 107, 133, 197, 200. *See also* Green, Wimbeldon
Wollen, Peter, 65
Woolf, Virginia, 175
Worcester, Kent, 7
Wright, Doug, 163, 164, 166, 204

www.ingramcontent.com/pod-product-compliance
Lightning Source LLC
Chambersburg PA
CBHW052049220426
43663CB00012B/2498